Haunted Histories and Troubled Pasts

Haunted Histories and Troubled Pasts

Twenty-First-Century Screen Horror and the Historical Imagination

Edited by

Amanda Howell and Stephanie Green

BLOOMSBURY ACADEMIC
NEW YORK · LONDON · OXFORD · NEW DELHI · SYDNEY

BLOOMSBURY ACADEMIC

Bloomsbury Publishing Inc, 1359 Broadway, New York, NY 10018, USA
Bloomsbury Publishing Plc, 50 Bedford Square, London, WC1B 3DP, UK
Bloomsbury Publishing Ireland, 29 Earlsfort Terrace, Dublin 2, D02 AY28, Ireland

BLOOMSBURY, BLOOMSBURY ACADEMIC and the Diana logo are
trademarks of Bloomsbury Publishing Plc

First published in the United States of America 2024
Paperback edition published 2026

Volume Editor's Part of the Work © Amanda Howell and Stephanie Green, 2024

Each chapter © of Contributors, 2024

For legal purposes the Acknowledgements on pp. vii–viii constitute an
extension of this copyright page.

Cover design: Eleanor Rose
Cover image © Getty Images

All rights reserved. No part of this publication may be: i) reproduced or transmitted in any form, electronic or mechanical, including photocopying, recording or by means of any information storage or retrieval system without prior permission in writing from the publishers; or ii) used or reproduced in any way for the training, development or operation of artificial intelligence (AI) technologies, including generative AI technologies. The rights holders expressly reserve this publication from the text and data mining exception as per Article 4(3) of the Digital Single Market Directive (EU) 2019/790.

Bloomsbury Publishing Inc does not have any control over, or responsibility for, any third-party websites referred to or in this book. All internet addresses given in this book were correct at the time of going to press. The author and publisher regret any inconvenience caused if addresses have changed or sites have ceased to exist, but can accept no responsibility for any such changes.

Library of Congress Cataloging-in-Publication Data
Names: Howell, Amanda, editor. | Green, Stephanie, 1959- editor.
Title: Haunted histories and troubled pasts : twenty-first century screen horror and the historical imagination / edited by Amanda Howell and Stephanie Green.
Description: New York : Bloomsbury Academic, 2024. |
Includes bibliographical references and index.
Identifiers: LCCN 2023043100 (print) | LCCN 2023043101 (ebook) |
ISBN 9781501394409 (hardback) | ISBN 9781501394447 (paperback) |
ISBN 9781501394416 (ebook) | ISBN 9781501394423 (pdf)
Subjects: LCSH: Horror films–History and criticism. | Fantasy films–History and criticism.
Classification: LCC PN1995.9.H6 H445 2024 (print) | LCC PN1995.9.H6 (ebook) |
DDC 791.43/6164–dc23/eng/20231219
LC record available at https://lccn.loc.gov/2023043100
LC ebook record available at https://lccn.loc.gov/2023043101

ISBN:	HB:	978-1-5013-9440-9
	PB:	978-1-5013-9444-7
	ePDF:	978-1-5013-9442-3
	eBook:	978-1-5013-9441-6

Typeset by Integra Software Services Pvt. Ltd.

For product safety related questions contact productsafety@bloomsbury.com.

To find out more about our authors and books visit www.bloomsbury.com
and sign up for our newsletters.

Contents

Acknowledgements   vii
Notes on editors and contributors   ix

1   Introduction: History, historiography and horror in the twenty-first century *Amanda Howell and Stephanie Green*   1

Part One Spectral encounters and haunted histories

2   Ghosts, vampires and sacrilege in Warwick Thornton's *The Darkside*, *Firebite* and *The New Boy* *Felicity Collins*   23
3   Undead heritage: Environmental trauma and curses that never die in Takashi Shimizu's 'village' trilogy *Simon Bacon*   39
4   Deferred demons: Diasporizing the haunted home in Babak Anvari's *Under the Shadow* *David Ellison and Zach Karpinellison*   55

Part Two Found-footage horrors

5   'It's too late for all of us': Ritual, repression and the historical imagination in *Noroi: The Curse* *Jeremy Kingston*   71
6   Congruent apprehensions of history in Irish horror cinema *Stephen Joyce*   91

Part Three History and horror in televisual storyworlds

7   Lace collars and cowboy cravats: Gothic time-travelling with *Penny Dreadful* and *The Nevers* *Stephanie Green*   109
8   Pretty ballads, bastard truths: History, memory and the past in *The Witcher* *Agnieszka Stasiewicz-Bieńkowska*   129
9   'Brings back some memories': Spectres of history in *Twin Peaks: The Return* *Martin Fradley and John A. Riley*   145

Part Four Female monsters and revolting women

10 'We're Americans': Remembering the 'other America' in Jordan
    Peele's *Us* Amanda Howell   167
11 'Cut them up': Lily Frankenstein, Valerie Solanas and the reanimation
    of radical feminism in *Penny Dreadful* Anthea Taylor   187

Part Five Engaging the past through body horror

12 'Laden with human flesh': *Dying Breed* and Australia's engagement
    with its convict past Clare Burnett   207
13 Killing Private Zombie: *Overlord* and the twenty-first-century
    military horror film Brian E. Crim   225
14 Post-socialist body horror(s): On exhaustion and social death in
    The Life and Death of a Porno Gang and *A Serbian Film*
    Andrija Filipović   243

Index   259

Acknowledgements

We owe thanks to many colleagues who helped bring this book to fruition, but especially to our contributors whose expertise and ideas have been essential to its realization: Simon Bacon, Clare Burnett, Felicity Collins, Brian E. Crim, David Ellison, Andrija Filipović, Martin Fradley, Stephen Joyce, Zach Karpinellison, Jeremy Kingston, John A. Riley, Agnieszka Stasiewicz-Bieńkowska and Anthea Taylor.

Likewise, this work shows the influence of our participation in the research network *Imagining the Impossible: The Fantastic as Media Entertainment and Play,* which we were lucky to be a part of during 2018–21. Leader Rikke Schubart and the other members of the network (Anita Nell Bech Albertsen, Sara Mosberg Iversen, Jakob Ion Wille, Jesper Juul, Mathias Clasen, Stephen Joyce, Marc Malmdorf Andersen, Angela Ndalianis and Cristina Bacchilega) were all great sources of enlightenment and inspiration. Early versions of the ideas explored here were shared as presentations for the Network's Utopia & Dystopia Conference held in 2021.

In addition to these network participants and our contributors to this volume, many other friends, family members and colleagues have variously aided and encouraged our work here, including especially David Baker, Lucy Baker, Sarah Baker, Verena Bernardi, Trish FitzSimons, Sue Hess, Shilon Howell, Maryline Kassab, Chris Louttit, Jay McRoy, Mark David Ryan, Alison Taylor and Terrie Waddell.

Likewise, we are very grateful to the School of Humanities and Social Science at Griffith University in Australia, especially its heads/deputy heads of school for their assistance and encouragement during its development: Robbie Mason, Michael Ondaatje and Sue Trevaskes. The Griffith Centre for Social and Cultural Research funded the copy-editing and indexing of this work, and the Centre's director, Susan Forde, has long been a champion of support for researchers in our school. We also give our thanks to GCSCR's editor, Susan Jarvis, for her expert assistance.

We must also extend our thanks to our editor at Bloomsbury, Katie Gallof, for her ongoing belief in the value of our project from the genesis of this collection.

Finally, as this book was initially conceived during the years of the pandemic and under construction at the time of the catastrophic floods that hit Brisbane and Gold Coast regions in 2022, we extend our gratitude to those many people whose names we don't know who worked tirelessly in service roles keeping us safe and well.

This publication was completed on the lands of the Yugarabul, Yuggera, Jagera, Turrbal, Yugambeh and Kombumerri peoples, traditional custodians of the lands and waters of the Brisbane and Gold Coast regions. We pay our deep respect to their Elders past and present.

Amanda Howell
Stephanie Green

Notes on editors and contributors

Editors

Amanda Howell is Senior Lecturer in Screen Studies at Griffith University, Australia. Her most recent publications appear in *Continuum* and *The New Review of Film and Television Studies*, also edited collections *Screening the Gothic in Australia and New Zealand* (2022) and *Australian Genre Film* (2021). She is the co-author of *Monstrous Possibilities: The Female Monster in 21st Century Screen Horror* (2022), also author of *A Different Tune: Popular Music and Masculinity in Action* (2015).

Stephanie Green is Adjunct Senior Lecturer with Griffith University, Australia, and co-editor of *Hospitality, Rape and Consent in Vampire Popular Culture* (2017), with Agnieszka Stasiewicz-Bieńkowska and David Baker. She co-edited the special issues 'Vampiric Transformations', *Continuum* 35.2 (2021), and '"As if": Women in Genres of the Fantastic', *Continuum* 33.2 (2019). Her most recent papers are 'Violence and the Gothic New Woman', *FULGOR* 6.3 (2021) and 'Playing at Being a Superhero', *Imagining the Impossible* 1.1 (2022).

Contributors

Simon Bacon is an independent scholar based in Poznań, Poland. He has written and edited more than twenty-five books, including *Becoming Vampire* (2017), *The Gothic: A Reader* (2018), *Eco-vampires* (2019), *Toxic Cultures: A Companion* (2022), *The Evolution of Horror in the 21st Century* (2023), *1000 Vampires on Screen* (2 vols, 2023) and *The Palgrave Handbook of the Vampire* (2024).

Clare Burnett is an award-winning journalist and doctoral candidate in the School of Humanities, Languages and Social Science at Griffith University, Australia. After graduating from Trinity College Dublin, she worked across independent online publications before returning to academia. She is currently a sessional lecturer and tutor in journalism, history and literary studies. Her research focuses on Gothic, horror and digital humanities methodologies.

Felicity Collins is Reader/Associate Professor in Screen Studies in the Department of Creative Arts and English, La Trobe University, Australia. She is the author of *The Films of Gillian Armstrong* (1999) and *Australian Cinema After Mabo* (2011), and co-editor of *A Companion to Australian Cinema* (2019), with Jane Landman and Susan Bye.

Brian E. Crim is Professor of History and John Franklin East Chair in the Humanities at the University of Lynchburg, United States, where he teaches courses in European history, military history, Holocaust studies, film and history and intelligence analysis. Select publications include *Antisemitism in the German Military Community and the Jewish Response, 1914–1938* (2014), *Our Germans: Project Paperclip and the National Security State* (2018) and *Planet Auschwitz: Holocaust Representation in Science Fiction and Horror Film and Television* (2020). His current project, 'In the Shadows: Spy Fiction and the "War on Terror"', examines the cultural legacies of 9/11.

David Ellison is Senior Lecturer in the School of Humanities, Languages and Social Science at Griffith University. His research focuses on the literary and cultural histories of Victorian domesticity. He is the author of 'Australian Ghost Fiction', with Penelope Hone, in *The Routledge Handbook to the Ghost Story* (2017), and 'The Call Came from Inside the House: Supernatural Noise and Domestic Incivility', *Republics of Letters* 5. 2 (2017): 1–12. With Andrew Leach, he co-edited *On Discomfort: Moments in a Modern History of Architectural Culture* (2016).

Andrija Filipović is Associate Professor of Philosophy and Art & Media Theory at the Singidunum University, Serbia. Their books include *Ars ahumana: Anthropocene Ontographies in 21st Century Art and Culture* (2022), *Conditio ahumana: Immanence and the Ahuman in the Anthropocene* (2019), *Brian Massumi* (2016), *Gilles Deleuze* (2015) and several edited volumes, most recently *Plastics, Environment, Culture and the Politics of Waste* (2023), and *The Routledge Companion to Gender and Affect* (2022).

Martin Fradley taught Film and Television Studies in the UK for over two decades. He is co-editor of *Shane Meadows: Critical Essays* (2013) and has written for *Film Quarterly*, *Screen*, the *Journal of Popular Television* and the *Canadian Journal of Film Studies*. His previous work on the cultural politics of contemporary horror cinema has also appeared in the collections *American Horror Film: The Genre at the Turn of the Millennium* (2010), *Postfeminism and Contemporary Hollywood Cinema* (2013) and *Make America Hate Again: Trump-Era Horror and the Politics of Fear* (2019).

Stephen Joyce is Associate Professor at Aarhus University, Denmark. His current research focuses on transmedia world-building across the creative industries. He is the author of *A River of Han: Eastern Tragedy in a Western Land* (2015), *Transmedia Storytelling and the Apocalypse* (2018) and numerous articles on literature and contemporary media.

Zach Karpinellison is a PhD candidate in the Interdisciplinary Cross Cultural Research programme at the Australian National University. His work takes place at the intersection between screen and museum studies, and the subject of his research is the National Film and Sound Archive of Australia. He previously worked as a projectionist for the Sydney-based Golden Age Cinema, and was an organizing team member for the Persian Film Festival Australia, 2017–19.

Jeremy Kingston is a doctoral candidate with the School of Humanities, Languages and Social Science at Griffith University, Australia. He is interested in the spatiality of trauma – primarily in the fiction of the American South. He is currently writing his dissertation on the phenomenology of spatial experience and memory.

John A. Riley is Assistant Professor of English at SolBridge International School of Business, South Korea, where he teaches classes on film, drama and academic writing. His research focuses on cult auteurs, hauntology and intertextuality, and his previous writing has appeared in *The Journal of Film and Video* and *The Journal of Popular Culture*, among others. His monograph, a study of the films of Peter Strickland, is due to be published by Auteur Press.

Agnieszka Stasiewicz-Bieńkowska is Assistant Professor at the Institute of American Studies and Polish Diaspora, Jagiellonian University, Krakow, Poland. Her academic interests include girlhood, popular and young adult culture, gender representations and the fantastic. She is the author of *Girls in Contemporary Vampire Fiction* (2021), 'Love, Violence, and Consent in Young Adult Vampire Fiction', in *The Palgrave Handbook of the Vampire* (2023), 'Suicide,

Depression and Mental Disorder in Vampire Fiction', *Continuum* 35(2) (2021) and *Hospitality, Rape and Consent in Vampire Popular Culture* (2017), co-edited with Stephanie Green and David Baker.

Anthea Taylor is Associate Professor in Gender and Cultural Studies at the University of Sydney, Australia. She is the author of four monographs in feminist cultural studies, including *Celebrity and the Feminist Blockbuster* (2016) and co-editor of *Gendering Australian Celebrity* with Joanna McIntyre (2020).

1

Introduction: History, historiography and horror in the twenty-first century

Amanda Howell and Stephanie Green

This edited collection speaks to how a transnational array of recent screen entertainments participate, through horror, in the social and creative work of transforming 'the past into a meaningful and sense-bearing part of the present' (Rüsen 2006: 17). It is motivated by the recognition that twenty-first-century film and television narrative has been characterized by a growing, popular engagement with history, memory and the past – including a worldwide movement to reconcile past losses and injuries with present legacies. Of course, the horror genre's fascination with – and fear of – the past is nothing new. For all that its entertainment value turns on keeping audiences emotionally in the moment, dreading what comes next, horror also commonly figures the past as a monstrous, revenant thing: restless, undead, abject, with a nasty habit of violently breaking into a tense and fragile present. This lurking sense of a past distinctly other from, yet never quite done with, the present speaks strongly to the generic influence of the Gothic – descant voice of an emergent modernity's persistent anxieties – and its role in shaping horror into what it is now: one of the oldest and most enduringly marketable of screen genres. The relationship between the past and present in horror, as in the Gothic, conjures a space that is uncanny, an imaginary borderland, an interstitial zone of hauntings, paranoid fantasies, atavistic obsessions and traumatic confrontations. It is this persistent, fearful reimagining of the past's relationship with the present – which takes so many lurid, also sometimes tritely generic, forms in horror – that constitutes its historical imagination. Importantly, along with (and through) its capacity to inspire terror, dread and jump scares, the historical imagination of horror can have a critical – even historiographic – potential to expose the limits and distortions of dominant or official accounts of the past. This potential has compelled scholarly engagements with screen horror but it has also gained wider attention from the participatory publics of twenty-first-century screen cultures.

By the end of the last millennium, new representational and communications technologies had transformed screen cultures worldwide, reshaping popular engagements with history and the historical. In her introduction to *The Persistence of History*, Vivian Sobchack (2013 [1996]: 6) describes an escalating commodification of history in the United States, alongside 'widespread contentiousness around categories, boundaries, exclusions, and inclusions, ordering and remembering History, history, herstory, histories'. Working against the temptations of cynicism in the face of Disney's marketing of *Pocahontas* (1995), the news media's repetition compulsions and trivializations of the O. J. Simpson trial and the hubristic assertions of A&E's then new History Channel ('All of History. All in One Place'), Sobchack ends her survey on an optimistic note. She concludes:

> [A]udiences have become involved in and understand the stakes in historical representation, recognize 'history in the making', and see themselves not only as spectators of history, but also as participants in and adjudicators of it. Current debates around the nature, shape, and narration of history are no longer only the province of academic historians and scholars of film and literature. 'History happens' now in the public sphere where the search for a lost object has led not only to cheap substitutes but, in the process, also to the quickening of a new historical sense and perhaps a more active and reflective historical subject.
>
> (Sobchack 2013 [1996]: 7)

In the broader context of what Henry Jenkins (2006) labels 'convergence culture', where audiences are actively involved in the production of meaning across an increasingly complex mediascape, Sobchack's sketch of a public sphere animated by a 'new historical sense' has proved prescient. During a period of transnational growth, diversification and box office success for the genre, a number of high-profile horror films and television series have become vehicles for interrogating and reimagining the past in its relationship to the present. A global array of directors and show-runners self-identified as horror fans – including Guillermo del Toro, Warwick Thornton, Aislinn Clarke, Jennifer Kent, Babak Anvari, John Logan and Jordan Peele – have, over the past two decades, deliberately drawn upon the potential of horror to engage with history, memory and the past, prompting audiences' 'active and reflective' responses.

One of the most prominent examples of screen horror taking this role in the public sphere – demonstrating horror's capacity as a form of popular historiography, exposing and engaging with what has been silenced in historical understanding – is Jordan Peele's 2017 debut feature *Get Out*. It became a cultural phenomenon for its harrowing engagement with contemporary experiences of racism – especially through its widely meme-ified image of 'The Sunken Place', a state of hypnotic paralysis forced upon the film's protagonist, Chris (Daniel Kaluuya), visualized as an otherworldly space of marginalization where 'the system silences us' (@JordanPeele Twitter, 17 March 2017). Working on the generic premise of eugenicist mad science, the film's narrative of possession and body-snatching, where all-too-familiar micro-aggressions visited by a prosperous white family on their daughter's new Black boyfriend inexorably escalate to deadly threat, was immediately recognizable to fans as an allegory for the African-American experience of racism and slavery. And, writer-director Peele was quite straightforward about his intention to make the film an intervention into popular understandings of America's past and its connections to the present, warning his Brooklyn premiere's audience, 'The real thing at hand here is slavery … Not to bring down the room, but guys it's some dark shit' (quoted in Harris 2017). Kareem Abdul-Jabbar (2017) commences his review of Peele's film for *The Hollywood Reporter*, saying: 'I recently watched the highly entertaining thriller *Get Out* and the deeply disturbing documentary *I Am Not Your Negro*. Turns out they're the same movie.' Abdul-Jabbar explains that while Peele's film is 'Invasion of the Black Body Snatchers for the Trump Era' and Raoul Peck's documentary, based on an unfinished manuscript by James Baldwin, is a history of racism in America, essentially, they make the same point: 'unless the body is free from others trying to control its actions and free from constant threat of injury or death, that body, that person, that *people* are still enslaved' (2017).

On its release, *Get Out* seemingly eluded generic definition. Peele labelled it a 'social thriller', while – notoriously – distributor Universal Pictures and production company Blumhouse submitted the film to the Golden Globes under the category 'Musical or Comedy' instead of 'Drama' (a controversial but strategic move for a film blending satire and horror, since horror films have not historically been competitive for major awards). By drawing on horror classics such as *Rosemary's Baby* (1968) and *The Stepford Wives* (1975), *Get Out* stages its encounter between present-day racism and America's monstrous, revenant history of slavery. As Peele explains, these movies 'did with gender what I wanted to do with race' (quoted in Yuan and Harris 2018). Critical engagement with *Get Out*, the relevance of its horror to the past, present and future of the United States with respect to race and the historical experience of slavery, spread across social media, with hashtags, memes and GIFs from the film proliferating across multiple media platforms. The film's images of monstrously stolen and magically possessed bodies were integrated into everyday conversations about race, power and oppression (Yuan and Harris 2018) as fans reflected on histories of slavery and their relevance to contemporary social experience. Meanwhile, university academics quickly built new courses around the film's interventions into American public life and screen cultures (Yuan and Harris 2018), extending the critical work already in progress across social media outlets. *Get Out*, with its body-snatching metaphors of slavery, offers an exceptionally vivid example of how screen horror can engage with history, highlighting the possibilities of creative and audience investment in the 'historiographic value of popular cultural objects' (Sobchack 1997: 10). The keen awareness of the genre's critical potential on the part of writer-director Peele, as well as audiences and critics, underlines the shifting status of horror entertainment over the last several decades while exemplifying the pop cultural 'quickening of a new historical sense' within transformed screen cultures of the twenty-first century. It is an example that bids us to take another look at contemporary screen horrors in terms of what their historical imagination might bring to our understanding of the past, and its relationship with the present and future.

Horror and the historical imagination

The lurid appeals of screen horror being what they are, nothing would seem further from its popular entertainments than history – which is to say, History – in the sense of a systematic branch of knowledge reliant on rationalist epistemologies for engaging with and understanding the past. Yet the historical imagination – the active, creative, interpretive work of engaging with the past – is something a wide array of history-focused entertainments, including horror, and the discipline of history have in common. In 1973, Hayden White controversially made a case for history as more art than science in *Metahistory* (2014), identifying the 'deep structure' of historical imagination as being, like literature (and film), poetic, figurative and narrative in character, with ideology and aesthetics closely aligned in its chosen modes of 'emplotment'. Decades later, in surveying the evolution of history-as-practice in academic institutions, including the various epistemological challenges brought by minority historians and practitioners of 'history from below', Sarah Maza (2017: 179) confirmed a shift 'away from an earlier belief that a stance of complete objectivity toward their material was, for historians, both possible and the ultimate professional goal'. Yet Maza also notes that the historical imagination remains a site of contention for the field, where, 'One historian's lapse into "fiction" is another one's act of sympathetic and responsible imagination' (2017: 208). Similarly, David Staley (2020: 2) offers students of history a cautionary description of the 'historical imagination' as a 'boundary' or 'threshold' between history and what he terms 'historical malpractice'.

Beyond the academic cultures and professional practices of history, a twenty-first-century boom in pop historical, para-historical and heritage-focused entertainments has confirmed the market potential of soliciting audiences' historical imaginations, a culmination of the late twentieth century's growing sense of 'future possibilities for representation (and commodification) of the historical past' (Sobchack 2013 [1996]: 4). Whereas academic practice approaches the historical imagination with care and caution, its excesses get free rein in entertainment cultures, which have expanded beyond the long-established film and television genres of the blockbuster historical epic, costume dramas and classic novel adaptations. What was formerly known as the History Channel is now, as of 2023, simply known as 'History', signified by a monumental golden 'H' under which it serves up a variety of reality programming and documentaries, including a long-running and controversial series that gives airtime to science sceptics, *Ancient Aliens* (2009–present). On screen and in real life, one can choose from a range of history-themed entertainments, including live-action role-play and role-play video-games, with various social groups and organizations – such as Australia's long-established Society for Creative Anachronism, with its focus on pre-seventeenth-century arts and cultures – all offering opportunities for performative engagements with the past. Likewise, popular interest in genealogy has inspired television series, databases, conferences, social media groups and DNA tests specifically geared towards family ethnicity and migration histories. As Jerome De Groot (2009: 4) observes, what counts as 'historical' in public discourses and popular cultures in the twenty-first century is 'multiple, multiplying, and unstable'. Focusing on film and television fictions, De Groot (2016: 2) notes the 'complexity' of a popular historical imaginary capable of encompassing everything from Steve McQueen's *12 Years a Slave* (2013) and *Downton Abbey* (ITV, 2010–15) to *Abraham Lincoln: Vampire Hunter* (2012). Acknowledging that many contemporary historical fictions are easy to disregard as 'excessive, unrealistic, sensationalist, experimental, pulp, cheap, or popular', De Groot (2016: 2) also emphasizes how they

> open up discursive spaces where ideas about the past, desire, time, horror, nationhood, identity, chaos, legitimacy, and historical authority are debated .... Fundamental to the purpose of these works are just the qualities that are often disregarded ... their 'perversity', in contrast to the rationalism expected of true historical engagement.

Critically engaged with its 'perversity', De Groot argues for screen entertainment's role in those wide-ranging social and cultural processes where time gains sense and meaning to become history.

An emergent awareness of and insistence upon the contribution that alternative modes of historical engagement might make have prompted a range of creative interventions through screen horror, as well as ground-breaking academic analyses. Adam Lowenstein's (2005) *Shocking Representation* and Linnie Blake's (2008) *The Wounds of Nations* reflect on how screen horrors might expose the limits of dominant ideologies and historical verities in service of the nation. Working through various national contexts, with an emphasis on cultural wounds of war, Lowenstein (2005) closely analyses how twentieth-century horror films and other filmic evocations of the horrific have engaged with historical trauma. Pursuing his concept of an aesthetic of 'shock', Lowenstein sees these cinematic horrors as a way of giving voice to 'unspeakable' historical events through allegory, drawing on Walter Benjamin's (2020 [1989]) notion of how *Jetztzeit*, or 'now-time', might 'blast open the continuum of history'. Similarly, Blake (2008) draws on the interdisciplinary field of trauma studies to discuss genre films from Japan, Germany, the United States and the UK, and their response to legacies of the Second World War, the Vietnam War and 9/11. Importantly, in contrast to the narrative and textual character of the historical imagination as theorized by Hayden White, Blake (2008: 189) emphasizes how screen horror, unlike 'more "respectable" branches of the culture industry', can offer 'a visceral and frequently non-linguistic lexicon' to challenge 'culturally sanctioned silence'. This argument is taken up by Briefel and Miller (2011) and Kevin Wetmore (2012), whose works – like Blake's *The Wounds of Nations* – engage with 9/11's impact on horror, and how horror might implicitly or explicitly provide a framework for negotiating its traumas.

A number of the chapters in this collection return to and look closely at screen horror's treatment of national wounds and traumas – those brought about by war, but also the challenges and transformations of modernization and globalization, the lingering impacts of colonialism and other sources of social and political repression and dislocation, oppression and abuse. Others reflect more broadly on how concerns about history have been woven into the fabric of screen entertainments – for instance, in the televisual building of worlds that speak, through horror and the past to the anxious and unsettled present of their audiences. Therefore, as 'perverse' as the cinematic and televisual fictions explored by this collection may be in their various engagements with history, they nevertheless form part of what Jörn Rüsen (2002: 3) calls 'historical culture', that 'totality of discourses in which a society understands itself and its future by interpreting its past'. As Rüsen (2005: 1) elaborates, these discursive engagements are not just a matter of 'historical studies', but 'an essential cultural factor in everybody's life'. Horror's imaginative uses of the past are clearly part of a broad trend towards increased commodification of history in entertainment cultures, but they also form a significant part of those public discourses of history likewise on the rise during this century, reshaping popular understandings of the present and future through the lens of the past.

Transnational trends in twenty-first-century horror

Horror has long been one of the most lucrative genres of screen entertainment (Gomery 1996: 49), with global popularity and a transnational aesthetic evident in its patterns of influence, adaptation and reinvention from the silent era onwards. Distinctively, however, the twenty-first century has witnessed a significant boom in horror production worldwide. Annual production grew from 200 films in 2000 to more than 1,000 as of 2016, with significantly more horror films showing a profit globally than other popular genres (Follows 2017: 8, 193). Global horror production has long been dominated by the United States – and still is – but one can no longer say, as Graeme Turner (1993) once did in the Australian context, 'Genres are American', thanks to what *Variety* dubbed the 'G-boom' (Hopewell 2008). This 'G-boom' produced Spain's 'Creepwave' of horror production (Hopewell 2008), Canada's 'mini boom' of horror (Kelly 2010) and the opening of Latin America's 'Blood Window' – the horror-focused niche of its *Ventana Sur* (Southern Window) movie market (Hopewell 2013). In the wake of what Dana Och and Kirsten Strayer (2014: 1) observe to be an 'explosion of non-Hollywood, national or regional successes', they see screen horror transformed by transnational circuits of influence, 'a constant flow of affinities and ideas'. This can be seen in both a Hollywood cycle of Asian horror remakes (Choi and Wada-Marciano 2009), and the way its own generic tropes have been recirculated and reimagined in the horror productions of diverse national cinemas during this period. Such transnational interdependencies have been heightened by what Jon Towlson (2021) identifies as the increasingly globalized character of media companies, with co-production encouraged by funding bodies such as the Council of Europe's Eurimages.

Developments in distribution and exhibition sectors have further intensified opportunities for transnational exchange and global consumption, reshaping horror productions and their place in screen cultures. A proliferation of international festivals devoted to horror, such as ScreamFest LA (founded in 2001), Australia's A Night of Horror International Film Festival (founded in 2007), Nightmares Film Festival and GenreBlast (both founded in 2016), to name just a few, has served as both marketplaces and sites for fostering filmmaker and fan communities. One outcome of this has been the 'rise of the female horror filmmaker-fan' (Sonia Lupher 2020: 223), as exemplified by Aislinn Clarke, the first Irish woman to direct a feature-length horror film, *The Devil's Doorway* (2018), discussed in Chapter 6. Parallel to the boom in horror cinema, production of horror television has also increased, largely due to a period of unprecedented growth in US-produced scripted television (Press 2018). And, making this growing volume of globally produced screen horror available to world audiences, video-on-demand services and specialist Blu-ray and DVD labels have opened new exhibition windows over the last two decades. Netflix in particular has positioned itself as a 'global network' expanding to 190 countries as of 2019 (Gaynor 2022: 121), giving audiences access to an international mix of horrific entertainments (Abbott and Jowett 2021: 5) including *The Witcher*, an adaptation of the popular Polish fantasy franchise discussed in Chapter 8. Likewise, new dedicated streaming services for horror have also contributed to growth of its transnational screen cultures. For instance, Koji Shiraishi's 2005 *Noroi: The Curse*, discussed in Chapter 5, was mostly just known in the West by reputation before Shudder acquired it as a streaming title in 2017.

These increases in and diversifications of production, distribution and exhibition have resulted in 'intensified critical engagement with horror cinema' (Falvey, Wroot and Hickinbottom 2021: 2), lending a newly prominent role in expanded public spheres to what has often been regarded as niche entertainment. Contributing to this trend is the unexpected international crossover success of two critically lauded and widely discussed films, *Pan's Labyrinth* (2006) and

Let the Right One In (2008), both credited with galvanizing horror production regionally and abroad (Hopewell 2008; Rehlin 2009). Confirming the importance of generic innovation and variation to screen horror's marketable pleasures (Hills 2005), both films weave a path between the local and the global, the art-house niche and commercial entertainments, challenging conventional boundaries between art and genre-based storytelling and aesthetics to capture international audiences. Notably, in their focus on child protagonists, both speak to what Rosalind Galt and Karl Schoonover (2010: 15) see as contemporary art cinema's inherited 'moral prerogative' towards 'representation of the underrepresented' and 'embrace [of] the socially excluded'. This is particularly important to the reimagining of the Spanish Civil War in *Pan's Labyrinth*, where horror's ability to speak to history results in not just a perverse, but a distinctly 'disobedient', account of the past (Orme 2010), resistant to the fascist, Francoist, dominance of Spain's historical narrative which demanded the silencing of the Republican dead. By emphasizing horror's power to speak to history here and in its 2001 'sibling', *The Devil's Backbone*, their writer-director Guillermo del Toro has played a key role in bringing horror's historiographic potential to public attention worldwide.

In response to these and other innovative productions, labels such as 'art horror', 'art house horror', 'elevated horror', 'smart horror', 'prestige horror' and the somewhat counter-intuitive 'post-horror' (Church 2021) have become commonplace in critical and reception discourses since the 2010s. These descriptors assert the hybrid character of high-profile horror productions, and insist on their prestige, while keeping in view horror's long-standing reputation as 'the most disreputable of the genres' (Wood 2018: 41). This book includes discussions of film and television productions marketed explicitly in such terms, notably Babak Anvari's *Under the Shadow* (2016) in Chapter 4 and *Twin Peaks: The Return*, the series for which the term 'art-house tv' was coined (Lyons 2017; Nordine 2016), in Chapter 9. However, perhaps most significant to the work undertaken in this collection is not so much the prestige of such labels, but rather how they draw attention to those features that arthouse and horror cinemas have long held in common. As Joan Hawkins' (2000) study *Cutting Edge*, which looks at alignments between arthouse and grindhouse entertainments through the lens of cult fandoms, makes clear, art and horror cinemas share a similar reputation for endeavouring to represent the unrepresentable by exploring the uncensored and the forbidden. Expanding on Hawkins' argument in their reflection on the 'impurity' of contemporary art cinema, Galt and Schoonover (2010: 15) usefully observe the way that 'the industrial history of exploitation and titillation intersects with textual strategies of realism, grounding art cinema's theoretical claims to truth in the revelation of the imperilled or impassioned body'. The insights of these scholars point to how, even in its seemingly least 'elevated', most disreputably exploitative and confrontational forms of violence and gore, horror – like art cinema – can engage with historical experience outside the comfort zone of the mainstream by asserting its own form of embodied truths. Though certainly no grindhouse film, we see this impulse at work in del Toro's use of horror to transform the conventionally family-friendly fairy-tale film into a darkly confrontational counter-history of the Spanish Civil War in *Pan's Labyrinth*. Likewise, films not so self-consciously aimed at historical trauma in the manner of del Toro's might nevertheless also speak to history through confronting violence and the visceral obsessions of body horror, as evidenced by controversial Serbian productions *The Life and Death of a Porno Gang* and *A Serbian Film*, which are the focus of Chapter 14.

Horror and history in Guillermo del Toro's Spanish Civil War films

In the midst of these larger developments, del Toro's films *The Devil's Backbone* and *Pan's Labyrinth* are significant for the way they drew popular attention to horror's capacity to engage with history, to make its silences speak, and bring these concerns into the public sphere. Both rework generic tropes popularized by Hollywood to engage with concerns at the forefront of public consciousness during Spain's 'memory boom' at the end of the 1990s, which was driven by rising popular concern with those lost to Francoist political violence – 'the disappeared'. Anticipating the trauma-focused work of scholars Lowenstein and Blake a few years later, del Toro's 2001 film *The Devil's Backbone* speaks to Spain's traumatic relationship with the Civil War through the Gothic trope of haunting and the ominous image of an unexploded bomb. Commencing with the open question 'What is a ghost?', *Backbone* uses Gothic horror to remember the forgotten and avenge the murdered. Never closing these wounds of the war, its image of the ghost instead insists that there is 'something still unsymbolized about national history' (Brinks 2004: 308). Refusing in this way the assurances of what Greil Marcus (1995: 18) describes in *The Dustbin of History* as history's 'smooth surface' where 'everything makes sense', del Toro's film deliberately uses Gothic uncertainties and anxieties to make a different sort of sense of Spanish national identity in its relation to the past (Ibarra 2012: 58).

The Devil's Backbone garnered critical acclaim after its world premiere at the Toronto Film Festival on 9 September 2001, but its success was immediately overshadowed by 9/11 – that moment of rupture in the narrative of Western culture, when history itself seemed near collapse. Del Toro recalls, on seeing the attack on the Twin Towers, feeling that 'everything I had to say about brutality and innocence, about war and innocence became obsolete' (quoted in Haddu 2014: 152), and explains that *Pan's Labyrinth*, with its heroically resistant, dying girl protagonist, came out of these feelings. Where *The Devil's Backbone* locates its exploration of a violent past in the figure of the ghost as something suspended in time, 'a fly in amber', the entire narrative of *Pan's Labyrinth* appears to be played out in the moment of a child's death. Within her death-dream, the war film's historical verisimilitude and fairy tale fantasy entwine in parallel narratives of Republican guerrilla action against the Francoist state, and childish resistance to monstrous appetites, cruelties and violence – both equally horror-filled modes of storytelling, both equally valid in narrating a doomed, idealistic refusal to capitulate. Through its hybridized account of the past, it leverages the abject possibilities of fairy-tale horrors against the fascist project of what Captain Vidal (Sergi Lopez) describes as 'a clean, new Spain', to 'propose a reconfigured social response to the past' (Ibarra 2013: 153). In the wake of *Pan's Labyrinth*'s international success, in interviews del Toro emphasized the political nature of horror and its status as an 'underestimated genre' with an 'important cultural and social function' (quoted in Merin 2006).

As in the case of Peele's *Get Out* a decade later, *Pan's Labyrinth* sparked both public debate and a significant cycle of scholarship centred on the political, cultural and historiographic role of fantasy and horror. The significance of the film was heightened by the timing of its release during debates over Spain's controversial 'Ley de Memoria Histórica' (Historical Memory Law), passed in 2007. Condemning Francoist repression and recognizing victims on both sides of the Civil War, similar to the legislative outcomes of 'truth commissions' established across the globe at the turn of the millennium, the law's aim was recuperative remembering for the purpose of reconciliation as the social and political means of moving forward, collectively, into the future. Del Toro's Spanish Civil War films are very much framed by similar goals: through horror and fantasy, they make an account of Spain's violent history; through child protagonists and victims, they return the Republican dead to memory and register the need for justice and peace. But with their images of repetition and suspension in time, and especially in their emphasis on recurrent cycles of innocent suffering (Brown

2015: 71–2), they focus on traumas that are not entirely reconcilable – that cannot entirely be contained by a revised national history or consigned to the past. Similarly, as discussed in Chapter 2, Australian Blak Wave writer-director Warwick Thornton's 'uncanny disruptions to the iconography of colonization' (Collins 2017) in *The Darkside* (2013), *Firebite* (2021–22) and *The New Boy* (2023) speak to those longstanding traumas, unresolved political tensions and divergent temporalities that shape the relationship between the settler nation and Indigenous Australia.

The structure of this book

Part One: Spectral encounters and haunted histories

The first three chapters in this book deal with ghosts and spirit worlds, recalling the Gothic tradition where a monstrous past hauntingly lingers on, but also where spectral interventions can signify and speak to alienation and 'indicate a certain disaffection with the present' (Botting 1996: 83). In Chapter 2, Felicity Collins reflects on how Thornton's conjuring of ghosts, vampires and supernatural mysteries in *The Darkside*, *Firebite* and *The New Boy* seeks to engage a new audience for Australian Blak Wave productions, one that is open to their spectres of difference. In Chapter 3, Simon Bacon considers Takashi Shimizu's recent trilogy of films *Howling Village* (2019), *Suicide Forest Village* (2021) and *Ox-Head Village* (2022) whose hauntings, based on popular urban legends, speak to the disconnect between modern Japan and the rural traditions of the past, identified with a land animated by human and ecological trauma. Both Collins and Bacon address ghosts and spirits which haunt and possess spaces that consequently cannot be entirely colonized, secularized or modernized. But as David Ellison and Zach Karpinellison point out in Chapter 4, the *djinn* in Anvari's *Under the Shadow* plays a rather different role, as the supernatural means by which not just a space or dwelling but the entire idea of home is transformed by the traumas and dislocations of diaspora.

Part Two: Found-footage horrors

Found-footage is a sub-genre of horror that both invokes and undermines empiricist epistemologies associated with practices of history by making the material of documentation, of evidence itself a source of horror – a variation on the genre's longstanding interest in destabilizing the image in order to strike terror in the viewer. The chapters in this section speak to how these particular qualities of found-footage might serve as the basis for horror's engagement with traumatic national histories. In Chapter 5, reading Shiraishi's *Noroi: The Curse* in terms of what Ayelet Zohar calls 'performative recollection', Jeremy Kingston argues for it as the means of 'memory-work', wherein video footage constitutes a performative third-space of recollection, generating dialogic encounters with what has been lost or silenced in Japan's path to modernization and secularization. In Chapter 6, Stephen Joyce coins the term 'congruent apprehensions' and, using Clarke's *The Devil's Doorway* as a case study, explores how structures of meaning making in found-footage horror might align – or prove 'congruent' – with those required to uncover, comprehend and communicate the traumatic history of Ireland's Magdalene institutions.

Part Three: History and horror in televisual storyworlds

The most visible result of this century's boom in scripted television has been a marked increase in so-called quality or prestige TV, characterized by narrative complexity, high production values, knowing engagements with literary or screen entertainments of the past, and a brand of thematic sophistication that translates into 'darkness literal and figurative' (Wildermuth 2019). This recurrent darkness of tone, theme and imagery allows horror a newly important role in a range of televisual offerings, including but not limited to what Janani Subramanian and Jorie Lagerwey (2016: 181) dub 'quality TV horror'. In this section, contributors attend to how connections between history and horror are foundational to the storyworlds of a range of television offerings. In Chapter 7, Stephanie Green draws on Marcia Landy's (2015) concept of 'counter-history' to reflect on how a combination of densely textured authenticity and expressionist theatricality shapes the horror-shaded neo-Victorian worlds of *Penny Dreadful* (2014–16) and sci-fi fantasy *The Nevers* (2021) whose narrative conflicts are at once historical yet also uncannily prescient of contemporary social concerns. In Chapter 8, Agnieszka Stasiewicz-Bieńkowska details how themes of history, memory and a haunting past pervade and serve as an organizing principle in the storyworld of Netflix's adaptation of Polish fantasy franchise, *The Witcher*, whose narrative structure relies on a Gothic sense of the past as a violent and threatening space of horror. In Chapter 9, Martin Fradley and John A. Riley address the long-awaited third season of *Twin Peaks: The Return*, which, in contrast to the playfully apolitical and archly post-modernist original series, uses horror tropes and imagery – from *doppelgängers* to gory violence to Lovecraftian grotesquerie and paranormal phenomena – to interrogate American socio-political realities.

Part Four: Female monsters and revolting women

In this section, female monsters with activist – and apocalyptic – aims conjure alternative views of the past and future when the oppressed return and the downtrodden rise. In Chapter 10, Amanda Howell reads the *doppelgänger* horror of Jordan Peele's *Us* – with its twinned monstrous mothers – through the lens of its historical allusions to New Hollywood film and Reagan-era social movements as an allegory for those oppositional logics of poverty inherited from the past that govern America's understanding of itself in the present. In Chapter 11, Anthea Taylor engages with *Penny Dreadful*'s reimagining of Mary Shelley's never-finished bride of Frankenstein, viewing her as a reanimation of radical feminism and her increasingly apocalyptic story arc as the means of opening a dialogue between the present day and what Taylor identifies as the 'unfinished business of second-wave feminism'.

Part Five: Engaging the past through body horror

In this final section, our contributors address *Dying Breed*, *Overlord* and the controversial and confrontational *The Life and Death of a Porno Gang* and *A Serbian Film* as harrowingly visceral responses to traumatic national histories. In Chapter 12, Clare Burnett reads *Dying Breed* – which focuses on the cannibalistic descendants of Irish convict Alexander Pearce – as both an example of 'Ozploitation' horror exporting monstrous images of Australian larrikinism, and evidence of Australian cinema's new willingness to put the darker, more violent aspects of its settler colonial past on screen for a global audience. While Burnett views the inbred Pearce clan of *Dying Breed* as the embodiment of a warped alternative history of Australia, overwriting Indigenous histories with monstrous white victims, in Chapter 13 Brian Crim considers a different sort of alternative history in the revisionist 'Nazisploitation' film *Overlord* which offers a monstrous revision of the Invasion of Normandy. Unlike earlier Nazisploitation fare, Crim argues, its aims are deliberately anti-fascist and a timely counterpoint to resurgent white supremacism in the Trump era. In the final chapter of the collection, Andrija Filipović speaks to how controversial horror films *The*

Life and Death of a Porno Gang and *A Serbian Film* speak in different ways to the excesses of Serbian history, viscerally expressing the cruel 'exhaustion' of Serbia's body politic in a period of increased social and economic precarity and inequality.

Together, these chapters explore horror's ability to speak to the unspoken, pushing the boundaries and probing the faultlines and ideological impositions of historical narrative. From spectral occupation to the visceral threat of body trauma, and from repressed social identities to the ruptures and impositions of nationhood, these discussions consider how twenty-first-century screen horror reimagines the past's relationship with the present. Trauma is a key theme in this book, examined through screen stories of war, ghostly invasion, institutionalized abuse, colonialization and environmental destruction. Underlying these concerns is the spectre of perpetual apocalypse, whether characterized as a close sense of impending doom or as the legacy of its aftermath. A trope that has long haunted the horror narrative, giving 'symbolic form to universal human fears' (Clasen 2010: 314), it has persistently reshaped our understanding of the past's relationship with the future, evoking the terrors of humanity's worst actions, but with the capacity to prompt us towards the powers and possibilities of our communal lives.

References

Abbott, S. and L. Jowett (2021), *Global TV Horror*, Cardiff: University of Wales Press.

Abdul-Jabbar, K. (2017), 'Why *Get Out* Is *Invasion of the Black Body Snatchers* for the Trump Era', *Hollywood Reporter*, 17 March. Available online: https://www.hollywoodreporter.com/tv/tv-news/kareem-abdul-jabbar-why-get-is-invasion-black-body-snatchers-trump-985449 (accessed 1 July 2023).

Benjamin, W. (2020 [1989]), 'Theses on the Philosophy of History', in *Critical Theory and Society: A Reader*, edited by S.E. Bronner and D. M. Kellner, 255–63, London: Routledge.

Blake, L. (2008), *The Wounds of Nations: Horror Cinema, Historical Trauma, and National Identity*, Manchester: Manchester University Press.

Botting, F. (1996), *Gothic*, London: Routledge.

Briefel, A. and S.J. Miller (eds) (2011), *Horror after 9/11: World of Fear, Cinema of Terror*, Austin, TX: University of Texas Press.

Brinks, E. (2004), '"Nobody's Children": Gothic Representation and Traumatic History in *The Devil's Backbone*', *JAC*, 24 (2): 291–312.

Brown, K. (2015), '"Time Out of Joint": Traumatic Hauntings in the Spanish Civil War Films', in *The Supernatural Cinema of Guillermo del Toro: Critical Essays*, edited by J.W. Morehead, 58–75, Jefferson, NC: McFarland.

Choi, J. and M. Wada-Marciano (eds) (2009), *Horror to the Extreme: Changing Boundaries in Asian Cinema*, Hong Kong: Hong Kong University Press.

Church, D. (2021), *Post-Horror: Art, Genre and Cultural Elevation*, Edinburgh: Edinburgh University Press.

Clasen, M. (2010), 'Vampire Apocalypse: A Biocultural Critique of Richard Matheson's *I Am Legend*', *Philosophy and Literature*, 34 (2): 313–28.

Collins, F. (2017), 'Disturbing the Peace: The Ghost in *beDevil* and *The Darkside*', *Critical Arts*, 31 (5): 107–13.

De Groot, J. (2009), *Consuming History: Historians and Heritage in Contemporary Popular Culture*, New York: Routledge.

De Groot, J. (2016), *Remaking History: The Past in Contemporary Historical Fictions*, New York: Routledge.

Falvey, E., J. Wroot and J. Hickinbottom (2021), *New Blood: Critical Approaches to Contemporary Horror*, Chicago: Chicago University Press.

Follows, S. (2017), *The Horror Report*, N.P. Film Data Fund. Available online: https://stephenfollows.com/reports/the-horror-report (accessed 1 July 2023).

Galt, R. and K. Schoonover (2010), 'Introduction: The Impurity of Art Cinema', in *Global Art Cinema: New Theories and Histories*, edited by R. Galt and K. Schoonover, 3–28, Oxford: Oxford University Press.

Gaynor, S.M. (2022), *Rethinking Horror in the New Economies of Television*, London: Palgrave Macmillan.

Gomery, D. (1996), 'The Economics of the Horror Film', in *Horror Films: Current Research on Audience Preferences and Reactions*, edited by J.B. Weaver and R. Tamborini, 49–62, New York: Routledge.

Haddu, M. (2014), 'Reflected Horrors: Violence, War, and the Image in Guillermo del Toro's *El espinazo del diablo/The Devil's Backbone* (2001)', in *The Transnational Fantasies of Guillermo del Toro*, edited by A Davies, D. Shaw and D. Tierney, 143–59, New York: Palgrave Macmillan.

Harris, B. (2017), 'The Giant Leap Forward of Jordan Peele's *Get Out*', *The New Yorker*, 4 March. Available online: https://www.newyorker.com/culture/culture-desk/review-the-giant-leap-forward-of-jordan-peeles-get-out (accessed 1 July 2023).

Hawkins, J. (2000), *Cutting Edge: Art-Horror and the Horrific Avant-Garde*, Minneapolis: University of Minnesota Press.

Hills, M. (2005), *The Pleasures of Horror*, London: Bloomsbury.

Hopewell, J. (2008), 'Spain Turns to Genre, Arthouse Films', *Variety*, 16 May. Available online: https://variety.com/2008/film/markets-festivals/spain-turns-to-genre-arthouse-films-1117985902 (accessed 1 July 2023).

Hopewell, J. (2013), 'Latin American Horror Booming at Blood Window Market', *Variety*, 20 November. Available online: https://variety.com/2013/biz/global/scarefare-surges-in-latin-america-1200857018 (accessed 1 July 2023).

Ibarra, E.A. (2012), 'Permanent Hauntings: Spectral Fantasies and National Trauma in Guillermo del Toro's *El espinazo del diablo* [*The Devil's Backbone*]', *Journal of Romance Studies*, 12 (1): 56–71.

Ibarra, E.A. (2013), 'History through the Fairy Tale', in *Bringing History to Life through Film: The Art of Cinematic Storytelling*, edited by K.A. Morey, 153–70, Lanham, MD: Rowman & Littlefield.

Jenkins, H. (2006), *Convergence Culture: Where Old and New Media Collide*, New York: New York University Press.

Kelly, B. (2010), 'Canadian Horror Hits Mini Boom', *Variety*, 22 January. Available online: https://variety.com/2010/film/news/canadian-horror-hits-mini-boom-1118014116 (accessed 1 July 2023).

Landy, M. (2015), *Cinema & Counter-History*, Bloomington, IN: Indiana University Press.

Lowenstein, A. (2005), *Shocking Representation: Historical Trauma, National Cinema, and the Modern Horror Film*, New York: Columbia University Press.

Lupher, S. (2020), 'The Rise of the Female Horror Filmmaker-Fan', in *Women Make Horror: Filmmaking, Feminism, Genre*, edited by A. Peirse, 222–35. New Brunswick, NJ: Rutgers University Press.

Lyons, M. (2017), 'Art-house TV and the Challenge Facing the New *Twin Peaks*', *The New York Times*, 27 June. Available online: https://www.nytimes.com/2017/06/27/watching/twin-peaks-the-return-episode-8-art-house-tv.html (accessed 1 July 2023).

Marcus, G. (1995), *The Dustbin of History*, Cambridge, MA: Harvard University Press.

Maza, S. (2017), *Thinking about History*, Chicago: University of Chicago Press.

Merin, J. (2006), 'Jennifer Merin Interviews Guillermo del Toro re *Pan's Labyrinth*', *Alliance of Women Film Journalists*, 29 December. Available online: https://awfj.org/blog/2006/12/29/jennifer-merin-interviews-guillermo-del-toro-re-pans-labyrinth (accessed 1 July 2023).

Nordine, M. (2016), 'David Lynch on *Twin Peaks* Return: "Cable Television Is the New Art-House"', *IndieWire*, 22 September. Available online: https://www.indiewire.com/features/general/david-lynch-twin-peaks-return-cable-television-new-art-house-1201729748 (accessed 1 July 2023).

Och, D. and K. Strayer (eds) (2014), *Transnational Horror across Visual Media: Fragmented Bodies*, New York: Routledge.

Orme, J. (2010), 'Narrative Desire and Disobedience in "Pan's Labyrinth"', *Marvels & Tales*, 24 (1): 219–34. Available online: https://www.jstor.org/stable/41388953 (accessed 1 November 2023).

Press, J. (2018), 'Peak TV Is Still Drowning Us in Content, Says TV Prophet John Landgraf', *Vanity Fair*, 3 August. Available online: https://www.vanityfair.com/hollywood/2018/08/peak-tv-fx-john-landgraf-tca-donald-glover-chris-rock (accessed 6 May 2023).

Rehlin, G. (2009), 'Horror Pics Get Swedish Massage', *Variety*, 27 March. Available online: https://variety.com/2009/scene/markets-festivals/horror-pics-get-swedish-massage-1118001772 (accessed 1 July 2023).

Rüsen, J. (2002), *Geschichte im Kulturprozess*, Cologne: Böhlau Books.

Rüsen, J. (2005), *History: Narration, Interpretation, Orientation*, Oxford: Berghahn Books.

Rüsen, J. (2006), 'What Does "Making Sense of History" Mean?' in *Meaning and Representation in History*, edited by J. Rüsen, 1–8, Oxford: Berghahn Books.

Seitz, M.Z. and S. Abrams (2017), *Guillermo Del Toro's The Devil's Backbone*, Berkeley, CA: Insight Editions.

Sobchack, V. (1997), 'The Insistent Fringe: Moving Images and Historical Consciousness', *History and Theory*, 36 (4): 4–20.

Sobchack, V. (ed.) (2013 [1996]), *The Persistence of History: Cinema, Television and the Modern Event*, New York: Routledge.

Staley, D.J. (2020), *Historical Imagination*, London: Routledge.

Subramanian, J. and J. Lagerwey (2016), 'Teen Terrors: Race, Gender, and Horrifying Girlhood in *The Vampire Diaries*', in *Reading in the Dark: Horror in Children's Literature and Culture*, edited by J.R. McCort, 180–200, Jackson, MI: University of Mississippi Press.

Towlson, J. (2021), *Global Horror Cinema Today: 28 Representative Films from 17 Countries*, Jefferson, NC: McFarland.

Turner, G. (1993), 'The Genres Are American: Australian Narrative, Australian Film, and the Problem of Genre', *Literature/Film Quarterly*, 21 (2): 102–11.

Wetmore, K. (2012), *Post-9/11 Horror in American Cinema*, London: Continuum.

White, H. (2014 [1973]), *Metahistory: The Historical Imagination in Nineteenth-century Europe*, Baltimore, MD: Johns Hopkins University Press.

Wildermuth, R. (2019), 'Trauma and Nostalgia: Youth and the Darkness of Quality in Stranger Things', *Refractory: Journal of Entertainment Media*, 26 February. Available online: https://refractoryjournal.net/trauma-and-nostalgia-youth-and-the-darkness-of-quality-in-stranger-things (accessed 31 July 2023).

Wood, R. (2018), *Robin Wood on the Horror Film: Collected Essays and Reviews*, Detroit, MI: Wayne State University Press.

Yuan, J. and H. Harris (2018), 'The First Great Movie of the Trump Era', *Vulture*, 22 February. Available online: https://www.vulture.com/article/get-out-oral-history-jordan-peele.html (accessed 1 July 2023).

Films and television series

Abraham Lincoln: Vampire Hunter (2012), directed by Timur Bekmambetov [film], Los Angeles and Moscow: 20th Century Studios and Bazelevs Company.

The Darkside (2013), directed by Warwick Thornton [film], Sydney: Scarlett Pictures.
The Devil's Backbone (2001), directed by Guillermo del Toro [film], Spain: Canal + España.
The Devil's Doorway (2018), directed by Aislinn Clarke [film], Ireland: 23ten.
Downton Abbey (ITV, 2010–15), produced by Julian Fellowes [TV series], United Kingdom: Carnival Films, WGBH-TV.
Dying Breed (2008), directed by Jody Dwyer [film], Australia: Ambience Entertainment.
Firebite (2021–2), directed by Warwick Thornton and Brendan Fletcher [TV Series], Australia: See-Saw Films.
Get Out (2017), directed by Jordan Peele [film], Los Angeles: Blumhouse Productions and Monkeypaw Productions.
Howling Village [Inunaki Mura] (2019), directed by Takashi Shimizu [film], Tokyo: Toei Company.
I Am Not Your Negro (2016), directed by Raoul Peck [film], United States, Germany: Velvet Film, Artemis Productions, Close Up Films.
Let the Right One In (2008), directed by Tomas Alfredson [film], Sweden: EFTI.
The Life and Death of a Porno Gang (2009), directed by Mladen Đorđević [film], Belgrade, Serbia: Film House Baš Čelik.
The Nevers (2021), directed by Joss Whedon, Phillipa Goslett [television series], United States: HBO.
The New Boy (2023), directed by Warwick Thornton [film], Australia: Dirty Films, Scarlett Pictures.
Noroi: The Curse (2005), directed by Kōji Shiraishi [film], Japan: Xanadeux Company.
Overlord (2018), directed by Julius Avery [film], Hollywood: Paramount Pictures.
Ox-Head Village [Ushikubi-Mura] (2022), directed by Takashi Shimizu [film], Tokyo: Toei Company.
Pan's Labyrinth (2006), directed by Guillermo del Toro [film], Madrid, London, Mexico City: Estudios Picasso and the Tequila Gang.
Penny Dreadful (2014–16), directed by John Logan [TV series], United States: Sky/Atlantic.
Pocahontas (1995), directed by Eric Goldberg and Mike Gabriel [film], Los Angeles: Walt Disney Studios.
Rosemary's Baby (1968), directed by Roman Polanski [film], Hollywood: Paramount Pictures and William Castle Productions.
A Serbian Film (2010), directed by Srđan Spasojević [film], Belgrade: Contra Film Production.
Stepford Wives (1975), directed by Bryan Forbes [film], Los Angeles: Palomar Pictures.
Suicide Forest Village [Jukai Mura] (2021), directed by Takashi Shimizu [film], Tokyo: Toei Company.
12 Years a Slave (2013), directed by Steve McQueen [film], Beverly Hills, CA: Plan B Entertainment.

Twin Peaks: The Return (2017), directed by David Lynch [TV series], New York: Showtime.

Under the Shadow (2016), directed by Babak Anvari [film], London: Wigwam Films.

Us (2019), directed by Jordan Peele [film], Los Angeles: Blumhouse Productions and Monkeypaw Productions.

The Witcher (2019–), produced by Lauren Schmidt Hissrich [TV series], United States, Poland: Little Schmidt Productions, Hivemind.

Part One

Spectral encounters and haunted histories

2

Ghosts, vampires and sacrilege in Warwick Thornton's *The Darkside*, *Firebite* and *The New Boy*

Felicity Collins

When Warwick Thornton's anthology of ghost stories, *The Darkside*, was released in 2013, it took audiences by surprise. When did the telling of ghost stories become so intimate, so tender? Where were the scary stories from Indigenous Australia that would haunt our dreams, send shivers down our spines and trash our belief systems? For Thornton, telling ghost stories in *The Darkside* is about 'a connection we have to keep to be Aboriginal … to appease ancestors … and keep collectively strong', while 'showing non-Indigenous people the way … reconciling from the other side' (*AWAYE!* 2013).

If fear and repulsion, rather than tenderness and connection, are what we seek, why have we been slow to embrace *Firebite*, Thornton's deep dive (with Brendan Fletcher) into the vampire genre, streamed on AMC+ in 2021? Surely the occupation of Coober Pedy's underground caves and mineshafts by the last of the vampires (rumoured to have arrived in Australia in 1788 with the First Fleet), and the emergence of Tyson (Rob Collins) and Shanika (Shantae Barnes-Cowan) as charismatic vampire-slayers, offers a fresh take on both the vampire genre and the genocidal violence of British colonization of country belonging to Aboriginal and Torres Strait Islander peoples?

And what are we to make of Thornton's third feature film, *The New Boy* (2023), set in an isolated monastery facing a numinous horizon of golden wheatfields, where the eerie sense of spaciousness is enhanced by the film's soundtrack, composed by Nick Cave and Warren Ellis? How might we understand the opaque world of an Aboriginal boy (Aswan Reid) who arrives in a hessian sack and brings his wordless perceptions to bear on the religious icons and furtive rituals that preoccupy heretical nun Sister Eileen (Cate Blanchett)? Is there room in our secular twenty-first-century imaginary for this fragmented, allegorical retelling of a Stolen Generations story set in the 1940s?

The Blak Wave, a hungry public and agonistic politics

In *The Darkside*, *Firebite* and *The New Boy*, Warwick Thornton wields the camera as a technology of the fantastic. He follows in the footsteps of Tracey Moffatt, who broke new ground with *Nice Coloured Girls* (1987) and *Night Cries: A Rural Tragedy* (1990), combining realism and melodrama to create uncanny disruptions to the iconography of colonization and its persistence into the twentieth century. Moffatt's two short films laid the groundwork for *beDevil* (1993), a feature-length trilogy of ghost stories that bring an aura of unreality to contemporary sites of colonization, including Sydney's Kings Cross, a railway track and weatherboard house in outback Australia, a murky swamp troubling a modern housing estate on Bribie Island and unhappy spirits refusing to vacate a derelict warehouse district ripe for development. While Moffatt's shift in the 1990s from filmmaking to the production of photographic artworks and site-specific installations has enabled her to address international and Australian art worlds – most recently with *Portals* (2019) and *A Haunting* (2021–3) – a new public has emerged in Australia, 'hungry' for the Blak Wave of screen production (*AWAYE!* 2013). This 'hungry public' has taken shape slowly over three decades, in response not only to the Blak Wave but also to feature films by non-Indigenous filmmakers that revise key tropes in the settler-colonial imaginary – notably, a frontier hanging in *The Tracker* (2002), stolen children on the run in *Rabbit-Proof Fence* (2002) and the flogging of an Irish convict in *The Proposition* (2005).

Alongside settler colonial revisions of the past on screen, The Blak Wave and its 'hungry public' emerged in constellation with a series of paradigm-shifting political events: the 1992 High Court's *Mabo* decision recognizing native title; the 1990s Decade of Reconciliation; the 1997 *Bringing Them Home* report on the Stolen Generations (Human Rights Commission 1997) and the long-delayed 2008 apology; and, most recently, the *Uluru Statement from the Heart* (2017), advocating for Voice, Treaty and Truth, rejected outright by conservative forces within the media and the Turnbull government (2015–18). At the time of writing, the Albanese Labor government (elected in 2022) has announced the 2023 referendum on a constitutionally enshrined Aboriginal and Torres Strait Islander Voice to Parliament. In tandem with these events in the political sphere, an unprecedented shift has taken place in Australian screen culture during the decades that separate Moffatt's *beDevil*, Thornton's *The Darkside* and the ground-breaking television series, *Redfern Now* (Blackfella Films, 2012, 2013, 2015).

In the decades since *beDevil* challenged cinema audiences to look with new eyes, a Blak Wave of film and television production has produced a new public, open to an 'agonistic' or 'performative politics of conflicting perspectives' (Collins 2016, 2017: 109). In Andrew Schaap's (2005: 67) words, what defines an agonistic politics is 'an openness and ongoing responsiveness to others and to the world, a willingness to share the world with different others'. Moreover, what agonism values is not the instrumental or expressive act, but rather 'its revelatory quality, its power to illuminate our life in common' (Schaap 2005: 67). However, a 'life in common' cannot be taken for granted in settler-colonial nations. Drawing on her family's long involvement with Warlpiri and Walmajarri communities in Central and Northern Australia, artist and writer Kim Mahood (2015: 50) insists on 'the spectre of differences' that cannot presume a 'life in common' between urban Australia and remote Aboriginal Australia, 'where cultural beliefs include the primacy of sorcery and the imperative of payback, where the landscape is seething with presences that are mischievous at best and malevolent at worst'. Rather than two worlds, 'what Mahood gives us is three worlds: a white Australia attempting to intervene in a black Australia that has enough on its plate dealing with kinship, law, and country, as well as a pressing world of sorcery, spirits and ancestors' (Collins 2017: 110).

How, then, might we conceive of the Blak Wave of screen production as a space where 'a white Australia', 'a black Australia' and 'a pressing world of sorcery, spirits and ancestors' might converge? Here, I draw on Bonnie Honig's (2013: 60) argument that, in response to capitalism's catastrophic forms of exclusion – including colonial dispossession, assimilation and genocide – we need new 'public things' around which to gather. In what follows, I argue that Thornton's ghost stories in *The Darkside*, vampire hunters in *Firebite* and discordant encounters with the sacred in *The New Boy* have brought something new and unexpected to the Blak Wave of screen production. Moving between genres and platforms, Thornton's conjuring of ghosts, vampires and the sacred enables mediated access for Indigenous and non-Indigenous publics to counterworlds – while insisting on the brief tenancy of the settler-colonial state and the enduring temporality of Indigenous polities (Collins 2017: 112).

In the remainder of this chapter, I explore the unreconciled or 'fugitive energies' (Hirsch 2012: 93) of colonization that give rise to three ghost stories performed by Sacha Horler, Romaine Moreton and Jack Charles in *The Darkside*. I then engage with anti-colonial vampire slayers Tyson and Shanika in *Firebite*, a series developed by Thornton and Fletcher, and produced by See-Saw Films (a British-Australian company) for streaming on the American platform AMC+. Finally, I delve into how Thornton's third feature film, *The New Boy*, tests my capacity to distinguish sacrilege from the sacred in an allegorical narrative featuring a captive Aboriginal boy and a nonconformist Catholic nun.

Retelling ghost stories in *The Darkside*

Twenty years after the 1993 release of Moffatt's *beDevil*, Thornton's *The Darkside* offered a 'hungry public' an anthology of thirteen performances selected from 150 audio-recordings of ghost stories submitted to *The Otherside*. In an interview with the National Film and Sound Archive (https://www.nfsa.gov.au/latest/darkside-force), Thornton talks about growing up 'with spirits and ancestors around you always'. He describes 'sitting under a tree, telling a story [for] ... the next generation' as the inspiration for keeping storytelling in *The Darkside* 'simple' and 'much more truthful'. Selecting thirteen stories from 150 audio-recordings involved condensing the original stories 'to make them flow in a three-act structure'. On bringing actors, locations and a visual track to transcripts of the audio-recordings, Thornton said, 'The stories told me how they should be directed and portrayed.' On working as a director with professional actors retelling ten of the thirteen stories to camera, he said:

> I had a little bit of phobia towards actors, so I thought the best way to go through 'rehab' ... was to cast ten of the best in Australia and work with them. They're all very different ... so being able to direct them was a fantastic workshop and learning curve for me.
>
> (NFSA 2023)

The actors 'were given the original recording so they could hear the voice' and keep the truth of the original storytellers in the re-scripted version. Thornton also discloses that 'the locations where we filmed weren't really the locations in the stories, but they had their own vibes. Old hospitals, cliff tops looking over the sea, etc.'

Of the thirteen ghost stories featured in *The Darkside*, I have selected two performed by professional actors and one narrated in voice-over by a writer-scholar. I begin with non-Indigenous actor Sacha Horler, who performs Kim's story standing on a shadowy beach with the sea and cliffs behind her. Addressing the camera, Kim grapples with a question her sister and brother-in-law have refused to countenance: who was here before the 'original white people' (including her brother-in-law's family) who came down from Adelaide to the Yorke Peninsula and 'settled in the area'? Off camera, we hear director Thornton respond, 'They *call* it settling.' Kim continues: 'I kept asking [and they kept saying] "No, no one was here". I didn't feel like that was right ... there had probably been massacres on the Yorke Peninsula ... you know, like everywhere else in Australia.' The frame cuts from a long shot to a close-up of Kim as she confesses to 'a feeling, you know, that something had happened ... in their family's past, what with claiming the land'.

Kim's hesitant storytelling continues in long shot. We hear that, on a cold and beautiful night, she wakes up and goes outside to the toilet. The clouds have cleared and for a minute Kim just stands there, looking. 'And all of a sudden these people started to appear.' In close-up, Kim says, 'I wasn't scared or anything. It was more like, oh, there you are ... I knew you were there. So, thank you.' She continues, 'Even as I was looking at them I was thinking that something had happened to them, you know. So, yeah.' Wind ruffles her hair as Kim attempts to describe the 'main fellow' in front, a woman nearby and boys and girls to the side. In a medium-long shot, she says, 'They sort of appeared, stayed there for a while and then just faded out.' Kim pauses, arms folded and head to one side, in shadow. She adds, 'And I had the sense that this was their country.' Off camera, Thornton responds, 'And you wanted to know.' In medium close-up, Kim returns to the question of denial, 'How could there be no one?' The frame shifts to a medium-long shot, and Kim is emboldened to say, 'From what people have told me, the ancestors chose to show themselves to me because I was curious.' Hands in pockets, she concludes, 'I'm just lucky ... I guess. So, it was a real honour. Yeah.'

My second storyteller is Indigenous writer and scholar Romaine Moreton, who does not appear on screen but narrates the story of her violent encounter with the ghost of Colin MacKenzie (former Head of the Australian Institute of Anatomy), in a building that now houses the National Film and Sound Archive (NFSA). We learn that in 2009 Moreton was doing research at the NFSA and living next door, in MacKenzie's former house. Watching film footage passing through an editing machine and being loaded onto a projector, we hear Moreton say, 'I got to learn more about this man, Colin MacKenzie ... then, more and more, I felt like I was being watched.' Off screen, Thornton comments, 'Studied almost.' Moreton continues:

> Each night I was terrified to go to sleep. It had built up so much, the energy around Colin MacKenzie and his work. [On screen, blinding lights begin to flash] And I was dozing in and out of sleep. I saw this man walking towards me. He just got closer and closer ... and he walked into my room. And in his right hand he had a scalpel. And he raised his hand and he sliced the scalpel through my body ... I jolted awake. From that moment on, the research I was originally there to do changed.

As Moreton recounts her discovery of McKenzie's anatomical dissection of the bodies of Aboriginal people, and the storage of their skeletal remains in what is now the NSFA, we are shown (projected into a small space at the centre of a large screen) archival footage of scientists taking physical measurements of the body of a woman and making a plaster cast of the head of a young man. We hear Moreton, off camera, speaking to Thornton, beside the camera, about the 'yet to be repatriated remains of Indigenous people' now sitting in storage containers in the National Museum of Australia. Moreton says, 'To me those voices are clear.' Thornton responds, 'Yeah, it is searching for connection.' Moreton responds, voice breaking, 'They've got to be returned home.' The screen fills with the flashing light of a projector, and Moreton says: 'This awful thing of having a scalpel cut through my body, being jarred awake by Colin MacKenzie led me on this path ... to the very people [who needed to be heard]. [I need] to work harder to take them home.' This most searing of the thirteen ghost stories ends with the image of a skull, flashing urgently in the darkness. In Faye Ginsburg's words, Moreton's 'encounters lead her to a ghostly kinship imaginary, experienced as both immediate and ancestral, summoning up a sense of awe as well as a sense of historical relationship and familial/historical obligation' (Ginsburg 2018: 73).

My third storyteller is Jack Charles, a member of the Stolen Generations and a founder of Indigenous theatre in the 1970s. In the documentary *Bastardy* (2008), he tells his story of juggling addiction and prison time with a long career on stage and screen. He became a much-loved Elder or 'Uncle', whose passing in 2022 was widely mourned. In *The Darkside*, he brings his larrikin and wise-elder qualities to the screen in the role of Ken. A diminutive and compelling figure, Ken sits alone at the bar of an empty pub and tells the story of working as a canecutter, staying in a shed with his wife and being spooked by a light coming down the hill and going back up. The frame shifts to a close-up and Ken describes going up the hill and finding a hut burnt to the ground. A 'fella' at work tells Ken that the husband, his wife and their child were burnt to death. At the bar, in an extreme close-up, Ken says, 'This woman, she was a keen gardener … only young, about twenty when she died.' In a wide shot, we learn from Ken that it was Amelia, his wife, who had brought home the flowers from the top of the hill. In an extreme close-up, Ken tells us he took the flowers, went back up the hill to the abandoned site and said, 'I'm sorry, my wife didn't know what she was doing.' And he 'never saw that light again'. But that is not the end of the episode. In the final wide shot, we become privy to Uncle Jack Charles as a wise Elder who, as he picks up his glass, stands, looks off screen, reaches over the bar and tops up his beer, says:

> So, I believe.
> I believe that when we die
> Our body goes into the ground
> Our soul goes to meet with our creator
> And our spirits remain.
> And I believe that spirit is still around that house
> Because that woman didn't like us taking her flowers.

We pause with Ken as he sips his beer and the episode ends. What remains is the voice, the presence and the enduring spirit of Uncle Jack Charles.

What *The Darkside* offers, then, is a safe holding environment in which to encounter thirteen ghost stories, mediated by Thornton's steady presence off-screen and a sense of our co-presence with the storytellers on-screen. To enter this space is to experience the possibility of listening and hearing across the divide between different polities. Below, I continue with a brief discussion of Thornton's 2021 vampire series, *Firebite* before turning to his 2023 allegorical feature film *The New Boy*. What *Firebite* and *The New Boy* share is the power of 'unreconcilable' or 'fugitive energies' (Hirsch 2012) to disrupt the sense of (or desire for) a shared space and a life-in-common with different polities.

Blood hunters, blood suckers and fugitive energies in *Firebite*

At the time of writing, Trumpian modes of disinformation and scare tactics, together with the emergence of discourses of Indigenous sovereign personhood (as opposed to Australian citizenship) are eroding support for the forthcoming

2023 Referendum on an Aboriginal and Torres Strait Islander Voice to Parliament. In this context, I propose that *Firebite*'s vampire-slayers – the Blood Hunters Tyson (Rob Collins) and Shanika (Shantae Barnes-Cowan) – speak to the unreconciled or 'fugitive energies' of the past that are causing a 'wild and disorderly rupture' (Hirsch 2012: 93) in contemporary Australian politics.

Produced by British-Australian company See-Saw Films, and released on US platform AMC+ in 2021, *Firebite* (Series 1, eight episodes) is currently streaming on the Australian multicultural television platform, SBS On Demand. On working with AMC, Thornton says, 'They [AMC+] knew there was going to be so much shit they do not understand. But what they are good at is story.' As *FilmInk* (2023) comments, *Firebite* is 'very Australian … one character says about the hero Tyson: "He's a dickhead, but he's not an arsehole." It's a compliment.' On *Firebite*'s mix of comedy and violence, Brendan Fletcher says, 'There's anger in this show, "let's just kill them, kill 'em all" … and on the other side of it is "we wanna have fun."' Thornton agrees that *Firebite* offers 'some fun bro' with a mix of 'vampire gothic and real-world outback', 'fast cars' and 'cool weapons'. For viewers, Thornton suggests, it is 'a great '70s rock'n'roll album where you can just dance to it or you can sit down and read the fuckin' lyrics'.

At another level, *Firebite* is a response to British colonization and the belief that in 1788 the First Fleet arrived in Eora country (New South Wales) with eleven vials of smallpox onboard, a claim explored in the archival documentary series, *First Australians* (Rachel Perkins and Beck Cole, 2008). The impact of colonization is given a wider context in the documentation of massacres and frontier violence in *The Australian Wars* (Perkins 2022). In this context, the hunting of vampires in *Firebite* can be viewed, in Thornton and Fletcher's words, as an act of decolonization 'with a very large body count'.

A review in *IndieWire* (Obenson 2021) offers an American lens, recognizing *Firebite* as 'a celebration of Aboriginal agency [and] a biting take on manifest destiny'. As 'a revisionist history tale wrapped in vampire lore', Obenson points out that *Firebite* 'isn't a relitigation of Australia's colonial past or reconciliation with the present. Instead, the series upends Australian history, replacing vials of smallpox with vampires who became addicted to Aboriginal blood and never left.' Obenson concludes, 'It isn't dissimilar from America's history of atrocities committed by non-Indigenous people against Native Americans, with ramifications the country continues to wrestle with today.'

For what follows, I want to borrow the term 'fugitive energies' from Alexander Hirsch (2012: 93), who claims that such energies have the power to transform reconciliation into a 'wild and disorderly rupture' that would allow the victims of atrocity to 'split open the present'. At first viewing, it might seem that *Firebite* is all colour and movement, darkness and light, action and respite, accompanied by a pumping music track and the squeal of car tyres doing wheelies in pools of light. But a closer look at Episode 4, 'Vampire Mythology Bulls**t' and Episode 5, 'I Wanna Go Home', reveals a dynamic between an underground world of 'bleeders' in a labyrinth of caves and mineshafts ruled by ancient vampire King (played by Callan Mulvey) and the desert community above-ground, where survival depends on who you trust among police, teachers, child protection agents, family or the attractive bar staff at the local pub.

In Episode 4, teenage Shanika breaks all the rules, dropping out of school, arming herself with makeshift weaponry (including wooden stakes) and descending alone into Opal City's labyrinth of tunnels and caves that she hopes will lead her to her captive mother, Rona. Her adult protector, Tyson, tracks her down, following her bare footprints into a cave where, together, they are confronted by a monumental wall of white skulls, arranged in the shape of vampire batwings. Climbing the wall-of-skulls in her bare feet, Shanika leads Tyson through a series of caves. Closing in on King's gruesome lair, Shanika and Tyson fight off less-than-human creatures in chains, clash with a lab worker and arrive at their destination, bloodstained and wary, to discover barely human 'bleeders' and a hospital-like space filled with rows of intravenous bags. Their attempt to escape with Shanika's cadaver-like mother, Rona, is foiled by the vampire King (who, mid-battle, fills up on blood from a human wrist). Only Shanika and Tyson make it out, their escape heightened by a pressing mob of cadaverous bodies and blinding lights.

In Episode 5, the vampire world recedes but, above ground in the world of police and welfare, there is no respite to be found. Shanika finds herself in protective custody, where a predatory boy has to be fought off. Meanwhile, haunted by a scene from his past, Tyson gets drunk at the pub, discovers his love-interest, Eleona, is 'one of them', survives a fight and gashes his own forehead with a beer glass, goading a drinker to suck his blood. The episode ends with Shanika, safe at last, in the home of a woman we think she can trust. The woman is called away and the episode ends with Shanika seated on the couch, back to camera. The frame moves and we see a predator approaching from behind and wrapping a yellow cord around Shanika's neck.

Above or below ground, there is no respite from the 'fugitive energies' that haunt Opal City. The ruptured past and the disorderly present offer no prospect of reconciliation or restoration. The only game in town is survival to fight another day. *Firebite* offers Australian viewers, in particular, an immersive experience of a parallel world where a community of bleeders, vampires and blood hunters resonate with frequent news stories of 'remote' communities 'plagued' by youthful gangs roaming the streets after nightfall, on the lookout for high-adrenaline moments, often involving stolen vehicles and police chases. Through a wider lens, *Firebite* insists on the 'unreconciled' or 'fugitive energies' of a haunted history of colonization and resistance – a history that, at the time of writing, seeks to be addressed through processes of treaty-making, truth-telling and an Indigenous Voice to Parliament on Indigenous issues.

Allegorical truth, sacrilege and the sacred in *The New Boy*

My first viewing of *The New Boy* in July 2023 left me, and others seated with me in the cinema, flummoxed. What did we just see? A young Aboriginal boy (Aswan Reid) with a mop of bleached hair, captured (in extreme wide shots) by two men on horses and delivered in a hessian sack to an isolated church-school in the middle of a vast expanse of wheatfields. A dim interior where the new boy makes a space under his dormitory bed for a mattress and the magical circle of light he generates with his fingers. Cate Blanchett in the role of a Catholic nun, concealing the death of a priest and conducting furtive rituals in place of the sacraments that only priests are ordained to deliver. Deborah Mailman in the role of Sister Mum, bereft of her own children while caring for a group of young boys being prepared for work or war. And Kelton Pell in the role of George, taking charge of the boys as they march off into the wheatfields for a day's work, a Sunday picnic, or to fight a raging bushfire.

Deprived of narrative cues, we observe these scenes in full expectation of a Stolen Generations narrative of discipline and punishment that fails to eventuate. Instead, after the lull of discovering an unfolding world of daily rituals, from the perspective of the new boy, the film shifts mode, from narrative to allegory. When a large black crate is delivered on the back of a dray, Sister Eileen and Sister Mum connive in signing for the delivery in the name of Dom Peter (whose death they are hiding). We are plunged into an allegorical world where the iconography of Christ on the Cross disrupts our expectations of a new take on the story of the stolen child. Herein lies the power of a second viewing to attune us to the film's unexpected shift into allegorical mode as the new boy (with his mice and snakes) and the heretical nun (with her wine and secrets) turn their attention to Christ on the Cross with an intensity and abandon that takes us by surprise.

One of the challenges of *The New Boy* is that it resolutely refuses to explain or elaborate on what we are shown. Like the new boy, we observe Sister Eileen from a distance as she engages in private, opaque rituals that derive from Christian practices of prayer, confession and acts of contrition. Here, our recognition of Sister Eileen as sacrilegious depends on our knowledge of the sacraments (including baptism, confession and communion) as rites conducted not by nuns but by ordained priests. In contrast, we witness rather than question the behaviour of the new boy as he interacts with Christ on the Cross in a series of scenes – climbing up the cross to embrace the suffering Christ, crashing to the ground with Christ in his arms, un-nailing Christ's cast-iron body from the cross and driving the nails through his own blood-soaked hands. There is an allegorical force to these scenes that defies conventional narrative exposition. But if we look at these scenes through the eyes of Walter Benjamin (Buck-Morss 1995), and more recently Ismail Xavier (1997, 1999), we might better understand the force of allegory (and the lack of narrative coherence) that drives the literal embrace of the body of Christ by the new boy, and the unorthodox rites or sacraments performed by Sister Eileen.

For Susan Buck-Morss (1995: 159–201), Benjamin's allegorical mode offers a way of engaging with the past, as the origin of the present, through cultural debris, fossils and ruins. For Ismail Xavier (1997: 349), modern allegory is fragmented and incomplete, with 'old facts like old signs losing their "original" meaning when looked at from a new perspective'. This new perspective is precisely what Warwick Thornton and his creative collaborators bring to *The New Boy*, detonating the narrative coherence of the classic, Stolen Generations story in Phillip Noyce's *Rabbit-Proof Fence* (2002). What *The New Boy* offers cinema audiences in 2023 is an elliptical, allegorical mode of engaging with Thornton's own story (first drafted as a screenplay eighteen years ago) of being an unruly youth, sent by his mother to a distant boarding school in New Norcia, Australia's only monastic town, founded by Spanish Benedictine monks in the Western Australia wheatbelt in 1847.

Filmed in a single, remote location where cast and crew lived together for the duration of the shoot, *The New Boy*'s allegorical form entails a shift from narrative coherence (as the boy discovers his new environment and its opaque rules and rituals) to something more fragmented and elliptical with the delivery of the cast-iron body of Christ. This fragmentation is evident in a decisive act, very late in the film, that did not register with me until my second viewing. Recognizing how far the new boy (with his hands wrapped in blood-soaked rags) has gone towards embodying Christ's crucifixion, in a moment of panic at the fate of his mortal soul, Sister Eileen baptizes him and names him Francis. In the closing sequence, the new boy, now Francis, undergoes a makeover and emerges, for the first time, neat and tidy in the school uniform. In the final scene of the film, Francis joins two boys in a race (rolling tin cans down the dirt road and uphill to the far horizon) and we are aligned with the onlookers, shouting 'come back' or 'keep going'.

Coming back to the film for a second viewing, I am struck, for the first time, by the significance of the boy's new name. A little research reveals that Francis of Assisi, Sister Eileen and the new boy have quite a lot in common. According to an extensively footnoted entry in Wikipedia, Francis of Assisi (1181–1226) is associated with birds, animals, stigmata and the crucifix. Like Sister Eileen and Sister Mum, Francis of Assisi wore a woollen tunic and a knotted rope belt. The story goes that Christ on the Cross spoke to Francis of Assisi in a country chapel and that Francis received the stigmata during a forty-day fast. The new boy's affinity with mice, snakes and the raging bushfire that threatens to engulf the small, monastic community speaks, then, to the ecology movement initiated by Pope Francis, who took his papal name from Francis of Assisi.

In *The New Boy*, the supernatural does not scare us. We might, however, find ourselves haunted by the disparity between Christ on the Cross as an emblem of suffering and resurrection, and Francis the new boy as a figure of 'Indigenous insistence' (Smith 2020). Unlike his namesake, the new boy does not convert to Christianity, but rather engages with a (living, breathing) body of Christ on his own terms. What *The New Boy* offers, then, is not a classical narrative but the allegorical fragmentation of a spacious storyworld that speaks to an 'agonistic politics' of 'conflicting perspectives' (Collins 2017: 109). The soundtrack by Nick Cave and Warren Ellis affirms and holds us within the agonism of the film's allegorical mode.

Conclusion: Unreconciled energies

Warwick Thornton's ghost stories in *The Darkside*, blood hunters in *Firebite* and secret rites in *The New Boy* are part of a Blak Wave of film and television production that is transforming Australian screen culture into a space of 'stranger relationality' or 'strangerhood' (Warner 2002: 74–5), where 'unreconciled energies' reappear and demand recognition of what cannot be redeemed or repaired in the present (Collins 2017: 112). For Alexander Hirsch (2012: 93), it is precisely these 'fugitive' energies, understood as 'wild and disorderly' ruptures, that have the capacity to 'split open the present'.

In 2013, the telling of ghost stories in *The Darkside* opened up a space of careful listening between Indigenous and settler-colonial polities. In 2021, *Firebite* offered an original First Nations take on the vampire genre, transforming Coober Pedy/Opal City into the final frontier in the underground war against colonization. In 2023, the collaboration between Warwick Thornton and Cate Blanchett on *The New Boy* has challenged audiences to grasp the deep chasm between First Nations and settler-colonial peoples, in relation to 'haunted histories' and 'the sacred'. It is precisely this space of 'the unreconciled' that Warwick Thornton has brought to our attention, across genres and platforms, in a body of screen-work that is both a provocation and a gift.

References

AWAYE! (2013), '*The Darkside*: Interview with Warwick Thornton, Radio National', 23 November. Available online: http://mpegmedia.abc.net.au/rn/podcast/2013/11/aye_20131123_1807.mp3 (accessed 10 January 2015).

Buck-Morss, S. (1995), *The Dialectics of Seeing: Walter Benjamin and the Arcades Project*, Cambridge, MA: MIT Press.

Collins, F. (2016), 'A Hungry Public: Stranger Relationality and the Blak Wave', in *Contemporary Publics: Shifting Boundaries in New Media Technology and Culture*, edited by P.D. Marshall, G. D'Cruz, S. McDonald and K. Lee, 27–42, London: Palgrave Macmillan.

Collins, F. (2017), 'Disturbing the Peace: The Ghost in *beDevil* and *The Darkside*', *Critical Arts*, 31 (5): 107–13.

FilmInk (2023), '*Firebite*: Warwick Thornton and Brendan Fletcher on Fire', 17 December. Available online: https://www.filmink.com.au/firebitewarwick-thornton-and-brendan-fletcher-on-fire (accessed 2 August 2023).

Ginsburg, F. (2018), 'The Indigenous Uncanny: Accounting for Ghosts in Recent Indigenous Australian Experimental Media', *Visual Anthropology Review*, 34 (1): 67–76.

Hirsch, A.K. (2012), 'Fugitive Reconciliation', in *Theorizing Post-Conflict Reconciliation: Agonism, Restitution and Repair*, edited by A.K. Hirsch, 79–99, London: Routledge.

Honig, B. (2013), 'The Politics of Public Things: Neoliberalism and the Routine of Privatization', *No Foundations*, 10, 59–76. Available online: http://www.helsinki.fi/nofo/NoFo10HONIG.pdf (accessed 6 January 2015).

Human Rights Commission (1997), *Bringing Them Home: Report of the National Enquiry into the Separation of Aboriginal and Torres Strait Islander Children from Their Families*. Available online: https://bth.humanrights.gov.au/the-report/bringing-them-home-report (accessed 8 August 2023).

Mahood, K. (2015), 'Review: Emma Kowal, Trapped in the Gap: Doing Good in Indigenous Australia', *The Monthly*, August, 50–1.

National Film and Sound Archive of Australia (NFSA) (2023), 'Warwick Thornton on *The Darkside*: From Darkness to Healing by Miguel Gonzalez'. Available online: https://www.nfsa.gov.au/latest/darkside-force (accessed 30 July 2023).

Obenson, T. (2021), '*Firebite* Review: Indigenous Vampire Hunters Protect the Outback in AMC Plus's Bouyant Indigenous Romp', *IndieWire*, 17 December. Available online: https://www.indiewire.com/criticism/shows/firebite-review-amc-plus-1234685391 (accessed 2 August 2023).

Schaap, A. (2005), *Political Reconciliation*, London: Routledge.

Smith, J. (2020), 'Indigenous Insistence on Film', in *Routledge Handbook of Critical Indigenous Studies*, edited by B. Hokowhitu, A. Moreton-Robinson, L. Tuhiwai-Smith, C. Andersen and C. Larkin, Ch. 36, London: Routledge.

The Uluru Statement from the Heart (2017), Available online: https://ulurustatement.org/the-statement (accessed 2 August 2023).

Warner, M. (2002), *Publics and Counterpublics*, New York: Zone Books.

Wikipedia (2023), 'Francis of Assisi'. Available online: https://en.wikipedia.org/wiki/Francis_of_Assisi (accessed 10 August 2023).

Xavier, I. (1997), *Allegories of Underdevelopment: Aesthetics and Politics in Modern Brazilian Cinema*, Minneapolis: University of Minnesota Press.

Xavier, I. (1999), 'Historical Allegory', in *A Companion to Film Theory*, edited by T. Miller and R. Stam, 333–62, Malden, MA: Blackwell.

Films and television series

The Australian Wars (2022), directed by Rachel Perkin [TV series], Australia: SBS.

Bastardy (2008), directed by Amiel Courtin-Wilson [documentary], Australia: Film Camp.

The Darkside (2013), directed by Warwick Thornton [film], Australia: Scarlett Pictures.

Firebite (2021–22), directed by Warwick Thornton and Brendan Fletcher [TV Series], Australia: See-Saw Films.

First Australians (2008), directed by Rachel Perkins and Beck Cole [TV Series], Australia: SBS.

The New Boy (2023), directed by Warwick Thornton [film], Australia: Dirty Films, Scarlett Pictures.

Nice Coloured Girls (1987), directed by Tracey Moffatt [film], Australia: Ronin Films.
Night Cries: A Rural Tragedy (1990), directed by Tracey Moffatt [film], Australia: Ronin Films.
The Proposition (2005), directed by John Hillcoat [film], Australia: Surefire Films.
Rabbit-Proof Fence (2002), directed by Phillip Noyce [film], Australia: Rumbalara Films.
Redfern Now (2012, 2013, 2015), directed by Rachel Perkins et. al. [TV series], Australia: Blackfella Films.
Samson and Delilah (2009), directed by Warwick Thornton [film], Australia: Scarlett Pictures.
The Tracker (2002), directed by Rolf de Heer [film], Australia: Umbrella Entertainment.

3

Undead heritage: Environmental trauma and curses that never die in Takashi Shimizu's 'village' trilogy

Simon Bacon

Japanese director Takashi Shimizu, creator of the *Ju-On* (*The Grudge*) franchise, is well versed in the viral nature of curses and how actions in the past can infect the present. His recent trilogy of 'village' films – *Howling Village* (2019), *Suicide Forest Village* (2021) and *Ox-Head Village* (2022) – is no exception, and all of three films link to familial heritage and a landscape tainted by trauma, where the former acts as a bridge to/from the latter. Indeed, it is the literal bloodline of family that fuels the original and ongoing traumas of the environments in question.

This chapter argues that the three films purposely create equivalences between terms such as 'traditional', 'non-urban' and 'the past', and 'curse', 'trauma' and 'bloodline', to show how modern Japan, as symbolized by the city, has irreparably damaged its connection to the natural world through multiple familial and ecological traumas. This entanglement between human and environmental trauma nevertheless reveals an intimate relationship between the land and those who have lived there for many generations. While the films seem to superficially suggest that it might be possible for female descendants to break the curses created by a patriarchal bloodline, as will be shown here, the spectres of a traumatic past can never be satiated and will never leave the present in peace.

The village as symbol of a monstrous past

The idea of the village is central to Shimizu's trilogy. It is a place that is rural, outside of, or beyond the modern world, and inherently monstrous; as noted by Carol Clover (2015 [1992]: 124), the world outside the city in horror narratives is like the 'deep, dark forest in traditional fairy tales … [and] a place where the rules of civilization do not obtain'. In fact, within the trilogy's narrative world the village is only founded because its would-be members are cast out of 'normal' society and forced to live in uninhabited parts of the countryside or woodlands. However, the exact nature of their monstrosity changes in each case: in *Howling Village*, they are those who have forged a life capturing and eating wild dogs in the woodlands beyond the city, later labelled as bestial 'dog-people'; in *Suicide Forest Village*, it is the physically disabled, the mentally ill and the unwanted, who were left in the forest as offerings to the gods, later joined by failed suicides; and in *Ox-Head Village* the monstrous are twins, who are labelled as evil. Their enforced 'non-human' status seems to give them a natural affinity with their non-human surroundings. Consequently, the 'cursed' nature of the villagers – both cursed in the sense of being conceived of as monstrous and cursed by the gods – endows the landscape with their monstrosity. It is how this original curse is exponentially compounded by trauma, however, that turns the villages themselves, as sites of misfortune and exile, into an open wound that consumes all who come into contact with it. This trauma is constructed differently in each film, but is intimately connected to family and environmental heritage in all three. Indeed, trauma and heritage become almost synonymous, so that all periods before the modernization of Japan are seen as traumatic in some way and as attempting to consume the present.

Before examining the three films, it is worth defining exactly what is meant by trauma here, as it was originally applied to individuals rather than landscape. Trauma was first used in relation to nineteenth-century train journeys and the possible effects of humans travelling at excessive speeds and/or crashing (Luckhurst 2008: 27). In legal cases of the time, it was cited as a psychological disorder, and Sigmund Freud (2005) continued that usage in his work *Mourning and Melancholia*, originally published in 1917. For Freud, trauma was inherently bound to the idea of loss – the loss of a loved one, of who one was and of psychological energy (melancholia). Violence was often also central, either in terms of the psychological effects caused by an event or actual physical altercation(s) in the past. The past is also crucial here, as Freud was treating patients only because they had been unable in some way to move on from those events. Subsequently, he theorized that originary occurrence as a wound (2005: 212) – a cut or a gash – that drew psychic energies into itself, leaving the patient powerless to escape it. The past literally consumed that person's ability to experience and embrace a future. Later, in *Moses and Monotheism*, published in 1939, Freud (2013: 62) extended this idea to a group or culture so that a people can be thought of as suffering from a historical trauma. Subsequently, there has been much work done to validate the idea that events such as slavery, war and genocide caused collective trauma in the nations, sectarian or ethnic groups involved (e.g. Caruth 1996; LaCapra 2001). Such examples contain site-specific locations, so the trauma experienced by a collective can be triggered by or transferred to that place (Berberich, Campbell and Hudson 2016; Rapson 2015). This correlation or transference of individual and collective trauma to a landscape can be seen to have affective proof in those who know of their shared cultural history with it, yet this would seem less likely to have the same impact on those who are oblivious to events that have occurred on that spot – one need only think of visiting a Holocaust memorial and experiencing the arrival of a party of schoolchildren. However, Shimizu's films posit that sites of collective trauma are not just signifiers of those events; these places are also physically and psychically changed, capable of haunting dwellers and visitors.

While this might suggest that the landscape is collectively alive in some way, Shimizu appears to tend more towards the idea that we are so intimately connected to the environment that we transfer our own traumas on to it. Shintoism reinforces this idea with supernatural entities or spirits called *kami* that can inhabit all things, including objects and landscapes (Hardacre 2017: 49–70). These *kami* may have a vengeful state (*yōkai*), often caused by disrespect or neglect of their sites or places they inhabited, as reflected in the kinds of trauma narratives expressed in Shimizu's films. Such supernatural elements were part of the original *kaidan* (ghost stories) that became popular in the Edo period (1603–1867), which would form the basis of later Japanese horror. Shimizu himself is part of that tradition. While Japanese horror, or J-Horror, gained something of a name in the early 2000s for showing the dangers of the urban space and technology – see *Ringu* (1998–2017), *Ju-on* (2000–present), *Pulse* (2001–8) and *Dark Waters* (2002–5) – there was always an element of the rural, and the otherworldly, invading the urban. Indeed, Shimizu uses the idea that spirits/*kami* have always been part of the very matter of Japan and that what once possessed the landscape will naturally inhabit that which is built on top of it.

The Village Trilogy sees trauma and supernatural presences as entangled and reinforcing. Human trauma thus enlivens the *kami*, who then encourage and draw in more of spirits like themselves. In a sense they may even become traumatic objects themselves, creating and consuming the psychic energy of those with whom they come into contact. Further, at least for Shimizu's films, family heritage is connected to this entanglement, so that if someone becomes embroiled in the trauma – seemingly at any point – their bloodline is also implicated so that any children or grandchildren they have will also fall victim to, or be haunted/cursed by, the trauma.

Original trauma

Howling Village is the first in the trilogy and, perhaps because of that, is the most explicit about why historical trauma haunts the present, what caused it and why it searches out certain people. The film begins by establishing that it is set in present-day (twenty-first century) Japan by the use of a 'most haunted', found-footage-style livestream of a pair of self-styled ghost-hunters, Yuma (Ryôta Bandô) and his girlfriend Akina (Rinka Ôtani), who are looking for proof of the urban legend about the 'Howling Village'. Shimizu bases all three films on actual urban legends, although he employs poetic licence in their application (Boelman 2021; Hammond 2021). Although both subsequently die, Akina and her ghost-hunting internet livestreams feature in all three films, connecting them while providing a shorthand symbol for modern Japan and technology, suggesting that urban legend and folklore are interchangeable and that contradictory myths and traditions can exist in the same space. Indeed, the fact that across the series Akina is alive and dead at the same time reinforces the way the past never really dies and is always alive in the present. This is clearly seen in *Howling Village*, where the village itself appears and vanishes at will – although it is also suggested that 'gifted' people are able to see it along with other ghostly presences.

Howling Village was established in the very early twentieth century by those shunned by the townspeople; they were subsequently forced to hunt wild dogs to survive – the 'howling' coming from the noise of the captured animals. This was a period when Japan was modernizing, shifting to an industrialized and a more urban society, moving away from the traditions of the past. The industrialization of Japan began with the Meiji era in 1868, rapidly transforming the country into a nation-state with growing urban centres. Not everyone was included or accepting of the changes, including forced adoption of Western standards, as Japan emerged as a regional superpower with a nationalist, colonial imperative.

Shimizu represents this shift from the rural to the urban as a traumatic moment in Japan's history, symbolized in the building of a dam that flooded the land on which Howling Village stood. This environmental trauma is given literal form in the villagers, who are not moved on by the construction builders but rather beaten and tied up in their wooden shacks so they drown as the newly created reservoir fills up. This event, which kills all the villagers – apart from one newborn baby – entangles their anguish and trauma with that of the drowned landscape upon which they depended, and of which they are now a part forever. The spectres of this trauma take two forms in the present: first, the villagers reappear as zombie-like corpses; and second, victims are possessed by something more elemental that makes them behave like dogs or dog-humans. Derogatory rumours were spread by the authorities before the dam was built that the villagers bred with dogs and were already un-human and not worth saving.

One hundred years later the traumatic wound this created now presses a claim on the descendants of the people who oversaw the construction of the dam, particularly the Morita family. This is slightly different from much J-Horror, where the victims are just unfortunate to be noticed by whatever supernatural force is at play (Strusiewicz 2021). Here they are actively sought out. The family appears to be deeply embroiled with the original trauma, whose expression in the present reveals it as a curse made manifest, not just in location but also in blood: the father, Akira (Masanobu Takashima), runs a company that was involved with the original dam project; his wife is possibly a direct descendent of the lone child who survived the drowning of Howling Village; his eldest son, Yuma, and his girlfriend, Akina, are the aforementioned 'ghost hunters' who stumble into the tunnel that leads to the village; his younger son, Kota (Hinata Kaizu), is making a model of the village for a school project and later goes missing in the haunted tunnel with Yuma; and finally his daughter, Kanata (Ayaka Miyoshi), who works as a psychologist in the local hospital, begins to see the ghosts and spirits created by the trauma.

Kanata is 'gifted' – this features in all three films where the female protagonists are supernaturally 'sensitive' in some way – something of which she has only recently become aware. This means she sees glimpses of ghosts or entities who are trapped within the hospital where she works. It also allows the trauma of Howling Village to reach out to her. In fact, it seems that this 'gift' originates in the sunken village itself and has passed through the female line of her family back to her great-grandmother, who was drowned in the rising waters of the reservoir – although not before giving birth to a daughter who was the sole survivor of the event.

In a now-classic horror trope, it appears that the trauma of her great-grandmother's death, and what happened to the village, is calling for Kanata to discover the truth of what has been covered up by her family and reveal it to the world, thus healing the trauma and interpreting it back into linear time. However, Shimizu does not allow for such an easy resolution to the narrative, as environmental and collective traumas are never easily healed or their psychic 'wounds' satiated. In trying to save her brothers, who have been 'taken' by the village, Kanata discovers that she, her mother and her grandmother are all connected to the traumatic event and their shared gift sees them possessed by it. As she uncovers the horrific events perpetrated by her family and how her great-grandmother might have been possessed by the spirit of the environment when she gave birth, Kanata herself begins to take on dog features and characteristics. This traumatic ancestral regression also begins to affect the environment around Kanata, allowing her to go (return) to Howling Village just before it was drowned, rescue her great grandmother's baby, escape the settlement and fall exhausted outside a nearby house. When she awakens, she is back in the present, but the house has become that of her mother's family and she has rescued her own grandmother. This time-bending element of the story conforms to Anne Whitehead's (2004: 3) description of the experience of trauma, where 'temporality and chronology collapse' – which here not only reveals the intergenerational aspect of the original trauma that reverberates along the maternal bloodline, but also how the environmental past still 'lives' in the city's present.

Just as the trauma seems to find its completion with Kanata saving her own grandmother – thus, ensuring her own birth – and burying her great-grandmother's remains in the family plot, it becomes apparent that it is not just a familial curse at play. As the film ends, we see Kanata back at work in the hospital and waving goodbye to a young patient, but as she turns to go back to work, she wipes her mouth, which suddenly has elongated canine teeth, with the back of her hand that now is held like a dog's paw, just like those possessed by the spirits/*kami* of Howling Village. The film never explicitly mentions the spirits or *kami*, or any shrines to such entities, yet the way the narrative constructs the village as a place of myth and old ways is highly suggestive. This is retrospectively confirmed in the next film in the series, *Suicide Forest Village*, which explicitly mentions ancient gods and spirits.

A cursed landscape, a cursed history

The plot of *Suicide Forest Village* comes from a well-established myth on which multiple films and novels have been based – although its designation as a place to kill oneself only came about after the Second World War. Prior to that, the forest on the north-western side of Mount Fuji, known as Aokigahara ('Blue Tree Meadow' or the 'Sea of Trees'), was said to contain the ghosts of the dead – due to the density of trees and the porous lava rock on which they grow, parts of the forest are very sound absorbent, heightening a sense of loneliness within them. Shimizu takes this myth further, suggesting that gods or spirits – *kami* – have always been there and that the first inhabitants would sacrifice 'special ones' to them to ensure their favour – special ones being those who were physically disabled or mentally ill. However, over time this became a way for nearby settlements to rid themselves of burdensome members who were led into the forest and abandoned to die. At some point the survivors formed a village of sorts, finding strength in their need for revenge on those who had left them there and empowered by the nature spirits around them. It is unclear in the film exactly when or how this took form, but the 'wound' created by this original collective trauma attracted others, designating it as a place where the terminally depressed would go to commit suicide. The film further suggests that those who failed to kill themselves also lived in the forest, or had somehow become part of it.

Again we see an entanglement between human trauma and the landscape that cannot be unpicked and that becomes stronger and more engrained over time. Indeed, the traditions and spirits of the past are so strong that they are pulling modern, urbanized Japan back into the mythic past, one person at a time. Unlike in *Howling Village*, there is no environmental trauma as such, but humankind's inhumanity to its own is enough to create ecological wounds in the landscape – human suffering literally bleeds into the landscape, feeding the *kami* who live there. Similar to the previous film in the trilogy, the ostracized villagers seem to become the monsters they were labelled as, and the inhabitants of Suicide Village facilitate their revenge on the outside world by creating a cursed box that they fill with the dismembered little fingers of all the new members of their encampment, constituting a brutal initiation rite that compounds the trauma of the site and the power of the curse contained within the box, which is then subsequently used to carry the trauma of the location out into the rest of Japan.

As with *Howling Village*, it is once the myth turns into urban legend that it spreads itself further into the outside world, when physical place becomes virtual space. Once again, it establishes a break between Japan's pre-modern era, when the country was a predominantly rural, traditional culture, and the post-modern era, when it became increasingly urban and technology based, and eschewed old beliefs. In the world of urban myth, it is this superstitious rural past that invades the present, drawing it back into the traumatic wound of the nation's forgotten history. The idea of a forgotten Japan seems even more pronounced with the predominantly youthful characters seemingly only knowledgeable about urban legends or 'creepy pasta' they find online. Supporting this the film opens with the reappearance of Akina, who is making another live-stream recording of her investigating a 'spooky' environment. This time she is alone, but the recording is more sophisticated than before. It is never explained how she is alive again or how this relates to the events of the first film – although we do discover that the hospital where Kanata works is near the forest; rather, she acts as a signifier of twenty-first-century youth, who are heavily connected to modern technology but completely disconnected from the rural environment outside of the city. Technology is shown to have no power over the traumas of the past and is rather a means for them to move into the present so the spectres of the past will haunt Japan no matter how technologically advanced or futuristic it becomes.

The aforementioned box is then used by the forest dwellers to target new victims by making it mysteriously appear in the vicinity of their house. Once found, the concentration of trauma in the box is so intense that anyone who touches it will die – usually via a freak accident or a possessed perpetrator who cannot control their actions. In *Suicide Forest Village*, that person is Mei (Mayu Yamaguchi)who, along with her sister Hibiki (Anna Yamada), lives with their grandmother – neither sibling knows what happened to their mother. Like Kanata before her, Hibiki is 'gifted' and seems to have a special connection to both the box and the village in the forest. When the box first appears in the film, it is hidden under the house of a friend, but she senses that it is there, and in fact draws the attention of others to it. The house is not part of a town but located nearby, which is suggestive of the urban space constantly encroaching on what rural space there is left – less than 10 per cent of Japan is not urbanized (O'Neill 2023) – so the appearance of the box is arguably as much about preserving the rural habitat and the 'old ways' as it is about enacting a curse.

Hibiki is an introverted young woman who spends most of her time in online chat groups. She follows Akina's livestream show, and is among a group of devotees who try to find the 'ghost hunter' when she goes missing in the forest. Although Hibiki escapes, the other members of the group are killed, following a pattern throughout the film where she seems to be a witness to or cause of multiple deaths because of the traumatic influence of the village. As the narrative unfolds, it becomes clear that the sisters are connected to the forest and that when they were little children, Mei, with Hibiki, found the box in the family garage. Their mother walked in before Mei had time to touch it, but knew what the object meant and so went to the forest herself to return it to the village and save her children. Unfortunately the two girls were with her, and although they escaped, they were marked from that day to join the inhabitants of the village.

Hibiki's increasingly erratic behaviour sees her placed in a mental health facility, leaving Mei to wonder why bad things are still happening. She goes to see the old man who acts as a warden of the forest and who found them wandering out from the trees many years ago. In all three films, only the old people are still connected to the past and the old myths. He tells her of the history of the forest and about the village created by the failed suicides who cannot leave. She goes back to the house where they found the box and discovers a map showing the village's location carved into the wooden floor underneath the carpet. This suggests the notion that the traumas of the past are indelibly written in the ground beneath our feet and remain 'alive' no matter how much we try to cover them over. This aliveness is seen when Mei takes photos of the map and the gruesome tale of the settlement's creation flashes into her mind, entangling the past in the present and, as with Kanata before her, revealing how trauma concentrates time and space into a single, never-ending moment. This convinces her that she needs to go there, find their mother and save Hibiki. Unsurprisingly, things do not go to plan: although she finds her mother and they escape the settlement, the forest comes alive to prevent them leaving its domain.

The aliveness of the forest – an indication of how the past is alive in the present – is hinted at throughout the film, from suddenly looming trees to branches appearing to grip people's feet, but once Hibiki is incarcerated in the medical facility it becomes far more obvious. Hibiki's hospital is some distance from the forest, yet shadows of its trees seem to find their way into her room at night. As she sleeps, the shadows of branches take on a life of their own and slowly stretch down the walls and grab at her clothes and body – one is reminded of the embodied shadow scene in Murnau's *Nosferatu*. Although she manages to save herself, when she projects herself into the forest to save her sister – another sign of the temporal and spatial collapse experienced in trauma – the forest becomes a completely different entity. As Mei and her mother run from the village, they fall down a hole into a small cavern – the same hole her mother was trapped in when she and Hibiki were younger. As Whitehead (2004: 3) notes, repetition is an important component of experience of trauma. As the young girl tries to escape, the tree roots protruding from the walls grow longer, becoming the arms, legs and bodies of people who are all intent on grabbing her. At this point, Hibiki projects herself from her hospital cell into the underground cavern to save Mei, sacrificing herself and pushing her sister up through an opening and out of the hole. As Hibiki does that, the plant/people grab her, their rapidly entwining bodies growing into a tall moss-covered tree trunk; Hibiki becomes one with the forest, just as the forest is one with the villagers and all those who entered its traumatic environment and remained.

In *Suicide Forest Village* those claimed by the forest seem to retain who they are, even as they have been incorporated into the trees and roots: the environment is literally 'alive' with the dead. The trauma of the past does not just include those who were immediately affected by it but everyone who has been touched by it since. As with *Howling Village*, family and heritage determine the victims chosen. As a representation of the break between Japan's past and present, the children have no connection with their ancestors and myths, and consequently no defence against them when they erupt into the everyday. It also becomes increasingly obvious that, although these two films share many details, such as the rural settings, Akina's ghost hunting and the hospital where Kanata works, the respective traumatic pasts and the 'wounds' are different. What begins to form through the trilogy is the idea that what is left of rural Japan consists of a patchwork of traumatic environments that are increasingly stretching out to the metropolitan areas via urban legends, just as the cities are expanding and encroaching on the natural landscape around them. This is reinforced by the last film in the trilogy, *Ox-Head Village*.

The past will not be forgotten

The location of *Ox-Head Village* is distant from that of the first two films. Even though it once again features a main female protagonist who is drawn into the grip of a traumatic past through shared blood, its focus on twins and an abandoned hotel building sets it apart. However, even more than its immediate predecessor, it foregrounds the idea of nature spirits and how they draw on, and resonate with, human trauma.

Once again, the film starts with Akina filming a livestream video investigating a haunted location – in this instance, an abandoned hotel in the middle of the countryside – and a related urban legend regarding an ox-head. The ox-head is connected to a roadside shrine and those that hear the noise of the ox-head are doomed to be cursed – this is the only film of the trilogy that explicitly links to the instance of a *kami*. Akina's video feed has the same level of sophistication as in the previous film, but this time she is blonde rather than black-haired, with two female friends and in a completely different part of Japan. This reinforces the idea that she is a signifier of twenty-first-century Japan rather than an actual person and suggests the idea of *doppelgängers*, which is central to this narrative. They discover something of interest on one of the upper floors of the building and one of their number, Shion (Koki), goes into the elevator next to it wearing an ox-head mask to re-enact the unexplained death that had caused the hotel to close – there is an urban legend about the ox-head, but it is not connected to a deserted hotel (Rosser 2022). The lift then crashes, killing the girl; the other two go missing.

All this is witnessed online by Kanon (Koki), who is shocked to see that the girl who died in the video looked exactly like her. As with Kanata's brother, Kota, and Hibiki, the internet becomes a means for the trauma to reach out to its intended victim and after watching the events on her phone, Kanon begins to have vivid dreams – which might also be memories – and a mysterious set of wounds appear on her arm that were also on the dead girl. This connection to a person and place of which she has no knowledge is so strong that she decides to go to the hotel where the death occurred to investigate and so boards a bus with her friend Ren (Riku Hagiwara) to travel to Toyoma, 300 kilometres away on the other side of Japan – although the name of the town where Kanon lives is not mentioned, we are led to assume that it is in the vicinity of the previous two films largely by the appearance of Ryotaro (Akira Sasamoto), the boy treated by Kanata in *Howling Village*, sitting near her on the bus.

Once she arrives in Toyoma, the nature of the trauma from the past and how it fits into the overall narrative of the trilogy become clearer. Kanon and Ren get off the bus at a location famed for the mirages produced across the bay when the sun is at its highest. As Kanon looks out over the water, figures begin to emerge with their reflections. As she turns around, everyone in the car park has a *doppelgänger* as the world seemingly splits in two before her eyes. Although reality snaps back into its regular singularity, Kanon is left with the feeling that a dark other is waiting to appear at any time. This gives a heightened sense to all reflections and mirrors in the film, with windows showing looming faces, and even puddles revealing past events that are not visible in the present – as mentioned earlier, the version of Akina in this instalment also mirrors her appearance in the other two films.

She and Ren find the abandoned hotel, but learn nothing. Back at the ocean, they find Shion's boyfriend, Shota (Fumiya Takahashi), who takes them to a house outside the town. The house is Shion's and, when her mother comes out, she instantly recognizes Kanon for who she is. It transpires that the girls are twins, but that her mother decided to send Kanon as far away as possible when she was six years old to save her from the archaic tradition that has taken place in the village since it was founded. On the edge of the village is a shrine to an ox-headed spirit suggesting, as earlier seen in *Suicide Forest Village*, that the area was originally inhabited by a nature spirit or *kami* of some kind. Those who lived in the village decided twins were an abomination to the gods and so elected to give one of the twins as an offering to the ox-head deity – the child had to be between six and seven years of age and wearing an ox-head mask before being cast down a large hole at the edge of the village where the spirit would come and claim them. However, the trauma suffered by the victims empowered the spirit (again like *Suicide Forest Village*), which subsequently infected the surrounding environment and also the uncanny bond between the twins who were born there. In fact, nearly everyone in the village appears to have a twin or *doppelgänger* – this is of importance because, when we finally see all the twins appear near the end of the film, it is clearly supernatural in nature (not unlike the mirages of doubles across the bay) with an inherent menace and intent to harm on their minds; this equally suggests that the rural landscape of Japan is a dark, albeit hidden, double to the urban terrain built upon it.

This actually gives a very different complexion to Kanon's connection to her twin sister, Shion, and her death. The supernatural nature of Shion's death in the elevator while helping Akina make her 'ghost hunter' film – the reflections with a life of their own, the lift plummeting down the shaft and a mysterious hand grabbing her from the ceiling with its nails digging into her arm – can be read as the ox-head spirit claiming what was denied it when Kanon was sent away (the past righting the 'wrongs' of the present). Further, the fact that the wounds on Shion's arm were replicated on Kanon's over 300 kilometres away is not so much suggestive of a special bond between twin sisters as a supernatural force trying to pull the other sister back into the traumatic wound of the Ox-Head Village. As Kanon discovers more, she meets her grandmother who, like the other old people in the previous two films, knows and is involved in what is going on. It seems that her grandmother was a twin and as a child she was the one chosen to be offered to the ox-head spirit, but her sister, Ayako, took the ox-head mask off her while she slept and was given to the god instead. However, she did not die when cast down the hole but turned into a malignant spirit energized by the traumatic past while at the same time feeding it new victims. It was she who drew Kanon back, through their shared familial bloodline, and who is now giving the young girl visions of the traumatic events that occurred in the past. As with the other films, this 'past' would have been when modern Japan broke with its 'traditional' past and particularly the Second World War. Although urbanization began at the end of the nineteenth century and continued after the war, the rise of nationalism that accompanied it saw Japan as a single, immutable culture. Defeat in the war and the American colonization that followed changed that, instigating a renunciation of pre-war ideals so that any kind of return to them would again release the all-consuming nationalist and expansionist ideologies that previously set the country on the path to destruction. It is the hungry spirits of that past that now try to draw the young (the future) to them.

These visions that Kanon experiences are so strong that they literally transport her down the hole where her ancestor is still alive and looking like a young woman. Amazingly, Shion is still alive as well, and Kanon manages to get her out of the hole with the help of Shota and escape the structure built over the hole as the other long dead victims began to 'revive' and come after them. Running from the village, they come to a cliff edge where they discover Shion is not alone but possessed by Ayako, so Kanon holds onto her and throws herself off the edge, followed by Shota, with the intention of killing themselves and the spirit. However, they awaken in the elevator back in the hotel and as they get up to leave they discover a small stone ox-head that is part of a roadside shrine. Sometime later, we see Shion with her mother replacing the ox-head on the figure at the shrine on the edge of the village as she receives a phone call from her sister Kanon, who is coming to meet them. As they walk back towards home, Shion allows her mother to walk ahead, and when the young girl turns towards us we see she is still possessed by Ayako and that the traumatic wound of the ox-head curse is still open and ready to draw in more victims.

Conclusion

Shimizu is well known for his 'curse' films and the ongoing impacts of traumatic events, which gain an undead and undying life of their own, but his 'Village Trilogy' shifts his normal focus of an individual person or event being the cause of this to it being about the nation itself. More specifically, it is about the dramatic shift in culture caused by the modernization of Japan and events that led up to the Second World War. Although this can be seen as a change meant to negate the possibility of the recreation of the nationalist and colonialist ideologies that founded Japan's expansionist policies, it has simultaneously caused a disconnect from the past and the rural traditions that form the cultural history of the Japanese people. The films express this separation in two ways: first creating a clear differentiation between the rural as a place outside of time and reason, and alive with myth and superstition, and the urban as technological, mundane and almost sterile in its controlled and regulated status; and second by the representation of the elderly as guardians of traditions and the past, and repositories of esoteric information about the land and the myths that invigorate it, and twenty-first-century youth who are inveterate city-dwellers who are dependent on technology and more at home in a virtual environment than in the real world.

As Shimizu shows, however, it is impossible to sustain this separation as the present is necessarily built on the past – the past being seen as any time before the Second World War – a point he shows by using family heritage and bloodlines where grandparents are both the only sources of information about the past and also part of the tradition or 'curse' that emanates from it. This inseparability of the past from the curse is embodied in the idea of twins or the *doppelgänger*, which is shown as not just the malignant other that exists alongside tradition, but as the dark undying reflection of modernity itself. The past, then, is viewed as a place of rural traditions and a world where humanity and the environment are inseparable, yet it is also where one's survival is often seen to be in the hands of the spirits of the land and doing whatever is necessary to appease them, no matter how violent and inhumane it might seem to modern eyes. For a present that denies any connection to this past, these traditions and their demands act like spectres that haunt the everyday world – ghosts that will not be forgotten and will continue to inhabit the land regardless.

This inescapable connection to the past – which is central to its undead nature – is represented in the films both in the idea of familial heritage (the traumatic past is literally passed on through blood) and in the conversion of myth into urban legend. In this sense, it is the 'blood' or heritage of the nation that is being passed from the rural past into the urban present. This last concept is vital to the films as it posits that the past is not a passive thing, or a palimpsest that can be easily written over and forgotten, but active and aggressive in its actions to be remembered and recognized. In this sense, the true trauma of Shimizu's films is not that of the violence of the past reverberating into the future, but that of a present that refuses to accept its past and find ways of living with it.

References

Berberich, C., N. Campbell and R. Hudson (eds) (2016), *Affective Landscapes in Literature, Art and Everyday Life: Memory, Place and the Senses*, London: Routledge.

Boelman, S. (2021), 'J-Horror Legend Takashi Shimizu Talks His New Film *Howling Village*', *disappointment media*, 11 August. Available online: https://www.disappointmentmedia.com/interviews/j-horror-legend-takashi-shimizu-talks-his-new-film-howling-village (accessed 28 April 2023).

Caruth, C. (1996), *Unclaimed Experience: Trauma, Narrative, and History*, Baltimore, MD: Johns Hopkins University Press.

Clover, C.J. (2015 [1992]), *Men, Women and Chain Saws: Gender and the Modern Horror Film*, London: BFI Publishing.

Freud, S. (2005 [1917]), 'Mourning and Melancholia', in *On Murder, Mourning and Melancholia*, translated by S. Whiteside, 201–18, Harmondsworth: Penguin.

Freud, S. (2013 [1937]), *Moses and Monotheism*, translated by K. Jones, Milton Keynes: Aziloth Books.

Hammond, C. (2021), 'A Short Interview with Takashi Shimizu (The Grudge, JU-ON) about His New Upcoming Release *Howling Village*', *Horror Patch*, 8 August. Available online: https://horrorpatch.com/2021/08/08/a-short-interview-with-takashi-shimizu-the-grudge-ju-on-about-his-new-upcoming-release-howling-village (accessed 28 April 2023).

Hardacre, H. (2017), *Shinto: A History*, Oxford: Oxford University Press.

LaCapra, D. (2001), *Writing History, Writing Trauma*, Baltimore, MD: Johns Hopkins University Press.

Luckhurst, R. (2008), *The Trauma Question*, London: Routledge.

O'Neill, A. (2023), 'Urbanization in Japan in 2021', *Statista.com*, 1 June. Available online: https://www.statista.com/statistics/270086/urbanization-in-japan/#:~:text=Urbanization%20in%20Japan%202021&text=In%20the%20past%20decade%2C%20Japan%27s,worldwide%2C%20which%20is%2055%20percent (accessed 6 June 2023).

Rapson, J. (2015), *Topographies of Suffering: Buchenwald*, Oxford: Berghahn Books.

Rosser, M. (2022), '"The Grudge" Creator Takashi Shimizu Talks Latest Horror and New Sci-fi Project', *Screen Daily*, 19 July. Available online: https://www.screendaily.com/features/the-grudge-creator-takashi-shimizu-talks-latest-horror-and-new-sci-fi-project/5172753.article (accessed 28 April 2023).

Strusiewicz, C.J. (2021), '*Suicide Forest Village* and the Anatomy of Japanese Horror', *Tokyo Weekender*, 24 February. Available online: https://www.tokyoweekender.com/art_and_culture/suicide-forest-village-and-the-anatomy-of-japanese-horror (accessed 6 June 2023).

Whitehead, A. (2004), *Trauma Fiction*, Edinburgh: Edinburgh University Press.

Films

Howling Village [*Inunaki Mura*] (2019), directed by Takashi Shimizu [film], Tokyo: Toei Company.

Nosferatu (1922), directed by F.W. Murnau [film], Germany: Prana Film.

Ox-Head Village [*Ushikubi-Mura*] (2022), directed by Takashi Shimizu [film], Tokyo: Toei Company.

Suicide Forest Village [*Jukai Mura*] (2021), directed by Takashi Shimizu [film], Tokyo: Toei Company.

4

Deferred demons: Diasporizing the haunted home in Babak Anvari's *Under the Shadow*

David Ellison and Zach Karpinellison

Babak Anvari's film *Under the Shadow* (2016) looks pointedly beyond haunted house tropes to envision a resentful, violent and restlessly haunted *home*. In his account of a *djinn*-infiltrated apartment, Anvari draws on memories of childhood, their vivacity sharpening and personalizing an account of domestic space at its least secure. Although the film's audience has proved to be international in scope, Anvari's complex imagining of home speaks with and to the specific register of diasporic experience. In this chapter, we consider Anvari's conception of haunted home through an analysis of the film and its allegorical devices. We also draw on Hamid Naficy's (2001) assessment of diasporic filmmaking, specifically the way members of the diaspora figure themselves in relation to departed homelands and host settlements. He recognizes the category of diaspora filmmaking in the company of 'exilic' and 'postcolonial' filmmaking, all of which form his broader category of 'accented cinema'. These sub-genres of accented filmmaking are all connected by displacement and the transplantation of cultural identities around the world. Speaking to the specific differences of diasporic filmmaking, however, he writes:

> People in diaspora, moreover, maintain a long-term sense of ethnic consciousness and distinctiveness, which is consolidated by the periodic hostility of either the original home or the host societies toward them. However, unlike the exiles whose identity entails a vertical and primary relationship with their homeland, diasporic consciousness is horizontal and multi-sited, involving not only the homeland but also the compatriot communities elsewhere ... diasporic cinema [is defined] by its vertical relationship to the homeland and by its lateral relationship to the diaspora communities and experiences.
>
> (Naficy 2001: 14, 15)

Here, Naficy demonstrates that, unlike the other categories he explores (exilic, postcolonial and ethnic), the diasporized person maintains the greatest interest in defining and redefining the *home*. Moreover, by continuing to practise a kind of reverence for an idealized version of their former homeland, as well as the faith in creating continuities through shared community experiences, the diasporic filmmaker perhaps has the greatest capacity to invent and construct a new *home*.

For Anvari, some of this discussion occurs beyond the bounds of the film proper, in paratextual interviews where he speculates on overlaps between his home and memories of it, and the home and its history constructed in *Under the Shadow*. The film, while not explicitly autobiographical, summons impressions, feelings and lingering traumas of the past. This is something to which Anvari returns in these interviews, linking the film's uneasy atmosphere of an ever-lurking presence with his boyhood anxieties triggered by his father's wartime absence. Indeed, Anvari's memory of this moment in Iranian history is itself located in a specific past. Rather than recreating specific events, Anvari recalls textures, fragments and sounds:

> The war was largely invisible to us because Tehran wasn't the frontline ... We were children, and we didn't really know what was happening. But I remember sirens wailing and running with my neighbours into the basement of the apartment block. I remember the arguments and rumours that would circulate down there, hearing these distant blasts of Iraqi missiles.
>
> (quoted in Seymour 2016)

Anvari's invocation of sense-memory and indirect narrativization of his past furnish a complex and burdened blend of the intimate and the historical, recollecting a home that is both fundamental shelter and the target of wildly violent impulses. Such troubled dwellings have proved a staple of horror, but they also offer the filmmaker a means to address the socio-political environment in which the film unfolds.

Under the Shadow is set in Tehran (its shooting location, Jordan, standing in for the city) during the Iran–Iraq conflict (1980–88). Shideh (Narges Rashidi), a former medical student, and her young daughter, Dorsa (Avin Manshadi), find themselves increasingly isolated as her husband, Iraj (Bobby Naderi), is called up for service and their apartment is pierced by a rocket that, while undetonated, may well have delivered a *djinn* as payload. For Shideh, a student forced out of medical school for her involvement in student leftist circles, home is subject to the baleful pressures of the theocratic state, the anxiety of the looming conflict and then, finally, to the *djinn* itself as if it were the apotheosis of the intrusions that preceded it. In an interview, Anvari likens the *djinn* to a poltergeist, speaking to the influence of Tobe Hooper's 1982 film. In the latter, the television set features as a malign portal for spirits that weaken the family's hold over their daughter, in much the same way that the *djinn* interposes between Shideh and Dorsa.

As the *djinn* arrives in an enemy weapon (an echo of *Dr Strangelove*), its destructive behaviour both anticipates and gives expression to regional geopolitics literally hitting home; however, rather than immediately laying waste to their building (that comes later), the *djinn*-missile attacks things – first, Dorsa's much-loved doll, Kimia, an object that supplements the parent–child relationship while also acting out its deficiencies. Shideh's nervy and distracted parenting finds a counterpoint in Dorsa's attentive intimacy with Kimia. But then the doll vanishes, and so does Shideh's late mother's medical textbook, which served as a memorial to a parent as much as to her own blighted career as a medical student. The *djinn*'s choice is revealing: these are enchanted things that hold vaster significance than their appearance would suggest. They are also, tellingly, portable objects, the essentials hastily gathered under conditions of diaspora. By *djinn*-logic, without them they cannot leave. As they are bound to their place (it can no longer be called home), Shideh and Dorsa are subject to the *djinn*'s punishing energies that cleave to, or mirror, those of Shideh's family's hostile response to her modernity, which in turn echoes state harassment and the war unfolding between states. In other words, while the *djinn* exists in its own recondite form, it also gives shape to other agendas – personal and political.

A new kind of haunting: Diasporic mobility

Anvari's haunted home subverts the haunted house trope by moving away from the dwelling as a singular site of paranormal and mystical activity in favour of the concept of home itself – as abstraction or memory – as inherently incapable of withstanding malign infiltration. By the film's third act, Shideh's apartment building is more or less destroyed; however, this proves no obstacle to the *djinn*'s capacity to haunt. It attaches itself inescapably to the realities of their newly exigent mobility, assuming the form, if not the purpose, of one of those sacred portable things from a home that no longer supports life.

Indeed, rather than treating the home as place sought out as a sanctuary or refuge, in this film the home is wholly doomed to mobility. This, we argue, aligns the home with the experience of the diasporic filmmaker, who must define, locate and then redefine and relocate their home under conditions of enforced movement. Naficy argues that, not unlike the trope of Chekov's gun, for an accented filmmaker houses and homes presumptively imply an eventual exodus:

> In the accented cinema, the house is an intensely charged place and a signifying trope. As a trope, it signifies deterritorialization more than reterritorialization, for displaced filmmakers are fully aware that in today's age of 'ethnic cleansing', possessing a house, a home, or a homeland seems to require first the expulsion of its current residents.
>
> (2001: 169)

In other words, if a house is depicted on screen in one of these films, we can assume that this house will likely be vacated in order to destabilize the location of this home. This cinematic depiction of the home treats it as a tool for the creation of suspense and anxiety. The home provides temporary shelter before becoming a menacing presence that seeks to expel its inhabitants. Anvari takes up this indicating trope in order to create the horror and suspense genre elements of his film. The *djinn*'s haunting codes the apartment space as insecure and fragile, but as the building literally begins to deteriorate, the *djinn*'s hold over the environment becomes more flexible and expansive. The destruction of the apartment and the expulsion of its residents in turn create the conditions for a new home.

Unlike the victims of films like *Halloween* (1978) and *Scream* (1996), where the suburban house and home exist as compromised, or false fortresses, proving to be more fragile than they initially realized, in *Under the Shadow* home is indestructible because of its incorporeal mobility – bound to the protagonists even as they leave their apartment building, their street and their homeland. In an interview with *Den of Geek*, Anvari, a British-Iranian who left Iran aged eighteen, describes aspiring to verisimilitude. When asked about casting, he explained his insistence on finding actors who spoke Farsi unaccented by the places in which the Iranian diaspora has spread (Dobbs 2016). Even before the film had begun shooting, Anvari had a particular vision of authenticity with respect to the past – presenting a challenge to the types of Iranian people he might otherwise cast. In using this film like a time capsule, it was Anvari's goal to accurately represent his memory of Iran in the 1980s. This dimension of accuracy, however, is of course also complicated by the fact that this memory no longer matches contemporary

Iran. As such, there is a dissonance between the idea of Jordan's frequent role as a generic Middle Eastern location (Mingant 2015), and the meticulous care with which Anvari attempts to recreate the detailed cultural specificity of Tehran in 1988. In this way Jordan becomes, in an unstated and perhaps even unintentional way, a key diasporic metanarrative that hangs over the film like a spectre. If the film is concerned with how to portray an inescapable connection to home, then this is expertly achieved by modifying modern-day Jordan to resemble a particularly melancholy and nostalgic vision of Tehran.

It is worth acknowledging that it would have proved very difficult to make this film in contemporary Iran. Under ever-changing censorship regulations in Iranian state-funded cinema, much of what is shown in Anvari's film would not have been permitted. This is why Jordan must suffice as a vision or impression of Tehran. Moreover, Anvari wants audiences to be drawn into his vivid memories. In his interview, he articulates a specific anxiety that audiences may disbelieve or challenge his recreation of the past:

> I was so worried – there are so many films, especially Hollywood films being made about Iran, that as an Iranian when I watch them I think, 'Whoa, this does not look anything like Iran!' Iranian audiences are very specific and I didn't want to annoy them. And I thought even an international audience will always find something's a bit phony if you don't get it right if you don't have that sense of authenticity. So that was really key for me.
>
> (quoted in Dobbs 2016)

The angst expressed about 'getting it right', we argue, is key also to the film's creation of tension and fear. Rather than necessarily being true to the experience of wartime Iran, the film's sense of authenticity is achieved in the specificity of Anvari's childhood memories. His concern is that other Iranian memories of this period will differ, so he recognizes an obligation to find and recreate shared textures and cultural memories that will prove recognizable to the greater community – both those in the diaspora and those still living in Iran. To this end, Anvari creates a shared approximation by drawing on, as discussed above, his own personal archive – photographs and family albums – framed by some of the key devices of the Iranian national cinema. This fusion of the intensely personal with the recognizably national can be seen in the way Dorsa embodies both innocence and wartime experience. Anvari draws on the allegorical tradition of using children in Iranian cinema to depict an emotional and social depth that, under conditions of state censorship, may not otherwise be shown in adult characters.

Film scholar Michelle Langford (2019) considers the allegorical deployment of children in *Allegory in Iranian Cinema: The Aesthetics and Poetry of Resistance*. She argues that children are a crucial tool for filmmakers to express both sympathetic and resistive sentiments about Iranian culture, history and theocratic government. As Anvari's film was made inside the diaspora, it was not subject to the censorship requirements of films shot within Iran. However, we argue that Dorsa's character, and her role within the film, is a decision that speaks to the tradition of child protagonists in Iranian national cinema. Langford (2019: 74) writes:

> [M]any of the child-centred films of the post-revolutionary period functioned as didactic parables delivering to viewers – young and old – practical lessons on how to take their place in the newly imagined community. In some cases, these parables take on an allegorical quality when characters are used to personify values and concepts such as patience, honesty, compassion and ethics, as well as becoming national allegories when these values and concepts tend towards the promotion of national belonging.

While the 'didactic' aspect of children in these films could be weaponized by filmmakers to attempt to create something propagandistic, or in service of cultural homogenization and assimilation, in Anvari's diasporic film he has experimented with this trope, using the character of Dorsa not only in this allegorical fashion (a beacon of innocence and a narrative shaped by the folkoric tradition) but also by deploying her as a meta-commentary on this kind of use of children in Iranian cinema.

The innocent, naïve and often resilient children in major Iranian films like *The Colour of Paradise* (1999) safely model ethical responses to confronting material. Langford (2019: 68) identifies the way that the political content thus embodied is both grounded and enhanced by the perception that child actors are inescapably children first. This 'reality effect' connects the viewer to a realism that exists beyond the diegetic realm of the film. Anvari's Dorsa literalizes this allegorical tradition of Iranian cinema by fluctuating between her existence as an actual curious and inquisitive child and as a vessel for the violent *djinn*. Anvari's Dorsa undermines the tradition of children furnishing a more or less safe space to articulate politics. Her unresolved fate points to an unsettling conclusion, that children are never exempt from harm – not in cinema, not in the Iranian folk culture of the *djinn*, not in reality or in its effects.

Djinn haunting

In Islamic theology, *djinn* are not unlike angels in the Judaeo-Christian tradition. Much as the latter exist on a spectrum from good to fallen, *djinn* are capable of benevolent action, but also of a terrible capacity to cause grief and pain. They are judged mostly invisible, but may make brief appearances. When they enter the home, they undermine the sureties of health and career. Where there is domestic tumult, there is reason to suspect the presence of *djinn*. Moreover, they impose a new and pitiless temporality of raw, permanently eventful insecurity. As such, human–*djinn* interactions illuminate and, importantly, domesticate the everyday realities of violence and dispossession. The *djinn*'s 'ghostly signals' give shape to fears and concerns that are 'contained or repressed or blocked from view' (Gordon 1997: 2; Lincoln and Lincoln 2015: 193). When Shideh receives a fine for leaving her home without her chador, her offence relies on home as a fixed point from which one might leave, and broad categories of citizens divisible into lawful and unlawful – a picture complicated by the presence of the *djinn*. While the *djinn*'s violence may align with the state, its actions undermine the coherence of the home as a site from which one might claim a space of exemption from persecution. Under *djinn* haunting, distinctions such as inside and outside differ only by their intensity of menace (Pandolfo 2019). Shideh and Dorsa's transgressions – even by virtue of negligence – only serve to further ensnare them in the inescapable grasp of the *djinn*. Once again, the home has become movable and, even as Shideh and Dorsa attempt to relocate, the home has left an indelible mark that brings punishment and torture – even in circumstances where the protagonists are unaware of the rule or tradition they have broken.

A detailed reckoning of the *djinn*'s powers does not appear until the halfway point of the film, prompted by Dorsa's sudden defiance of her mother. In one sense, there is a psychologically plausible explanation here: Dorsa's changed behaviour is triggered by her father leaving for the front line, but her symptoms – sleeplessness, compulsive behaviours, screaming – increase to such an extent that they call the adequacy of that explanation into question. Dorsa's insomnia serves as the occasion for tea parties that appear more real, more *attended*, than can comfortably fit within the symptomology of traumatic abandonment. When confronted by her mother during one of her outbursts, Dora recounts speaking to some sort of monster, negotiating the sharing of space, property and keepsakes. Shideh is unwilling to believe her daughter's descriptions of supernatural encounters, choosing instead to lay the blame at the feet of a child who has recently moved into the apartment above theirs. The neighbour harbouring the accused child accepts Shideh's premise, but speculatively shifts the blame onto the *djinn* who may well be tormenting both children. Rather than denying responsibility for the child's actions, the neighbour explains that this is a ward she has taken in from a relative, and that as far as she can tell the child is indeed deeply disturbed. But the neighbour goes further, conveying her fear about a *djinn* who inhabits the building and is likely the source of the havoc played on both children. In this moment, the neighbour emerges as a sort of folk expert, explaining that 'if they take something you treasure … there's no escape from them'. This moment, while subtle and occurring before the *djinn* has made its entrance, is an overt acknowledgement of the film's diasporic metaphor.

Anvari transmutes the diasporic trauma experience into a subverted trope of paranormal haunting. By applying distinct and culturally specific aspects to this otherwise Western tradition of Gothic horror and haunted houses, Anvari can dislodge the centrality of the house, or even the monster, in order to transform the terrifying spectre into the mobility of home itself. In the film's closing scene, as Shideh and Dorsa drive away, we are reminded of the personal belongings strewn among the rubble of their doubly wracked apartment, the target of both an Iraqi missile and the *djinn* itself. The camera cranes over the debris only to linger on the crucial mementos: Shideh's textbook and Dorsa's doll's decapitated head. The book is blown by the wind, urgently flipping its pages as though it were being rifled for clues. This final moment serves both to free the protagonists of the worldly objects that weighed them down and to announce that their treasuring of these objects, and the sentiment they inspired, in fact functions as a kind of memory tattoo – through which they are indefinitely stained and unable to escape. This closing image registers the paranormal realization of the symbiotic relationship of trauma and hauntings, memory and, in turn, the home and the objects to which it cleaves to: this is inescapable and forever a component and tool for building and understanding one's relationship with home.

Naficy (2001: 127) writes that the mother–daughter dynamic is one often explored in diasporic filmmaking:

> In both accented literature and cinema, conflict arises because mothers and daughters occupy different generational, cultural, class, linguistic, and imaginative worlds. While mothers tend to be preoccupied with the past and with their far-off homeland, their daughters are more apt to be concerned with the here and now.

In this film, however, Anvari achieves a more complex display of intergenerational conflict. Dorsa, who is both innocent and corruptible, is entranced by the presence of a *djinn*, a figure from the folk-past who is nonetheless 'real'. Conversely, as a rational adult, Shideh is learning that trust in a particular memory and mythology is necessary for her self-preservation. This serves to reveal some of the inherent tensions of diasporic filmmaking, which requires a perspective that is at once distrusting of the concept of home and also endlessly trying to define it, or secure it in the process of definition. Beyond the demonic education that Shideh receives, this also represents a moment when the audience is instructed on how best to understand the terms of the film. The conventions of the horror genre create an expectation that it is wise to believe the warnings of otherwise unreliable and superstitious characters – much like Bram Stoker's (2003 [1897]) *Dracula* where it is Van Helsing, the marginalized figure steeped in folklore, who is best placed to describe phenomena that do not sit well in modernity.

The house is alive – and it hurts

The undetonated missile penetrating Shideh's apartment is, among other things, the direct consequence of US military aid to Iraq. In this way, not only does the missile serve as a visceral warning of potential violence, it also opens a pathway through which Western culture, in one of its most familiar iterations, can enter. This literal penetration is paired with a more figurative infiltration of Western culture articulated through a bootleg copy of a Jane Fonda instructional aerobics VHS tape.

First, we will consider the more literal penetration. While some residents are harmed by this missile, including one death, the violence of its penetration is more sinister and subtle than a kind of direct confrontation. The missile further degrades the structural integrity of the building, generating a precarity that hangs over the rest of the film. However, it is the ongoing damage caused by the weapon that has the most profound impacts. In between the sequences of unexplained and unnatural events, as well as the more overt hauntings that happen in the film's final act, Anvari places ominous close-ups of the crack in the ceiling caused by the undetonated missile. These shots serve a dual purpose. On the one hand, they entrench the fragility of the apartment as structure. On the other, the associative editing of the crack with the supernatural events in the apartment transforms it from mere property damage into something fleshier. The crack is a wound: the invasive source of domestic pain. Shideh's constant – and clearly futile – exercise of taping and retaping vulnerable windows throughout the film further bolsters this sensation of house-pain. And as the various assaults on the home register in the creaks, groans and cracks expressed, it becomes clear that these injuries will inevitably extend to Shideh and Dorsa themselves.

Once the crack has caused the building to undergo an organic and emotional transformation, it places certain other images and ideas in the film into context – most notably, the use of a tarpaulin to cover the hole left by the undetonated missile. This tarpaulin gathers various reference points. First, it is a kind of camouflage. The large piece of beige fabric creates an outward impression that the structure remains intact. From outside the building, it would be difficult to notice the gaping hole left by the shelling. However, from the inside the tarpaulin's bandaging of an enormous wound is both obvious and profound. Cutaway shots feature the tarpaulin rippling in the wind, flowing against the stony walls. Here the tarpaulin assumes a skin-like quality. Like the crack in the ceiling, its relationship to something living registers, and with it the trauma stained into the war-torn apartment. Moreover, the tarpaulin indicates the way the *djinn* has chosen to become the apartment and also the building, haunting not just the space in which Dorsa and Shideh live, but the home in its totality. Again, this is an important subversion of tropes involving the home and house in horror films. Rather than taking aspects of the home that might otherwise seem reliable and proving them to be false, Anvari's *djinn* becomes the home, and uses its very texture and quality to persecute and torture the protagonists. In the film's final act, as Shideh and Dorsa confront the *djinn*, the tarpaulin transforms into the demonic presence, becoming in the process a shapeshifting chador, the very thing Shideh resisted outside the home, now returning – literally – with a vengeance. As a powerful metaphor for the diasporic experience, the attachment of this structural damage to the physical and mental wellbeing of Shideh and Dorsa serves to demonstrate that the physical, psychic and cultural experience of a home are all messily linked. Even to uproot and leave this place would not necessarily repair the damage already inflicted.

Shideh's repertoire of burdened objects includes that VHS tape of Jane Fonda teaching aerobics. This is an insupportable thing from the position of the regime, yet in Shideh's hands it becomes part of a domestic routine, a banal reprieve from the stress of the war. Shideh's sole comfort, however, seems to be interpreted by the *djinn* and Dorsa as forbidden. In using the cassette to claim time for herself, the VHS transforms into an object of forbidden pleasure, one that in the eyes of her djinn-possessed child creates the conditions of neglect. Eventually, either Dorsa or the *djinn* (Anvari leaves the matter undecided) retaliates and destroys the tape, unspooling it into a rubbish bin. The camera lingers on Shideh's hand slowly lifting the tape out of the trash, its contents like tangled intestines now intermingled with organic waste. The sequence comes the closest to providing the visual aftermath of a missile strike deferred above their heads.

Shortly after this sequence, Dorsa's mania sets in and the film's pace quickens to more terrifying effect. But the lead into this direct conflict with the *djinn* is to make the home itself a space of conflict, from both invited and uninvited transgressions of Western culture and ancestral folklore. Such liminality is recognized in Zahra Khosroshahi's (2019) 'Vampires, Jinn and the Magical in Iranian Horror Films':

> [*Under The Shadow* is] a diasporic film, engaging with the world of in-betweenness through its very form. The demonic forces that drive the plot … become a means through which the film explores the consequences and trauma of war and the religious state.

Key to Khosroshahi's assertion is that form plays a crucial role in creating the conditions through which the film functions as a diasporic horror. This focus on form is justified by the ways in which Anvari repeatedly subverts horror tropes that serve to illustrate aspects of the diasporic tension in relation to the definition of a home. Rather than organizing the film's politics around the plot, Anvari weaponizes and anthropomorphizes the insecure home as a space that speaks to the diasporic condition. Instead of providing the audience with an explicit monster terrorizing the characters for no apparent reason, Anvari fashions the *djinn*'s behaviours to animate their apartment and shadow the protagonists, exposing the inseparability of danger and comfort in a home filled with loved objects. The *djinn*-home is as if alive, capable of feeling rejection and remorse, and the pain it experiences – and, by turn, inflicts – can be read into the inhabitants of that home, to determine what they value and define as key parts of their identity. In other words, if Dorsa and Shideh are trapped in between a new life outside their home and the familiar life inside, it is the *djinn* and all the memories that this particular corporealizing of home (the apartment) makes real, and supernatural, that allow for a haunting full of resentment and disappointment.

Conclusion

Through *Under the Shadow*, Anvari probes the extent to which the diasporic experience can remake the haunted house trope by creating a monster – the *djinn* – that punishes its victims from a position of non-specific, but still pointed resentment. As the *djinn* challenges what can and cannot feel local, Anvari distils a framework for the horrors at play when building or maintaining a home – or, indeed, when leaving home behind. The mother and daughter duo of the film add further layers to this framework by distorting and texturing intergenerational conflict in strange and – crucially – difficult ways. Rather than simply anthropomorphizing the trauma and pain that members of the diaspora feel as a kind of monster from the past, Anvari goes further by offering a demon that challenges its protagonists to grapple with how they will cope with bringing the past to their present and future. Anvari asks us to consider what it means to remember a home you left behind if that home is still following you.

References

Dobbs, S. (2016), 'Babak Anvari Interview: *Under the Shadow*, Horror, Statham', *Den of Geek*, 7 October. Available online: https://www.denofgeek.com/movies/babak-anvari-interview-under-the-shadow-horror-statham (accessed 6 June 2023).

Gordon, A. (1997), *Ghostly Matters: Haunting and the Sociological Imagination*, Minneapolis: University of Minnesota Press.

Khosroshahi, Z. (2019), 'Vampires, Jinn and the Magical in Iranian Horror Films', *Frames Cinema Journal*, 16 December. Available online: http://framescinemajournal.com/article/vampires-jinn-and-the-magical-in-iranian-horror-films (accessed 6 June 2023).

Langford, M. (2019), *Allegory in Iranian Cinema: The Aesthetics of Poetry and Resistance*, London: Bloomsbury.

Lincoln, M. and B. Lincoln (2015), 'Toward a Critical Hauntology: Bare Afterlife and the Ghosts of Ba Chúc', *Comparative Studies in Society and History*, 57 (1): 191–220. Available online: https://doi.org/10.1017/S0010417514000644"https://doi.org/10.1017/S0010417514000644 (accessed 16 June 2023).

Mingant, N. (2015), 'A Peripheral Market? Hollywood Majors and the Middle East/North Africa Market', *The Velvet Light Trap*, 75: 73–87. Available online: https://doi.org/10.7560/VLT7506 (accessed 6 June 2023).

Naficy, H. (2001), *An Accented Cinema: Exilic and Diasporic Filmmaking*, Princeton, NJ: Princeton University Press.

Pandolfo, S. (2019), 'The Knot of the Soul: Postcolonial Conundrums, Madness, and the Imagination', in *Postcolonial Disorders*, edited by M. DelVecchio Good, S.T. Hyde, S. Pinto and B.J. Good, 329–58. Berkeley, CA: University of California Press.

Seymour, T. (2016), 'Terror in Tehran: Under the Shadow and the Politics of Horror', *The Guardian*, 29 September. Available online: https://www.theguardian.com/film/2016/sep/29/terror-in-tehran-babak-anvari-under-the-shadow (accessed 6 June 2023).

Stoker, B. (2003 [1897]), *Dracula*, New York: Penguin.

Films

The Colour of Paradise (1999), directed by Majid Majidi [film], Tehran: Varahonar Company.

Dr Strangelove (1964), directed by Stanley Kubrick [film], Los Angeles and London: Columbia Pictures and Hawk Films.

Halloween (1978), directed by John Carpenter [film], Los Angeles: Compass International Pictures Inc.

Scream (1996), directed by Wes Craven [film], New York: Dimension Films.

Under the Shadow (2016), directed by Babak Anvari [film], London: Wigwam Films.

Part Two

Found-footage horrors

5

'It's too late for all of us': Ritual, repression and the historical imagination in *Noroi: The Curse*

Jeremy Kingston

In Meiro Koizumi's art film *Where the Silence Fails (Double Projection #1)* (2013), two screens are projected – one partially overlapping the other – in which two men face each other. One wears brown military aviation goggles; the other is bare-headed. They are, in fact, the same person: Mr Tadamasa Itazu, an ex-kamikaze pilot (*tokkōtai*) whose plane crash-landed safely with engine trouble in 1945 when he was nineteen years old.[1] His fellow pilots successfully completed their mission and Itazu has lived with the 'ultimate shame' ever since (Koizumi n.d.). On the second screen, Koizumi, who is off-camera, asks Itazu to act as one of his fellow pilots, Mr Ashida, who died in the mission. This fictional dialogue is held by Itazu himself, who converses with the ghost of his friend as if he were present. The two projections overlap in thirds, creating a space in which these two presents collide. Koizumi's piece is not only a creative playing out of a ghostly encounter – with its implications of guilt, shame and the spectral address – but also allegorizes modern Japan's tendency to systematically subdue or 'delete' its imperialist past and discussion of the Asia-Pacific War (Zohar 2016: 117). An unlikely survivor, and therefore himself a type of ghostly subject, Itazu effectively plays the ghost, and under Koizumi's direction is performatively able to work through his survivor's guilt.

Koizumi's audible direction points to what Zohar (2016: 129) terms a 'performative recollection'. Through a self-consciously performative style, Koizumi's work 'permits a direct encounter with images pushed into oblivion' (2016: 119) and represents the ability to engage with history in 'a dislocated manner' (2016: 123). As the title of the work suggests, Itazu's recollections emerge 'where the silence fails', and refute the revisionism that characterizes Japan's relationship with its history of imperialism. By opening up this third space between the repressed past and dynamic present through the emblematic *tokkōtai* – a figure firmly fixed in the global imaginary – Koizumi transfixes a potent piece of Japanese military and cultural history and brings it into negotiation with the present: the living, breathing Itazu. In doing so, he critiques the cultural status of the *tokkōtai* as a figure crucial to the internal circuitry of Japanese 'conservative attitudes of nationalism, patriotism, and self-sacrifice' (2016: 124). While also a poignant rumination on guilt, shame and patriotism, the piece is also self-reflexive as a documentary. The viewer is privy to Koizumi's directions as he shapes this fictional dialogue, muddying the distinction between artistic intention and 'pure testimony' (2016: 128).

An example of this performative recollection is Kōji Shiraishi's *Noroi: The Curse* (2005), a film that serves to open up the dialogue of history by engaging with Japan's pre-modern spirits.[2] This chapter will discuss *Noroi* in terms of its explicit relation to truth and history – bound as it is by the rubrics and expectations of mockumentary and as it has emerged from the milieu of Japanese horror cinema. The film follows in the footsteps of the global popularity of found-footage horror after the release of *The Blair Witch Project* (1999), as well as a surge of interest in Japanese horror following Hideo Nakata's *Ringu* (1998), Takashi Shimizu's *Ju-On: The Grudge* (2002) and Takashi Miike's *One Missed Call* (2003) – all of which spurred speedy Hollywood remakes. Analyses of national allegory in Japanese horror have focused largely upon the after-images of Hiroshima – 'a master code for catastrophe in the twentieth century' (Yoneyama 1999: 15) – that have been burned into the historical imaginaries of Japan's filmmakers. Previtali (2017: 137) likens the effect to the nuclear shadows seared into surfaces in Hiroshima and Nagasaki after the flash of the atomic blasts on 6 and 9 August 1945 – images of 'excess' that have formed a seemingly indelible link between history and its representation, while also entailing the negative possibility of 'an imprint without a matrix, a shadow without a body' (Previtali 2017: 137). The paradox of the image without the body – crystallized and 'subtracted' from time – points to the difficulty of addressing traumatic history and disaster, events that 'can only be presented through allegory: the ruins of a history that is both "shattered and preserved"' (Lehman 2008: 243, quoting Benjamin 2007: 169).

Since the 1960s, Japan's horror cinema has tried to restore the body to the event, employing the 'monstrous feminine' of *onryou* (vengeful spirit) narratives to articulate the histories of those left behind by Japan's modernization and the country's disavowal of 'unpunished historical crimes' (Blake 2008: 44; Creed 1993). Terrifying in her retribution, the 'abject woman' functions as both sign and augury of death, calling her victims to acknowledge and witness what has been silenced (Blake 2008: 47). Yoneyama (1999: 32) argues that Japan's forgetfulness has been engrained in an 'ongoing reformulation of knowledge about the nation's recent past … a process of amnes(t)ic remembering whereby the past is tamed through the reinscription of memories'. As an antidote to amnesia, Shiraishi's film is a memory-work that utilizes the formal qualities of documentary to allegorize the silences surrounding Japan's path to nationalism in the early twentieth century.

In *Noroi*, the fragments of Japan's history are coded within a narrative of the demonic, figuring an ancient deity named Kagutaba as the spectre and sign of what has been lost to modernity. Kagutaba was the object of worship for Shimokage village, a community founded by sorcerers who developed a system of rites called Shimokage's Way. After a dam is built in 1978, the locals are forcibly removed to a neighbouring town and the village is submerged. During the final ritual for Kagutaba before the town's desertion, the demon – angry that the ritual should be left to fade away – possesses Junko Ishii (Tomono Kuga), who is participating in the ritual as a prosopopoeia, wearing an eery eyeless mask that we come to know as the face of Kagutaba. We later learn that she believes she has heard the voice of God and is spurred to attempt the demon's resurrection. The film follows a paranormal investigator who tries to piece together the uncanny traces of the curse that surround a series of people. Pigeons appear to follow those who are cursed and characters are haunted by images of repeated loops and compelled to construct them out of cord and rope – a motif that, in its circularity, echoes the scientific verification to which these spectral events are subjected throughout the film (Nelson 2021: 219–20). These traces all lead the investigator back to the village and the underlying event of its submersion that forms the traumatic site around which the curse (or *noroi*) is established. The village is buried by the necessity of expanding infrastructure in modern Japan and its spiritual economy is disrupted by this state interference. Rather than being an affirmative tabula rasa, the dam becomes ground-zero for a clash between the pre-modern past and a capitalist present.

Shimokage's submersion can be read allegorically as a breach in service of Japanese modernity proceeding from the 'spiritual violation[s]' enacted during the Meiji period from 1868 to 1912 (Figal 2000: 202). Gerald Figal traces the 'supernatural ideology' employed by the Japanese state during the Meiji period by way of shrine mergers, a policy that saw smaller hamlet shrines razed or decommissioned in favour of larger, centralized shrines – an action that 'possessed the ideological aim of channelling the people's respect for local Shintō deities and ancestors toward the imperial nation-state' (Figal 2000: 202). While providing the secular sub-stratum for Japan's nationalism in the early twentieth century, Meiji rulers inadvertently opened a deep wound on the level of the folk by interfering in its structures of memorialization, funerary rites and worship. Lowenstein (2005: 10) argues that culture's fascination with wounding has come to equate contemporary nations with their historical trauma: 'It is unthinkable to address the idea ... of contemporary "Japan" without Hiroshima.' Equally, it is unthinkable to address the idea of contemporary Japan without acknowledging the ideology that bolstered its nationalism in the late nineteenth and early twentieth centuries. In this sense, *Noroi* does not find its referent in the traumatic ground-zero of the atomic bombs; rather, Shiraishi distils the transgressions of modernity into the figure of an ancient deity cut loose in the service of progress, secularization and the unhindered development of modernity. The film delves further into the cultural imaginary, tracing the alienation of the folk, the amnesia for the ancient and the decimation of *kami* (deities or spirits) alongside the fashioning of Japanese Spirit. Rather than serving to close the open wound of Hiroshima and Nagasaki, *Noroi* uses an 'allegorical vision' (Lehman 2008: 241) to open up what Lowenstein (2005: 2) describes as the 'allegorical moment', illustrating the impossibility of forgetting the infraction of modernity by bringing forth the past to shock us in the present.

By laying bare the wounds of history, Japan's horror cinema since the 1960s has 'provided one of the most suitable mechanisms through which to articulate anxieties and concerns over the changing nature of Japanese society', as Balmain's (2008: 31) seminal analysis of the subject suggests. The belief is corroborated by Iles (2008: 109), who argues that anxieties are 'cathartically expunged through an almost ritualistic confrontation' with the monstrous. Such a remedy is not unique to the filmic mode, nor to any particular regional cinema, but can be seen throughout Japanese visual culture in the 'prodigious appearance' of the supernatural within its art during periods of political, social and national turmoil, as observed by cultural anthropologist Komatsu Kazuhiko (Figal 2000: 22). In this sense, monsters are not stable figures in Japan's cultural imaginary, but surface in times of unease, such as in the rise of *bakemono* (monsters) in the transition between the Tokugawa period (1603–1867) and the Meiji period (1868–1912), a passage that heralded Japan's rapid entrance into modernity (Figal 2000: 22). The most evocative example is Ishirō Honda's *Godzilla* (1954) – a film Balmain (2008: 37) argues is transparent as allegory of the ruin wrought by war and the atomic bombs, also reflecting a larger anxiety surrounding the 'erosion of pre-modern Japanese structures, or indeed over the very notion of "Japan" as a nation'. Japanese horror cinema thus emerges from a central tension between a strident, implacable modernity and the 'nostalgic imaginings' (McRoy 2008: 76) that drive the impulse to recover what has been lost (Balmain 2008: 31). Through its pseudo-factual narrative of the ancient demonic, *Noroi* serves Walter Benjamin's (2007: 262) notion of the allegorical imperative for the historical materialist – 'to blast open the continuum of history' – bringing the past into focus in the present through the 'allegorical mortification of time' (Lehman 2008: 246).

Found-footage horror, documentary and the 'spectacle of the real'

Noroi begins with a foreboding disclaimer: 'The names of persons and organizations in this movie have been partially changed … This video documentary is deemed too disturbing for public viewing.' Such a disclaimer, Wallace (2020: 522) argues, 'grounds the film's diegesis within our own world', suggesting that what is about to be revealed may pose a threat to our own safety. This prologue promises that the truth is 'too astounding for us to imagine'. The film proper begins with a quote from seasoned 'Reporter of the Supernatural' Masafumi Kobayashi (Jin Muraki): 'I want the truth. No matter how terrifying.' Unlike reality television's sober, black-clad, boisterous ghost-hunters, Kobayashi is a fumbling and earnest paranormal reporter. The narrator informs us that Kobayashi has since gone missing following a fire that claimed the life of his wife, Keiko (Miyoko Hanai). The footage has been assembled and edited by his cameraman, Miyajima (Hisashi Miyajima). Shiraishi furnishes the footage with hallmarks of documentary, utilizing its formal qualities to present what at first glance might be considered a mockumentary. Shiraishi's style, however, is more appropriately subsumed under Zohar's (2016: 123) rubric of 'performative recollection', sharing a testimonial impulse more attuned to the voids of a silenced history and the dialogic process of their exposure.

Documentary occupies a 'privileged position' in the cultural psyche due in part to its perceived indexical relationship with fact and a belief in the direct correlation between the image of an event and its truthfulness. As a narrative form, documentary retains a sense of '"fullness and completion" in its representations'

(Roscoe and Hight 2001: 6). This assumption betrays the fact that documentary is situated within a network of tensions of which the camera is only one alterable facet, a medium existing on a 'continuum between fact and fiction' (2001: 23). Koizumi's *'parafictional'* film operates on this same premise, sliding between fact and fiction in order to draw attention to the artificial mode of its telling (Zohar 2016: 126, emphasis in original). In a similar vein, mockumentary hijacks the narrative codes of documentary – archival or found-footage, interviews, extra-diegetic narration – in order to 'critique factual discourse' (Roscoe and Hight 2001: 53). In Koizumi's 'performative recollection', *Double Projection #1* (2013), Itazu's testimony is resolved and expanded through an element of fantasy not in order to undermine or critique his recollections but to create a ghostly third-space in which to confront Itazu's shame at having survived his mission, a shame that is embroiled in Japan's ongoing legacy of forgetting and silence around its imperial role in the Asia-Pacific (Zohar 2016: 120, 123).

Distinct from satirical modes of mockumentary that adopt a self-conscious posture in which truth is never truly at stake – found-footage horror in the documentary style capitalizes on documentary's veracity to calcify its representations as images of the real, satisfying horror audiences' 'desire for the authentication of the horrific experience' (Ancuta 2015: 149). The horror is not happening to actors embedded in flashes on a screen, but to real people (Sayad 2016: 45). It is part archival document, part 'survivor's log' (Reyes 2015: 122). Sayad (2016: 45) argues that found-footage dissembles the distinction between film and reality through the style's commitment to the 'frame's undoing': the film is 'presented not as mere artifact but as a fragment of the real world, and the implication is that its material might well spill over into it'. In the context of *Noroi*, this material is the silenced past – like Koizumi's film, *Noroi*'s 'performative recollection' sets the stage for a 'cultural visualization of the forgotten and repressed' (Zohar 2016: 119, 123).

The generic techniques of found-footage horror and fictional documentary horror – with its shaky camerawork, dizzying pans and bump-zooms, audio interference and 'precariously framed images' (Sayad 2016: 43) – are easily recognizable today some twenty-four years after the mainstream success of *The Blair Witch Project*. *Noroi* manipulates its audience through its feigned status as an investigative documentary, as glimpses of the paranormal are freeze-framed, zoomed in upon, enhanced, spectrographically analysed and replayed frame by frame in grainy texture. Discussing the found-footage space-horror *Apollo 18* (2011), Wallace (2020: 524) suggests that the filmic texture does not just point towards the veracity of the film's claim to be archival footage, but to the monstrous presence of the supernatural within the footage itself through aesthetic and physical disturbances such as degradation of the film-reels – an indicator that what is being shown, replete with 'excessive textures', can be believed as an historical artefact. These textures not only lend credibility to the text itself, but shorten the gap between the monstrous and the audience. Incursions into the real world are thematized by the prevalence in Japanese horror films of *nensha* (thought-images or psychic photography) – the ability to burn thoughts into photographic images (Kang and Kiyomi 2002: 53). Similar to *Ringu*'s Sadako, who possesses this skill, psychic images are inexplicably burned into the frames of Kobayashi's film. When he is reviewing some of the raw footage, the audio suddenly distorts wildly, pixels flutter across the screen before a tessellated image begins to form: a wall of demon masks lit eerily in deep blue. Shiraishi places the audience within dangerous reach of this image – an acute vulnerability generated by the curse's contagion and the immediacy of the shaky-cam (Ancuta 2015: 153).

While the same cannot be said for *The Blair Witch Project*, the pre-millennium appearance of which transposed the 'indeterminacy' (Mallin 2001: 112) and preparedness in the face of a rapidly approaching Y2K, found-footage horror in the twenty-first century situates its narratives within the type of 'amateur aesthetics' (Reyes 2015: 123) offered by the simulcast and replay of 9/11 (Wallace 2020: 521). As Wallace (2020: 521) argues, 'aesthetic signifiers of "terror" sit in tension with the continued erosion of epistemic faith in the documentary image to which they belong'. Found-footage monsters are evasive, with the medium operating through a system of obstruction by which the camera often fails to apprehend the object of horror due to aesthetic noise (2020: 531). Technology fails, frames are filled with 'dead pixels and dropout', data are corrupted, sweeping cuts drag the horrifying image into long strands of blurred visual matter (2020: 533). Occlusion brings into question 'the documentary's failure in the face of the existential challenges of post-modernity and post-truth' (2020: 531). Nelson (2021: 213) notes Shiraishi's tendency to 'both reveal and obscure occultish "hidden" worlds and entities, forcing the viewer to constantly question the version of "truth" that is presented on screen'. She concludes: 'Visibility does not equal knowability' (2021: 212). In the context of Japan's horror cinema and the confrontation with what has been wilfully forgotten through a national amnesia, occlusion and aesthetic noise also indicate a difficulty in confronting images of excess 'pushed into oblivion' (Zohar 2016: 117).

The found-footage phenomenon has its roots not in Eduardo Sánchez and Daniel Myrick's *The Blair Witch Project* (1999), but in Ruggero Deodato's *Cannibal Holocaust* (1980) (Sayad 2016: 44). Deodato's film follows a group of anthropologists as they attempt to contact and study a cannibal tribe. Their demise and the ultra-realistic depictions of death and cannibalism led to the film being used as evidence against Deodato, who was placed before a court to provide proof-of-life for his actors (Reyes 2015: 123). The same slippage between factual discourse and found-footage horror propelled the success of *The Blair Witch Project*, a production with a cost of $35,000 and a box-office pull of close to $150 million in 1999 alone (Telotte 2001: 32). The film's aggressive marketing campaign banked on its marketability as a factual document central to locating the teens who had seemingly disappeared following their encounter with the witch. Missing posters were hung, advertisements taken out in college gazettes and media spots secured with *MTV* and *Rolling Stone* (2001: 33). The elements of the film's marketing campaign, Telotte argues, 'suggest we see the film *not as film*, but as one more artifact ... which we might view in order to better understand a kind of repressed or hidden reality' (2001: 35, emphasis in original).

Noroi is situated within the pantheon of Japanese horror cinema that emerged on the cusp of the twenty-first century. Until recently, the film was mostly lost to the English-speaking world, available only through grainy reproductions or clandestine distributions over the internet, until horror streaming service Shudder acquired the rights some twelve years after its Japanese release. *Noroi* is not Shiraishi's only found-footage horror film – his later works in the genre include *Occult* (2009), *Cursed Violent People* (2010) and *Shirome* (2016). With its thematic links to Japanese pop-group 'idol culture' (Nelson 2016: 140), *Shirome* most explicitly engages with aspects of truth, actuality and artifice. As Nelson (2016: 141) argues, Japanese 'idol culture', with its painfully manufactured veneers, cookie-cutter imagery and acknowledged artificiality, shares a strain with found-footage horror in that both mediums 'base their appeal on a "mutual agreement" between fans and creators to maintain an illusion of reality'. Symptomatic of a media-saturated, audiovisually captured and disenchanted public caught within growing 'transnational power and influence', this 'spectacle of the real' is recourse against the breakdown of 'national myths and national identity' (2016: 142). As performative recollection, *Noroi* engages with spectacle to generate an encounter with the monstrous truth. The plot is complex, adhering to the piecemeal schematics of investigative journalism, while the ability to slow the framerate, freeze-frame and zoom into the horror allows Shiraishi to dwell in the still-image and initiate what Barthes would call a 'punctum' – the opening of a wound that dismantles the safety of the audience through the 'illusion' of the indexical image (Howell 2015: 84).

The end of ritual and the open wound

Lowenstein (2005: 95) argues that allegorizing the wounds of Hiroshima and Nagasaki requires a commitment to the 'politics underlying discourses of victimization and war responsibility' prevalent in the nation's post-war culture. The resonating images of Hiroshima and Nagasaki, burned into the cultural imaginary by the flash of the blasts and their resulting fallout (Previtali 2017), found their chief symbol in the city-razing devastation of *Godzilla* (Japanese *Gojira* 1954). Much like Figal's observation of the emergence of the grotesque in Meiji-era art (2000: 22), the arrival of *Godzilla* on Japanese screens came at a time of socio-cultural disturbance: 'the monstrous mutant reptile with its atomic breath functions as a reminder of the devastation caused by nuclear weapons and critiques modern technological warfare, whilst simultaneously mourning the loss of tradition' (Balmain 2008: 31). *Godzilla* drew attention to the enduring presence of the pre-modern embedded within traditional beliefs, while simultaneously representing 'a physical manifestation of the disruption of *wa*, or the harmony between man and nature' (Balmain 2008: 38). The monster was thus capable of addressing the lacunae left by Japan's traumatic history that had been repressed and diffused within its historical imaginings.

Found-footage horror is uniquely positioned to engage with these troubled and silenced histories, providing counter-memories against the 'obfuscation, denial or revisionism' that colour colonial and nationalist histories (Blake 2008: 23). Found-footage horror films disturb in two ways: by threatening to spill over into our world and by unsettling the notions of truth and history taken for granted within a 'post-truth' society reliant on audio-visual artefacts (Wallace 2020: 535). They erect documentary apparatuses only to witness their failure to contain or represent the true nature of the horror, often foregoing resolution in order to leave an 'open wound' that resists closing (2020: 535). For a national cinema so concerned with its ghosts, Japan's repressed history bleeds through its narrative forms. In Fredric Jameson's terms, what has been repressed is symptomatic of a political unconscious emerging through narrative. Allegory is critically positioned to rectify this type of repression and 'heals the gap, between the present and a disappearing past which, without interpretation, would be otherwise irretrievable and foreclosed' (Fineman 1980: 49). Lim (2001: 294) argues that as an anachronistic figure, the spectre 'estranges' the audience from linearity, offering the counter-notion that 'times other than the present contend with each other in the disputed Now' (2001: 294). This is denied in the 'historical revisionism' and cultural forgetting embedded within Japan's cultural imaginary (Law 2008: 269). The historical consciousness within *Noroi*'s generic codes and concerns is memorial in nature – willing the audience to remember in order to acknowledge the traces of the pre-modern that survived the cultural and spiritual upheaval of the Meiji period.

Blake (2008: 47) notes that *onryou* narratives 'granted a highly resonant insight not only into Japanese cultural trauma of the post-war period but the culturally silenced horrors of the pre-war and war-time years'. Silence, she argues, speaks. Like *Ringu*'s tape-hopping Sadako – the long-haired, watery ghost exploding into the world of the living through the crackling static of the television screen – the *onryou* speaks, unbinding the silences of history that are 'testimony to the existence of un-addressed and hence unassimilated horrific events in each nation's past' (2008: 21). While the decimation of Hiroshima and Nagasaki and the subsequent US occupation loom at the edges of Japan's cinema, it is the pre-war and wartime years that flow through *Noroi*'s narrative coding, captured by the after-images of modernity and the island-nation's path to a militarized nationalism. Balmain (2008: 168) locates in contemporary Japanese cinema a pervasive sense of alienation refracted across styles of techno-horror, exemplified by 'urban alienation in a society dominated by the image'. Since *Ringu*, the image in Japanese horror cinema has been primarily a visual contagion. Narratives of urban isolation, technology and loneliness, such as Kiyoshi Kurosawa's *Pulse* (2001) and Takashi Miike's *One Missed Call* (2003), suggest that science is both violent transgressor and the mode of an absent history's recovery and exposure – the 'ghosts within the machine' (Balmain 2008: 183). Much like *Pulse*, *Ringu* juxtaposes the traditional, 'folkloric' *onryou* narrative with a pathogenic videotape, thematizing the ever-present contrast of tradition and modern Japan (Teo 2013: 96–7).

Writing on the sentiments expressed during wartime intellectual debates in Japan – in particular, the 'Overcoming Modernity' symposium held in 1942 in Meguro, Tokyo (Krummel 2021: 87) – Anderson (2006: 21) echoes that Japan's modernity 'was to be mourned as a loss of spiritual presence'.[3] *Noroi* implements alienation as a symbol of the suffering generated by modernity's creative destructions. Throughout the course of his investigation, Kobayashi speaks with the 'Super Psychic' Mitsuo Hori (Satoru Jitsunashi). Hori is perpetually clad in crumbled sheets of aluminium foil and baffles his acquaintances, who laugh at his sporadic movements, hand-wringing, twitching eyes and terrified gaze. He is afraid, he tells Kobayashi, because he is receiving 'dangerous information' from ectoplasmic worms. As Kagutaba's curse spreads, he warns that the worms will increase if they are not dealt with. Radically alone, Hori is an outcast – which, more than being just a social status, is a 'metaphorical death' in a society defined by groupism (Balmain 2008: 174). His house – and the multiple houses of the medium, Junko Ishii – are marked by their mess and accumulation. Hori is doubly excluded from the world: through ridicule at the hands of others and due to an interminable paranoia that ejects him from the social fabric. His home is also glazed in foil, bright from the reflections of incandescent bulbs. Throughout the film, this space grows smaller. When Kobayashi later returns to Hori's house, the psychic has retreated to a foil-lined cardboard box. By the end of the film, Hori is found dead, trapped in a cramped, metallic air-duct. Apart from Kobayashi, who sees the potential for using the super-psychic to locate a missing girl – the medium, Kana (Rio Kanno) – through his abilities, Hori is assigned what Blake (2008: 50) would call 'psychotic meaningless' – a designation that signifies his exclusion from the normal.

Kagutaba's curse issues from a central site of trauma: the submerging of Shimokage and the end of the demon rituals. Isolated and ill-documented, Shimokage is already at risk of slipping into obscurity – even before its submersion it has already been forgotten. The only trace of the rituals' rites is a videotape harboured by a nearby town's historian. Performed regularly to 'pacify' Kagutaba, the ritual involves summoning the demon to possess a vessel. However, in the final ritual, the medium falls into a screaming fit. The ritual is prematurely ended and the footage freezes on the medium's demon-mask. This aborted ritual leaves an open wound, and Kagutaba becomes the Benjaminian monad, charged with the apparitional energy of the ghost, 'demanding a different kind of knowledge, a different kind of acknowledgement' – the death's head that shocks the historical materialist into the allegorical moment, reminding them that 'the past is alive enough in the present' (Gordon 2008: 64–5). Benjamin's way into history, writes Gordon (2008: 66), is through his blasting method, which 'might be conceived as entering through a different door, the door of the uncanny, the door of the fragment, the door of the shocking parallel'.

In his fifth thesis on the philosophy of history, Benjamin (2007: 255) writes: 'For every image of the past that is not recognized by the present as one of its own concerns threatens to disappear irretrievably.' This view is underwritten with the 'potential for encounters between the living and the dead' (Lincoln 2015: 193), an enervating impulse that recognizes 'the past's value for the present' (Lowenstein 2005: 16). In contrast, Japan's official memories since Hiroshima are built upon 'the grave obfuscation of the prewar Japanese Empire, its colonial practices, and their consequences' (Yoneyama 1999: 3). *Noroi* allegorizes the process of secularization that cemented Japan's growing nationalism during the Meiji period (1868–1912), which saw a decisive shift away from syncretic forms of Buddhism and Shintō – with its 'heterogeneous complexes of local beliefs' – towards a renewed emphasis on a secularized State Shintō, embodying filial devotion to the emperor and 'a homogenized belief in a unique *kokutai*' (Figal 2000: 199). Belief in 'unofficial' spirits was stripped of its religious efficacy and shoehorned into the lesser designation of 'folklore and superstition' (2000: 197). By suppressing the pre-modern elements of Japanese spiritual belief, the Meiji rulers sought to erase those elements of history that seemed contradictory to a deeply rational modernity (Tateishi 2003: 296). Historical erasures throughout the late-Meiji period and extending into the cultural amnesia of Japan's imperialism thus gave rise to uncanny repetitions.[4] Japan's pre-modern traces repeat and signify a re-emergent threat to its modern society, similar to Yoneyama's (1999: 37) note that the 'persistent yet undetectable traces of exposure to radiation' suffered by survivors of Hiroshima and Nagasaki resurface within the testimonial presence of the poisoned survivors.

Following the Russo-Japanese War of 1904–5, two concerted actions were undertaken by Meiji officials to bolster national spirit: 'the national enshrinement of the spirits of the war dead' at the infamously contentious Yasukuni Shrine and the shrine mergers that took place from 1906 to 1912 (Figal 2000: 200), whereby the state destroyed or merged thousands of provincial hamlet shrines in order to redirect worship towards larger, more centralized state shrines – effectively transforming the larger shrines into 'more effective instruments of national policy' (Fridell 1973: 11).[5]

While in theory the 'joint enshrinement' of the war dead at Yasukuni Shrine would seem to serve well the public sentiment towards the accelerating expansionism of Japan, it was just one aspect of a growing sense of 'spiritual violation' (Figal 2000: 202) in those who saw the state intervention in their spiritual affairs as too steep a price to pay for the Western-influenced modernity Japan was coming to emulate. By collectively enshrining the war dead, state officials sought not only to bind the 'would-be wandering spirits' produced by the large-scale casualties of the Russo-Japanese War, but also to bind the collective national Spirit in a state of mourning (2000: 200). However, in bypassing the rites traditionally bestowed by the dead's family, '88,243 spirits were not, strictly speaking, allowed to repose with the ancestral and clan *kami* of their respective home regions; nor could their spirits be properly memorialized as *hotoke* (a Buddha)' (2000: 200–1). The surviving families had 'no further authority' over the care bestowed upon their dead (Hardacre 1989: 148). By intervening in the 'spiritual economy' of local spiritual practice, officials attempted to bestow national significance upon the spirits of the dead, thus symbolically entwining the folk with 'national entities and with the ancestors of the imperial family itself' (Figal 2000: 201).

Local shrines that were demolished, with their contents sold or migrated, were mourned by locals who, out of allegiance to the local spirits that found their home there, attempted to rebuild (Susumu and Murphy 2009: 118). Their rituals, now performed upon spiritually empty grounds, had lost their object – the spirits were missing (Fridell 1973: 84–5). Fridell (1973: 82) writes of the 'melancholy loneliness' felt by locals who were forced to '[escort] their *ujigami* to their hamlet borders and there bid them farewell'. Citizens who worked in dangerous occupations such as ocean fishing had their guardian *kami* removed (Figal 2000: 206). *Ujigami*'s protection extended only to the hamlet borders, and in their absence citizens were left open to danger and illness (Fridell 1973: 83). The *kami* themselves were thought to have been dishonoured by the exodus – 'uprooted from the land and people with whom it had long been intimately associated ... dispatched to an alien place ... forced to accept hospitality from strangers' (1973: 83). Contrary to their conciliatory aims, Meiji officials decimated local shrine life and undermined piety towards the emperor, leading instead to a 'loss ... in patriotic spirit from the masses' (Figal 2000: 203).

The ancient ruins of Kagutaba's shrine provide *Noroi* with its allegorical energy – figuring the end of traditional ritual as a repressed wounding. Caught within the tensions of memorialization and the 'active destruction' of modernity, ruins speak to the complexities of decay and forgetting (Tateishi 2003: 296). Dower (2012: 144) argues that Hiroshima and Nagasaki re-centered Japanese memory to focus elegiacally on the horrors of nuclear devastation rather than on the 'countless Japanese atrocities' perpetrated by Japanese military operations in the Pacific Theatre. This spirit of mourning allowed Japan to view the war as 'fundamentally a *Japanese* tragedy' (2012: 144, emphasis in original). Trigg (2009: 89) aligns ruins with the possibility of the encounter with traumatic history, arguing that their spectrality 'undercuts a claim of temporal continuity, instead offering a counter-narrative in which testimony becomes guided by voids rather than points of presence'. Ruins speak precisely by being the void that marks what has been lost. As a location of testimony, ruins thus function 'in both an affective and evidential manner' (2009: 88). The Shimokage shrine and the Shikami dam, Lowenstein (2005: 102) would argue, function similarly as an 'allegorical ground zero' – a haunting absence around which the curse revolves, allowing past and present to collapse into a sensible, affective historical object.

The first encounter with Kagutaba comes when real-life celebrity Marika Matsumoto is shown on a ghost-hunting programme visiting a popular ghost-hunting site. The footage contains hallmarks of the spectral encounter – tingling on the back of the neck, sub-audible voices, possession – and the clip ends after Matsumoto collapses. It is later revealed that the footage has been edited to spare her the horror of what has been captured. The raw footage shows a ghostly, warped figure lurking in the background between two dead trees set apart from the vibrant, living forest. We learn that the voice that Matsumoto hears is that of Kagutaba. When the events surrounding Matsumoto intensify, Kobayashi agrees to visit the dam with her. They set out in a boat to the centre of the water and perform an abridged version of the demon ritual. On completion, Matstumoto no longer feels her attachment to the entity. They hear Hori screaming from the shore that they must come back before he runs into the forest. Kobayashi follows, and now in darkness, he and Hori hike into the forest where they find a shrine inscribed with the familiar looping patterns. Nearby, a magical field is tied with rope, bloody feathers and pigeon feet. As they approach the shrine, Hori screams and points; the camera whips towards a space of darkness before being flung into the green scape of night-vision, whereupon we see the medium girl Kana sitting beneath the shrine's *torii* amidst a crying, crawling, heaving mound of foetuses. Kobayashi switches to the flashlight and the scene vanishes – the *torii* is empty.

The *torii* is significant in that it marks a transitional territory – a movement from without or, perhaps more horribly, from within. As a liminal threshold space, the *torii* echoes the dread that is encoded within the architectural structures of *Noroi*. Boundaries are all too thin in its haunted spaces. There is a preoccupation with keeping evil out: buildings are lined with apotropaic objects such as sickles and rope and Hori's intense paranoia of the ectoplasmic worms sees his aluminium-foiled world shrunk into an air-vent. The *torii* marks a site of puncture. What was kept out is now inside and vice versa. Balmain

(2008: 34) stresses the Shintō belief that 'the inside (*uchi*) is associated with safety, the family and Japan as a whole' while the 'outside (*soto*) is a place of danger'. Located square on the threshold between the safety of the nation and the entropic pre-modern, the ritual marks a perforation in the lining between this world and Kagutaba's.

In her exile and infested with Kagutaba's influence, Junko Ishii uses her capacity as a nurse in abortion clinics to steal the discarded foetuses. These foetuses were fed to Kana as part of the ritual to resurrect Kagutaba; however, we are assured that this is only Kobayashi's 'speculation'. Law (2008: 273) argues that the foetus occupies a symbolic position within Japanese post-war cultural memory, figuring as the 'ultimate victim with no agency in the face of war', aligned with the horrific acts perpetrated by Japanese soldiers upon pregnant women during the Nanjing Massacre in the Second Sino-Japanese War. The image of the foetus confronts the 'historical revisionism' generated by Japanese nationalism and the unstable narratives of wartime memory chiefly symbolized by the Yasukuni Shrine (2008: 269). Junko Ishii's necromancy allows Kagutaba to represent a bifold antidote to cultural amnesia, recalling both the monstrous pre-modern and the spectre of war-crimes denied at Yasukuni Shrine even today. The horrific images, argues Law (2008: 272), 'utterly [explode] the careful counter-memory' of Japan's 'victimology'.

The failure of Kobayashi's ritual mimics a broader stroke of a troubled history that has been repressed: that which cannot be remedied against, appeased or bound, but rather transmitted through narrative. The demon is not yet depleted, not yet recognized. When Kobayashi returns to Junko Ishii's home, he finds both her and Kana dead. A boy sits beside her body, mute, and it is revealed through newspaper articles that he is not Ishii's child. Shiraishi feigns a resolution while instilling a sense of dread. Kobayashi interviews Matsumoto, who has seemingly recovered; however, the cameraman slowly zooms into a close-up, revealing a brief wavering of her smile. The documentary ends and the credits roll before cutting to another film made by an unknown person who explains that after Kobayashi's disappearance and his wife Keiko's death in the fire, a mysterious video-cassette surfaced – apparently sent by Kobayashi. The film shows the super-psychic Hori arriving at Kobayashi's house in the night then attacking the couple and the boy with a rock. Bloodied, the boy stands, and in a brief glimpse we see his face has morphed horrifically into the shape of the Kagutaba mask, while the hazy apparition of Kana lurks behind him. Hori and the boy leave, and in a fugue state Keiko sets herself and the house alight.

Conclusion

Hills (2005: 51) writes of the 'contrapuntal' tension between 'opposing and reinforcing repression/oppression' within horror films. What has been repressed is allowed to surface with the monstrous, only to be 'followed by the reactionary restoration of repression/suppression'. Where *Noroi* differs is in its commitment to the resistant wound. Repression is not restored, and the monster spills out of the frame after the failure of the ritual. The wound of modernity persists, resisting any narrative restoration to its place within the cultural unconscious. The demon in *Noroi* is those left behind, transfixed and excluded, suppressed by the creative destructions of modern Japan. The potency of the spectre is its capability as witness, bursting into the present with a keen 'nonsynchronism' (Lim 2001: 288) that troubles the historical narratives that have sedimented into fact. Lim (2001: 289) argues that the ghost film functions as historical allegory when it reinvigorates an 'almost-forgotten history' as a legible, meaningful object: 'In these ghost films, nostalgia and allegory coalesce, promoting a radicalized historical consciousness that counters the blinkeredness of historicism and modernity's homogenous time.' The found-footage trope of ghosts existing simultaneously with the present, only to be uncovered by night-vision or a certain shift in the light, speaks to the 'palimpsest' nature of allegory, a 'textual doubling that allows one stratum to be construed via another' (2001: 291) – a third-space in which two presents may coalesce into a sensible, affective object of history.

Notes

1. Zohar (2016: 121) distinguishes between the term 'kamikaze' ('associated with wartime propaganda language') and the contemporary 'honorific term *tokkōtai*' which translates as 'special attack unit'.
2. Hereafter referred to as *Noroi*.
3. This echoes Terry Castle's (2005: 693) indication that the Gothic novel emerged from an interest in the obscene as a result of the 'withdrawal of the numinous', symptomatic of 'the emotional void left by that complex and momentous historical transformation known as secularisation'.
4. Yoneyama (1999) writes of one such example of Japanese historical amnesia. The 'textbook controversy' in 1982 saw the Ministry of Education intervene

to 'euphemize the history of Japanese expansionism', seeking to replace the nomenclature of the term 'invasion' with the decidedly more sanitized, 'neutral' expression: 'advancement' (1999: 5).

5   In the pre-Meiji period, the practice of Shintō was a matter of personal reverence dedicated to local *kami* (Gordon 2014: 108). By the restoration of 1868, the Meiji government had established the Department of Divinity. By 1869 the department declared 'the nation was to be guided by the "way of the *kami*"' and by 1871 Shintō shrines were 'officially designated as government institutions for the observance of "national rites"' (2014: 108). In 1914, shrines across the country numbered 120,000, a significant decrease from the previous number of 200,000 (Susumu and Murphy 2009: 118).

References

Ancuta, K. (2015), 'Lost and Found: The Found Footage Phenomenon and Southeast Asian Supernatural Horror Film', *Plaridel*, 12 (2): 149–77.

Anderson, M. (2006), 'Mobilizing *Gojira*: Mourning Modernity as Monstrosity', in *In Godzilla's Footsteps: Japanese Pop Culture Icons on the Global Stage*, edited by W.M. Tsutsui and M. Ito, 21–40, New York: Palgrave Macmillan.

Balmain, C. (2008), *Introduction to Japanese Horror Film*, Edinburgh: Edinburgh University Press.

Benjamin, W. (2007), *Illuminations: Essays and Reflections*, New York: Schocken Books.

Blake, L. (2008), *The Wounds of Nations: Horror Cinema, Historical Trauma and National Identity*, Manchester: Manchester University Press.

Castle, T. (2005), 'The Gothic Novel', in *The Cambridge History of English Literature*, edited by J. Richetti, 673–706, Cambridge: Cambridge University Press.

Creed, B. (1993), *The Monstrous Feminine: Film, Feminism, Psychoanalysis*, London: Routledge.

Dower, J. (2012), *Ways of Forgetting, Ways of Remembering: Japan in the Modern World*, New York: The New Press.

Figal, G. (2000), *Civilisation and Monsters: Spirits of Modernity in Meiji Japan*, Durham, NC: Duke University Press.

Fineman, J. (1980), 'The Structure of Allegorical Desire', *October*, 12 (1): 46–66.

Fridell, W.M. (1973), *Japanese Shrine Mergers 1906–12: State Shinto Moves to the Grassroots*, Tokyo: Sophia University.

Gordon, A. (2008), *Ghostly Matters: Haunting and the Sociological Imagination*, Minneapolis: University of Minnesota Press.

Gordon, A. (2014), *A Modern History of Japan: From Tokugawa Times to the Present*, Oxford: Oxford University Press.

Hardacre, H. (1989), *Shintō and the State: 1868–1988*, Princeton, NJ: Princeton University Press.

Harootunian, H. (2006), 'Japan's Long Postwar: The Trick of Memory and the Ruse of History', in *Japan after Japan: Social and Cultural Life from the Recessionary 1990s to the Present*, edited by T. Yoda and H. Harootunian, 98–121, Durham, NC: Duke University Press.

Hills, M. (2005), *The Pleasures of Horror*, London: Continuum.

Howell, K. (2015), 'Time, Loss, and the Death of the (M)other in Roland Barthes' *Camera Lucida* and Sally Mann's *Deep South*', *Berkeley Undergraduate Journal*, 28 (1): 78–111.

Iles, T. (2008), *The Crisis of Identity in Contemporary Japanese Film: Personal, Cultural, National*, Leiden: Brill.

Kang, J. and Kiyomi, K. (2002), 'Orality and the Transforming Senses in Meiji Media: An Exploration of Kami-Shibai and Japanese Folklores', *Review of Japanese Culture and Society*, 14 (1): 49–59.

Koizumi, M. (2013), 'Where the Silence Falls (Double Projection #1)', *Meiro Koizumi*, 24 August. Available online: https://www.meirokoizumi.com/doubleprojection1 (accessed 24 August 2022).

Krummel, J.W.M. (2021), 'The Symposium on Overcoming Modernity and Discourse in Wartime Japan', *Historicka Sociologie*, 13 (2): 83–104.

Law, J.M. (2008), 'Out of Place: Fetal References in Japanese Mythology and Cultural Memory', in *Imagining the Fetus: the Unborn in Myth, Religion, and Culture*, edited by V. Sasson and J.M. Law, 259–74, Oxford: Oxford University Press.

Lehman, R. (2008), 'Allegories of Rending: Killing Time with Walter Benjamin', *New Literary History*, 39 (2): 233–50.

Lim, B.C. (2001), 'Spectral Times: The Ghost Film as Historical Allegory', *positions*, 9 (2): 287–329.

Lincoln, M. (2015), 'Toward a Critical Hauntology: Bare Afterlife and the Ghosts of Ba Chúc', *Comparative Studies in Society and History*, 57 (1): 191–220.

Lowenstein, A. (2005), *Shocking Representation: Historical Trauma, National Cinema, and the Modern Horror Film*, New York: Columbia University Press.

Mallin, E. (2001), '*The Blair Witch Project*, *Macbeth*, and the Indeterminate End', in *The End of Cinema as We Know It: American Film in the Nineties*, edited by J. Lewis, 105–14, New York: New York University Press.

McRoy, J. (2008), *Nightmare Japan: Contemporary Japanese Horror Cinema*, Leiden: Brill.

Nelson, L. (2016), 'Choosing Illusion: Mediated Reality and the Spectacle of the Idol in Kōji Shiraishi's *Shirome*', *Journal of Japanese and Korean Cinema*, 8 (2): 140–55.

Nelson, L. (2021), 'Obscure, Reveal, Repeat: Hidden Worlds and Uncertain Truths in Kōji Shiraishi's *The Curse* and *Occult*', in *Japanese Horror Culture: Critical Essays on Film, Literature, Anime, Video Games*, edited by F.G. Pagnoni Burns, S. Bhattercharjee and A. Saha, 211–26, Lanham, MD: Lexington Books.

Previtali, G. (2017), 'Spettri Nucleari. Sulla Memoria Di Hiroshima in Alcuni J-Horror Alle Soglie Del Duemila', *Cinergie II – Cinema E Le Altre Arti*, 6 (11): 135–44.
Reyes, X. (2015), 'Reel Evil: A Critical Reassessment of Found Footage Horror', *Gothic Studies*, 17 (2): 122–36.
Roscoe, J. and Hight, C. (2001), *Faking It: Mock-documentary and the Subversion of Factuality*, Manchester: Manchester University Press.
Sayad, C. (2016), 'Found-Footage Horror and the Frame's Undoing', *Cinema Journal*, 55 (2): 43–66.
Susumu, S. and Murphy, R.E. (2009), 'State Shinto in the Lives of the People: The Establishment of Emperor Worship, Modern Nationalism, and Shrine Shinto in Late Meiji', *Japanese Journal of Religious Studies*, 36 (1): 93–124.
Tateishi, R. (2003), 'The Japanese horror film series: *Ring* and *Eko Eko Azarak*', in *Fear Without Frontiers: Horror Cinema Across the Globe*, edited by J. Schneider, 295-304, Godalming: FAB Press.
Telotte, J.P. (2001), 'The *Blair Witch Project*: Film and the Internet', *Film Quarterly*, 54 (3): 32–9.
Teo, S. (2013), *The Asian Cinema Experience: Styles, Spaces, Theory*, London: Routledge.
Trigg, D. (2009), 'The Place of Trauma: Memory, Hauntings, and the Temporality of Ruins', *Memory Studies*, 2 (1): 87–101.
Wallace, R. (2020), 'Documentary Style as Post-Truth Monstrosity in the Mockumentary Horror Film', *Quarterly Review of Film and Video*, 38 (6): 519–40.
Yoneyama, L. (1999), *Hiroshima Traces: Time, Space, and the Dialectics of Memory*, Berkeley, CA: University of California Press.
Zohar, A. (2016), 'Performative Recollection: Koizumi Meiro Representations of Kamikaze Pilots and the Trauma of the Asia-Pacific War in Japan', in *Interdisciplinary Handbook of Trauma and Culture*, edited by Y. Ataria, D. Gurevitz, H. Pedaya and Y. Neria, 117–31, Cham: Springer.

Films

Apollo 18 (2011), directed by Gonzalo López-Gallego [film], United States and Canada: Bazelevs.
The Blair Witch Project (1999), directed by Daniel Myrick and Eduardo Sánchez [film], United States: Haxan Films.
Cannibal Holocaust (1980), directed by Ruggero Deodato [film], Italy, F.D.: Cinematografica.
Cursed Violent People (2010), directed by Kōji Shiraishi [film], Japan: Creative AXA.
Godzilla [Gojira] (1954), directed by Ishirō Honda [film], Tokyo: Toho Co.
Ju-On: The Grudge (2002), directed by Takashi Shimizu [film], Japan: Pioneer LDC, Nikkatsu, Oz Co., Xanadeux.

Noroi: The Curse (2005), directed by Kōji Shiraishi [film], Japan: Xanadeux.
Occult (2009), directed by Kōji Shiraishi [film], Japan: Creative Axa Company and Image Rings.
One Missed Call (2003), directed by Takashi Miike [film], Japan: Kadokawa-Daiei Eiga.
Pulse (2001), directed by Kiyoshi Kurosawa [film], Japan: Daiei Film, NTV Network, Hakuhodo, Imagica.
Ringu (1998), directed by Hideo Nakata [film], Japan: Ringu/Rasen Production Committee.
Shirome (2010), directed by Kōji Shiraishi [film], Japan: Shirome Project Partners and Stardust Promotion.

6

Congruent apprehensions of history in Irish horror cinema

Stephen Joyce

In Dan Simmons' (1991) short story 'All Dracula's Children', a team of foreign observers reflects on the banality of evil while visiting Romanian orphanages after the fall of Ceaușescu. One of the characters notes bitterly that the world would care more about these abandoned children if they could somehow connect these orphanages with vampires. The protagonist replies, 'Dracula would be a story. The plight of hundreds of thousands of victims of political madness, bureaucracy, stupidity … this is just an … inconvenience' (1991: 67). The story seems to criticize the use of the horror genre to represent horrific historical events – especially events that result from the habitual grinding of institutional machinery – but the narrative then doubles back on itself to reveal that the orphanages are being used as blood banks by a secret race of vampires, thus connecting real-life horror with the supernatural after all. With its interplay of genre conventions and historical trauma, the story raises some salient questions: Can the horror genre be used to make historical horrors meaningful for modern, more globally dispersed audiences? And can the synthesis of history and horror also be part of a cultural processing of these events?

These questions are particularly relevant for Irish culture, which over the past thirty years has been grappling with the legacy of institutional abuse. For decades, the Irish state and the Catholic Church combined to impose what James Smith (2007: 2) describes as an 'architecture of containment', a network of institutions that included 'industrial and reformatory schools, mother and baby homes, adoption agencies, and Magdalen asylums, among others'. These institutions were crucial in imposing a patriarchal religious morality that focused on repressing female sexuality, with victims of sexual abuse, unmarried mothers and their children effectively imprisoned in institutions run by Catholic religious orders. Since the 1990s, as survivor testimonies have emerged in Irish media – especially in a series of powerful documentaries – Irish society has been grappling with the legacy of these institutions and its own complicity in this disciplinary regime.

In this same period, Irish cinema has also experienced an unexpected boom in the horror genre. While Irish literature has produced renowned horror and Gothic authors such as Bram Stoker or Joseph Sheridan Le Fanu, Irish cinema had virtually no history of horror until the twenty-first century, when a new generation began creating films such as *The Devil's Woods* (2015), *The Hole in the Ground* (2019) or *Without Name* (2016). According to a leading scholar of Irish cinema, Ruth Barton (2019), 'It was the rise of the low budget Irish horror film that really defined the generational shift.' Typically, modern Irish horror plays on the tension between modern, urbanized characters confronting a wild countryside suffused with supernatural and mythological overtones, thus exploring the disjunction between Ireland's rural, agrarian, strongly Catholic past and its more cosmopolitan present. However, until recently these films have shied away from addressing the most obvious source of horror in Irish society: the legacy of Ireland's architecture of containment.

This chapter examines Aislinn Clarke's *The Devil's Doorway* (2018), the first Irish horror film directed by a woman and set inside one of Ireland's infamous Magdalen Laundries, institutions in which women were incarcerated for being seen to have violated the rigid sexual norms of Irish society. Drawing on found-footage horror, the film uses the recordings of two priests sent to investigate an alleged miracle in a Magdalen asylum, only to discover demonic forces at work. Reviews were mixed, with *Screen Daily* calling it 'a stylish, shuddering horror' (Hannigan 2018) and *The New York Times* a 'smart but uneven horror movie' (Catsoulis 2018), while *The LA Times* lamented how it fails to 'overcome the clichés of … the found-footage format' (Murray 2018) and *The Hollywood Reporter* how it becomes 'a compendium of horror-film clichés' (Scheck 2018). It is tempting to argue that reviewers who were more aware of the historical context were able to read more into the film, but most audiences understood the context well enough to grasp the main point. The central issue is mentioned at the beginning of Frank Scheck's critical review for *The Hollywood Reporter* when he writes, 'The well-documented infamies of Ireland's Magdalene Laundries would seem to hold diabolically effective potential for a horror film.' Do institutional histories of this type hold 'diabolically effective potential' for horror if these narratives are also bound by the conventions of the genre, which may be unsuitable for representing banal administrative processes?

Building on Adam Lowenstein's (2005: 2) concept of 'allegorical moments', this chapter introduces the idea of *congruent apprehensions* to describe how the conventions of particular horror sub-genres and the strategies they use to construct fearful representations may overlap with the dominant understanding of traumatic historical events; this congruency allows such genre films to be a meaningful exploration of those traumatic histories rather than a formulaic set of tropes imposed on historical raw material. At the same time, attention must also be paid to how these films deviate from genre conventions because these inflections are where the particularities of the local context may best be understood. I will first look at contemporary understandings of the Magdalen Laundries and the rise of Irish horror before examining how these congruent apprehensions can be seen in *The Devil's Doorway*.

Irish horror and the horrors of Irish history

In order to understand the traumatic legacy of the Magdalen Laundries and other institutions in Ireland's 'moral-industrial complex' (O'Toole 2017), it is necessary to see them not just in terms of perpetrators and victims but in the context of a wider society that stood by in shameful silence. The history of the Magdalen Laundries is not about secretive religious organizations inflicting punishment on innocents out of sight of decent society; rather, it is about how post-independence Irish society resorted to institutionalizing the vulnerable – particularly women and children – in the name of a postcolonial national identity. The struggle against British rule had led Irish nationalists to form a particular idea of Ireland, embodied in the symbol of Kathleen Ni Houlihan, a blameless female victim who cries out for young men to save her from British tyranny. After independence, the issue of how to deal with 'fallen women' was bound up with this construction of Ireland as a staunchly Catholic, morally pure counterpart to the British Empire. As Clara Fischer (2016: 822–3) explains, 'Women's potential *im*purity formed a substantial threat to the project of national identity formation, which required women's purity and virtue as the essential and differentiating features of Irish nationhood.' The existence of women who could be considered sexually impure thus had to be suppressed, even after death. In 1993, the bodies of 155 women were discovered in the convent grounds of one of the laundries, dozens of whom were never identified. Moreover, 'many infants and children died in these places and were buried anonymously and secretly by the nuns' (Haughton, McAuliffe and Pine 2021: 8). It was not enough that these women and children were punished; they had to be vanished, their names erased, their existence denied, their bodies hidden in unmarked graves.

However, it would be wrong to say that nobody knew what was going on inside these institutions. Ireland is a small country and these institutions were often among the biggest, most imposing buildings in town. According to Fischer (2016: 830), at its peak 'a staggering 1 percent of the population was institutionalized, despite significant emigration rates. This percentage was higher than the peak of penal confinement in the United States and in the Soviet Union at the time.' Rather than address the issues that led so many young women and children into distress, Ireland chose to institutionalize them in its very own gulag archipelago, thus sending a chilling message to the wider society. 'The threat of incarceration there also served to control girls and women outside the Laundry walls. While what *precisely* went on behind the high walls may not have been common knowledge, most people knew it was not a place in which anyone would wish to be' (Haughton, McAuliffe and Pine 2021: 10). Fintan O'Toole (2017) describes society's knowledge of what was going on in these institutions as Ireland's 'unknown known', a horror everyone understood but simply chose not to know, creating a double layer of 'malignant shame: the shame that made us lock up unwanted people and then the shame of having done so'. These layers of shameful silence, more so than the walls themselves, were what imprisoned so many for so long.

The symbiotic relationship between church and state facilitated this silence because the state could deny any responsibility for the 'penitents' within. Even as the courts turned distressed citizens over to Magdalen Laundries and the police returned escapees, 'the Magdalen asylums were never governed by state legislation. They never received state capitation grants. They resisted all forms of government regulation and inspection' (Smith 2007: 46). Even now, the state has no record of what happened inside these institutions, while the religious orders cannot be compelled to hand over their archives. This has created serious difficulties 'in breaking these silences given the absence of documentary and historical material because of lack of access to religious and other records' (Haughton, McAuliffe and Pine 2021: 3).

In such a context, the first wave of representations focused on telling these forgotten stories and allowing survivors to deliver public testimony about their experiences. Patricia Burke Brogan's 1992 play *Eclipsed* shone a light inside the Magdalen Laundries, while a growing number of memoirs and novels tackled the subject of institutional abuse. In particular, a wave of documentaries that focused on survivor testimony, including *Dear Daughter* (1996) and *Sex in a Cold Climate* (1998), began to break down the walls of silence. Peter Mullan's *The Magdalene Sisters* (2002), which won the Golden Lion at the Venice Film Festival, dramatized the experiences of the women incarcerated in these institutions. While all these works are open to criticism, Smith (2007: 88) argues that their collective significance is twofold: 'They give force to a history that Irish society traditionally prefers not to acknowledge, and they break the culturally imposed closed ranks and silence typically accompanying such sensitive issues as rape, incest, illegitimacy, and domestic, physical, and sexual abuse.'

What role can the horror genre play, though, when the ethical imperative seems to call for documentary realism, for giving voice to lived experiences? In the first place, one could argue that doing justice to experience means more than simply historical accuracy. Facts by themselves do not necessarily convey subjective emotional aspects, such as the fear and despair of the victims and the shame and anger inspired by the suffering inflicted on them. These emotions are as much a part of the historical experience as the raw details of what happened, but may require alternate means of representation. In *The Politics of Irish Memory*, Emilie Pine (2010: 5) argues that traumatic memory has become 'the dominant way of seeing, of understanding, and of communicating, the Irish past. We are obsessed with the past, and we are haunted by trauma.' What genre is better equipped to deal with questions of how we are haunted by the past than horror? For Emma Radley (2020: 390), 'the persistence of horror as a preferred generic form can itself be read, following Pine, as representing a need to find new narratives and structures to approach the traumatic reconfiguration of Ireland's national memory'.

The problem with using horror to address traumatic memory is less to do with the genre's capacities than with how a global medium like film promotes recognized conventions in order to make local content accessible to international audiences. As Pietari Kääpä (2018: 161) explains, 'Genre is thus a means to neutralize some of the obstacles facing producers from small nation film cultures. It functions as the means that allows these producers to speak the language understood by global distributors.' Attracting global distributors is essential for Irish filmmakers because Ireland's domestic market cannot sustain an indigenous film industry. According to Roddy Flynn (2020: 300), 'Since 2010,

Irish films have accounted for anything from less than 1% of the total local box office to ... up to 7% in 2014.' In order to foster production, Ireland offers a mix of favourable tax policies for multinationals, co-productions and state funding, but this also means that any significant production needs to have international audiences in mind, creating 'a political economy which perhaps tacitly encourages such genre-based production' (2020: 300). This may also require adherence to internationally understood genre conventions. Both *The LA Times* and *The Hollywood Reporter* make this point in their critiques of *The Devil's Doorway*, claiming that it submerges the horrific story of the Magdalen Laundries beneath the conventions of found-footage horror.

However, this may be a highly limiting perspective on the role horror can play in addressing historical trauma. For Adam Lowenstein (2005: 9), the key question is how such films 'access discourses of horror to confront the representations of historical trauma tied to the film's national and cultural context'. As Lowenstein (2005: 2) argues, the significance of such films lies in how they stage 'allegorical moments', which involve 'a shocking collision of film, spectator, and history where registers of bodily space and historical time are disrupted, confronted, and intertwined'. Linnie Blake (2008: 2) builds on Lowenstein's discussion to argue that, 'Horror cinema is ideally positioned to expose the psychological, social and cultural ramifications of the ideologically expedient will to "bind up the nation's wounds" that is promulgated by all aspects of the culture industry in post-traumatic contexts.' Both Lowenstein and Blake reject the idea that culture should play the role of therapist to the national psyche; rather, its role is to question how and why we remember the past the way we do.

Since the 1990s, the history of Ireland's moral-industrial complex has been narrated as a trauma haunting the present, and this mode of understanding aligns it with the horror genre. Yet we may go deeper than this. The uncovering of this history has involved the fight to gain access to hidden archives, the documentary testimony of survivors, their necessarily subjective viewpoint and the seeming powerlessness of individuals to affect events. These characteristics are all foundational elements of found-footage horror, which purports to be a recording of real events from an eyewitness perspective by individuals who will inevitably fall victim to the forces they are trying to document. Creating a found-footage horror of the Magdalen Laundries is thus not an opportunistic attempt to cash in on a popular genre but a recognition that there are *congruent apprehensions* between the historical trauma and the genre's conventions – that is, strong alignments between their shared strategies for knowing and representing a traumatic past. Acknowledging these apprehensions allows us to see moments when the film grapples with history through, and sometimes against, the genre's conventions.

The Devil's Doorway

In her director's statement, Clarke (2018: 3) explains that when she was approached about the film, she accepted because 'I couldn't let anyone else do it'. According to Clarke, 'My mother's best friend was dragged from home at thirteen and thrown into one of these institutions … my father, a breadman, delivered bread to the laundries every day, describing it, when he came home, as delivering straight to Hell' (2018: 3). Like many people in Ireland, Clarke had personal connections with the architecture of containment and knew that this history had to be central to the film. As she explains, 'It was important to me that the first horror feature made by a woman in Ireland confront the horrors of being a woman in Ireland, rather than exploiting that real horror' (2018: 3).

The film is set in the autumn of 1960, when Ireland's moral-industrial complex was at its peak. A bishop receives a letter with two photographs of a miracle – a statue of the Virgin Mary weeping blood – and sends two priests to investigate. In a reversal of the priestly duo in *The Exorcist*, it is the elder, Father Thomas Riley, who is jaded and disillusioned while the younger, Father John Thornton, is a naïve and enthusiastic believer. Their attempts to film the miracle on a 16mm camera are the source of the found-footage as the two priests discover other forces at work in the Magdalen Laundry. The women there suffer abuse at the hands of the tyrannical Mother Superior, and in the basement the priests find a 16-year-old girl called Kathleen chained up and seemingly possessed. She is also pregnant, despite being confirmed as a virgin by a local physician. Haunted at night by the sounds of ghost children, the priests discover evidence of a satanic Black Mass and some tunnels beneath the asylum, where they find the skeletons of numerous small children. Finally stumbling on a group of nuns, including the Mother Superior, performing a secret rite, the film ends in typical found-footage style as the priests are killed and there is no one left to continue filming.

This summary alone makes clear how much the film draws on existing horror conventions from *The Exorcist* (1973) to *The Blair Witch Project* (1999). In 2015, Xavier Aldana Reyes had already defined two main thematic strands of found-footage horror as 'the demonic possession film … [and] ghostly found footage horror centred on a specific building … which has given rise to the niche asylum subgenre' (Reyes 2015: 125–6). Yet what is of interest here are the ways in which these conventions align with the subject matter of the Magdalen Laundries.

The choice of genre is itself significant because of its mimicking of documentary realism. As Cecilia Sayad (2016: 45) explains, found-footage films 'are not presented to us as "inspired by" real events – they are supposed to constitute the audiovisual documentation of these events. What we see, we are told, are *real* people, not characters based on them.' This creates an immediate parallel with the documentaries that exposed the Magdalen Laundries, but where the documentaries drew on the testimony of the victims, *The Devil's Doorway* imagines something we do not have: the records of the Catholic Church, which refuses to make them available. By purporting to be an audio-visual record of events inside a Magdalen asylum by two Catholic priests, the film poses an important question to the audience: What could be in these records that the institutions are still hiding? Are there even worse horrors than those we know about from survivor testimony?

These gaps in the historical record are emphasized by an interesting feature of the found-footage genre. Because what we see is determined largely by the character holding the camera, who is simultaneously a participant in the action, found-footage is characterized by the limited perspective of a homodiegetic narrator. The camera is thus not in a position to show us all the important information in any given scene:

> Just like the characters with whom our vision is aligned, we as viewers know that there is always something outside the frame to which we are not privy. In these works, we are always aware that our spectatorial position is not a privileged one. These looks are uncertain of what they might find or where they might find it.
> (Hart 2019: 75)

Like the blanks in the historical record, the gaps in the film highlight everything we do not know, and the film uses this unreliability to show us things whose significance we are unable to assess. At one point, for example, the camera spies down a stairwell at an anonymous inmate weeping quietly. Why is she crying and is this relevant to the plot? The viewer never gets any answer to this question, but such moments of epistemic uncertainty pervade the film.

Some of the film's most interesting narrative sequences are those that deviate from found-footage conventions in order to give viewers a glimpse into these untold stories lurking outside the frame. Typically, found-footage is characterized by the synchronicity of sound and image – the camera may have a limited and potentially unreliable perspective, but we trust that the shots themselves come to us raw and unfiltered. In *The Devil's Doorway*, however, there are several montage sequences in which sound and image become disconnected, especially when one of the women in the asylum is giving testimony. In the first such sequence, we hear Father John interviewing an unnamed inmate while we see a montage of women toiling under the prison-guard watchfulness of the stalking nuns. In another sequence, the nun whose letter alerted the bishop gives anonymous testimony while we see different, unsmiling nuns waiting one by one to have a blood test. In both cases, we cannot tell which of these women is the one telling her story, but this motivates us to consider each woman in the sequence and what her story might be.

In this respect, the opening shots are particularly interesting. Some intertitles briefly introduce the history of the Magdalen Laundries, interspersed with footage of nuns and inmates posing for a group picture in front of the building. The grainy 16mm footage raises the possibility that this may be actual documentary footage, but even though we later recognize these women as minor characters, we are never introduced to most of them. Some close-ups focus on women we might expect to be significant for the plot, but we learn almost nothing about them. These montage sequences and isolated shots of other women throughout the film raise the possibility that the priests are investigating just one story among many in the asylum, but these other stories remain out of sight because these women belong to other tragedies.

These montage sequences emphasize the tighter connection between *The Devil's Doorway* and documentary than the cinéma vérité style of most found-footage horror, which fosters another key stylistic difference. According to Reyes (2015: 129), 'since found footage is often, although not exclusively, shot in first person POV, both establishing shots and close-ups are difficult to obtain'. *The Devil's Doorway*, however, is primarily a series of intimate close-ups as characters speak almost directly to the camera about their beliefs in the manner of documentary interviewees. Instead of trying to catch a clear glimpse of the monsters just out of shot, as in *Cloverfield* (2008) or *Paranormal Activity* (2007), this film is more about getting people to open up to the camera about the horrors they have already seen. The handheld pursuit of ghosts through catacombs is thus a distraction from the real source of horror, not the thing that is hidden but the forces that compel everyone to silence, to look away from the camera or cast only furtive, guilty glances in its direction.

Instead of the obvious generic tropes – demonic possession, devil worship, ghost children – the real evil in the film lies with the forces that created the institution and the silence that enshrouds it. This is signalled by Father Thomas when he declares, 'There's no evil in this world or the next that can surpass that done by human hand.' It is telling that the priests are sent to the asylum to investigate a supposed miracle rather than the abuses going on there. Whenever Father Thomas threatens the Mother Superior with exposure, she laughs with contempt. When he tells her, 'We've become concerned with how the girls are being treated in this home', she replies mockingly, 'Oh, you have, have you? You're concerned, are you?' They both know the girls are there because no one cares about them. Later, when Father Thomas accuses her of lying about what happened to the illegitimate children, he acts as if he is exposing a guilty secret but she answers forthrightly that she sold the children to pay for the upkeep of the institution. When Father Thomas threatens to tell the bishop, she looks at him in amusement and says, 'However you want.' The authorities are complicit in the ongoing crime so there is no one to whom they can report it. That the priests discover evidence of a Black Mass in the asylum is thus a horror genre red herring; the actual Catholic mass and the church it represents are the real threats to the people trapped inside.

The soul-crushing effect of living under the weight of these institutions is well captured by Lalor Roddy's fine performance as Father Thomas, a man whose stoic veneer hides a deep repugnance for the system he can neither extricate himself from nor stop. He became a priest because 'I wanted to become a good man. I wanted to get closer to God', but the institutions of the church repulse him: 'This place disgusts me. The people who run this place disgust me. This bishop who sent us here, the Vatican itself with its costumes and theatre and luxury, built on the back of ordinary people ... I'm sick of it.' His ever-widening indictment is also an indication of powerlessness because the system is vast and distant, while he is just one recalcitrant cog in the machinery of injustice. The twenty-five years he has spent disproving miracles can be seen as his futile attempt to undermine the blind faith that sustains these institutions, to encourage the faithful to see reality clearly, but his jaded cynicism reveals the extent of his failure.

Here, genre conventions align well with the film's themes, because Father Thomas's failure is presumed from the start. A basic premise of found-footage horror is that the narrator is already dead, which is why the footage is 'found' rather than revealed by the person who filmed it. As Hart (2019: 87) argues, 'the mimetic response to the diegetic camera is, in the end, one that presumes powerlessness ... our horror comes in part from our inability to act'. The lone good man will fail to save anyone because the evil he confronts is too powerful for him to stop. Yet the film also points out that we still have the power to bear witness to it. Any found-footage horror is based on the idea of eyewitness accounts of extreme events, but *The Devil's Doorway* emphasizes the importance of such testimony, in both the seemingly documentary footage and the interviews with inmates and nuns. When interviewing the anonymous 'good' nun, Father Thomas says, 'Bearing witness is not a sin, child. It depends on how we act on that'. If Ireland's architecture of containment flourished under cover of shameful silence, then the film emphasizes the importance of being able to speak about it. Fittingly, one of the final scenes is Father Thomas's confession to the camera, a convention that can be traced back to *The Blair Witch Project*, but that has extra resonance here because of the conjunction of form, subject and theme.

This conjunction also offers an alternative reading of the film's use of horror genre clichés, a primary source of disappointment for many reviewers. However, a genre novelty would have been a betrayal of history. There are no surprises in the film because there were no surprises in real life. Anyone familiar with the Magdalen Laundries would know the shameful secret has to do with abused women and abandoned children, which applies to both the investigating priests and the audience. Hence, finding an abused and demonically possessed girl is both clichéd and thematically appropriate because *The Devil's Doorway* is not really about shocking secrets coming to light; what was in these asylums was not a secret in the first place. The evil does not lie hidden in the basement but above ground, in the workings of the institution overhead. Instead of an aesthetic disappointment, we can read these genre clichés as pointing to Ireland's shameful history of 'unknown knowns' and our inability to acknowledge what everyone knew was happening.

Conclusion

From the foregoing discussion of *The Devil's Doorway*, some key points emerge regarding horror as a means to engage with historical trauma. The question is not whether horror is an appropriate form for historical tragedies, but to what extent it allows for *congruent apprehensions* – those moments when the structures of understanding for both a horror sub-genre and the particular historical trauma come into alignment. In *The Devil's Doorway*, these congruent apprehensions are the shared emphasis on previously inaccessible archival material, the necessarily limited viewpoint, the powerlessness of the narrator to affect events and the importance of testimony in making audiences aware of what happened.

The conventions of found-footage may have developed elsewhere for different reasons, but their resonance with the legacy of the Magdalen Laundries is apparent. However, these aspects also need to be understood alongside a film's deviations from genre conventions – those moments in which the influence of the local context may best be seen. In the case of *The Devil's Doorway*, these moments reside in the film's montage sequences and isolated shots of anonymous minor characters, offering a window to other stories that remain untold. In this light, we may also read the film's use of clichéd plot twists as a particular kind of adaptation to the local context, suggesting that these untold stories will not surprise us, but need to be told anyway.

Two serious critiques can be made of the film, however – one that is general to historical horror and the other specific to the particular film. The first is that historical horror films can be seen as a kind of anti-nostalgia. As Pine (2010: 8) explains, 'anti-nostalgia's vision frames the past as inherently unstable and traumatic, encouraging audiences to be grateful that they have escaped'. Rather than frame an allegorical moment in which the past and present are brought into shocking collision, anti-nostalgic cinema may set up 'a boundary between a traumatic past and the relative security of the present ... if the past is a foreign country then its victims are, by extension, foreigners to the present' (2010: 14). In this respect, the combination of historical and found-footage horror may be incapable of creating effective allegorical moments because, without some present-day framing story, its nature as fake archival footage keeps it permanently locked in the past. However, we may consider this attempt to represent the past as a foreign country in a more literal sense; if Irish films are increasingly co-produced for international audiences, then the material is already foreign to most audiences and the genre becomes a way of making the Irish past accessible to those who may have difficulty grasping local cultural references. Genre thus becomes a tool of explication rather than obfuscation, helping to convey some of Ireland's collective emotional response to the raw facts of history.

The second critique is that the film cannot resolve a tension between its feminist sympathies and its portrayal of the Mother Superior as the main antagonist. Throughout, the film emphasizes how these church-state institutions oppress women, something made clear by the title, which Eamon Byers (2020: 264) remarks is 'inherently suggestive of female genitalia, and misogynistic religious attitudes towards them'. The title itself is attributed to the early Christian author Tertullian (2003) in *De Cultu Feminarum*, when he accuses women of being *diaboli ianua*; given the film's harsh criticism of the church's patriarchal authority, there is something perversely admirable about the nuns rebelling against it by turning to Satan. They are at least not meekly submitting to church dogma, which the film strongly implies is the right attitude. At one point, we hear a conversation in which Father Thomas explains that his favourite piece of music is Verdi's 'Requiem': 'It's a mass but not a mass ... the whole thing is a challenge to the set order.' The nuns' Black Mass is at the furthest end of this continuum, the right impulse but taken too far in the other direction. Yet there is an inevitable tension at the climax when Father Thomas shouts at them, 'God the Father commands you! God the Son commands you!' because the invocation of patriarchal religion rings hollow after all we have seen. Setting the Mother Superior up as the chief villain thus runs counter to the film's overall themes.

However, we may also read this ending as the film's allegorical moment and its clichéd invocation of satanic nuns as a deliberate challenge to the viewer. The Magdalen Laundries existed because Irish society demonized 'fallen' women and made them responsible for crimes of others; will viewers of the film repeat the same error by simply demonizing another group of women? To return to the opening sequence, seeing the inmates and nuns together in the group photos encourages us to recognize both groups as victims of the same institutionalized discourses, forced to do things they did not want by a society that 'punished women for sexual transgressions while avoiding male culpability' (Smith 2007: 19). The film's ending challenges us to recognize how easily we fall into this trap – how conventional it is to blame everything on a group of women with sexual hang-ups and let the distant and unseen bishop off the hook. Perhaps those reviewers who were dissatisfied with the film were right, but we may add that this dissatisfaction is not necessarily a weakness. Instead, it may be read as an allegorical moment in which viewers are encouraged to see how the discourses that created the Magdalen Laundries are embedded still in popular culture and why it is important that we remain alert to those evils that seem most clichéd and banal.

References

Barton, R. (2019), 'Is There Such a Thing as an Irish Film Anymore? Does It Matter?', *Irish Times*, 29 June. Available online: https://www.irishtimes.com/culture/film/is-there-such-a-thing-as-an-irish-film-anymore-does-it-matter-1.3935680 (accessed 30 May 2022).

Blake, L. (2008), *The Wounds of Nations: Horror Cinema, Historical Trauma, and National Identity*, Manchester: Manchester University Press.

Byers, E. (2020), '"The Mother Who Eats Her Own": The Politics of Motherhood in Irish Horror', in *The Politics of Horror*, edited by D. Picariello, 249–66, London: Palgrave Macmillan.

Catsoulis, J. (2018), 'Review: Sinfulness and Scares behind *The Devil's Doorway*', *New York Times*, 12 July. Available online: https://www.nytimes.com/2018/07/12/movies/the-devils-doorway-review.html (accessed 30 May 2022).

Clarke, A. (2018), 'Director's Statement', *Grimmfest*, 3–4. Available online: http://grimmfest.com/grimmupnorth/wp-content/uploads/2018/08/The-Devils-Doorway-Production-Notes-Final.pdf (accessed 31 May 2022).

Fischer, C. (2016), 'Gender, Nation, and the Politics of Shame: Magdalen Laundries and the Institutionalization of Feminine Transgression in Modern Ireland', *Signs: Journal of Women in Culture and Society*, 41 (4): 821–43.

Flynn, R. (2020), 'Introduction: Irish Film and Television: Year in Review', *Estudios Irlandeses*, 15: 297–301.

Hannigan, F. (2018), '*The Devil's Doorway*: Galway Review', *Screen Daily*, 12 July. Available online: https://www.screendaily.com/reviews/the-devils-doorway-galway-review/5130875.article (accessed 30 May 2022).

Hart, A.C. (2019), 'The Searching Camera: First-Person Shooters, Found-Footage Horror Films, and the Documentary Tradition', *Journal of Cinema and Media Studies*, 58 (4): 73–91.

Haughton, M., M. McAuliffe and E. Pine (2021), 'Introduction: Commemoration, Gender, and the Postcolonial Carceral State', in *Legacies of the Magdalen Laundries: Commemoration, Gender, and the Postcolonial Carceral State*, edited by M. Haughton, M. McAuliffe and E. Pine, 1–26, Manchester: Manchester University Press.

Kääpä, P. (2018), 'From Nordic Gloom to Nordic Cool: Producing Genre Film for Global Markets', in *Rethinking Genre in Contemporary Global Cinema*, edited by S. Dibeltulo and C. Barrett, 151–64, London: Palgrave Macmillan.

Lowenstein, A. (2005), *Shocking Representation: Historical Trauma, National Cinema, and the Modern Horror Film*, New York: Columbia University Press.

Murray, N. (2018), 'Review: Irish Found-Footage Horror Film *The Devil's Doorway* Can't Escape Clichés', *LA Times*, 11 July. Available online: https://www.latimes.com/entertainment/movies/la-et-mn-mini-devils-doorway-review-20180711-story.html (accessed 30 May 2022).

O'Toole, F. (2017), 'Ireland Is Still Defined by the Church's Mindset', *Irish Times*, 14 July. Available online: https://www.irishtimes.com/opinion/fintan-o-toole-ireland-is-still-defined-by-the-church-s-mindset-1.3008295 (accessed 30 May 2022).

Pine, E. (2010), *The Politics of Irish Memory: Performing Remembrance in Contemporary Irish Culture*, London: Palgrave Macmillan.

Radley, E. (2020), 'Irish Media and Representations: New Critical Paradigms', in *Routledge International Handbook of Irish Studies*, edited by R. Fox, M. Cronin and B.Ó. Conchubhair, 379–92, London: Routledge.
Reyes, X.A. (2015), 'Reel Evil: A Critical Reassessment of Found Footage Horror', *Gothic Studies*, 17 (2): 122–36.
Sayad, C. (2016), 'Found-Footage Horror and the Frame's Undoing', *Cinema Journal*, 55 (2): 43–66.
Scheck, F. (2018), '*The Devil's Doorway*: Film Review', *Hollywood Reporter*, 9 July. Available online: https://www.hollywoodreporter.com/movies/movie-reviews/devils-doorway-1125600 (accessed 30 May 2022).
Simmons, D. (1991), 'All Dracula's Children', in *The Ultimate Dracula*, edited by B. Preiss, 45–74, New York: Brick Tower Press.
Smith, J. (2007), *Ireland's Magdalen Laundries and the Nation's Architecture of Containment*, Notre Dame, IN: University of Notre Dame Press.
Tertullian (2003), 'De Cultu Feminarum', trans. Marie Turcan, *The Latin Library*. Available online: https://www.thelatinlibrary.com/tertullian/tertullian.cultu1.shtml (accessed 31 May 2022).

Films

The Blair Witch Project (1999), directed by Daniel Myrick and Eduardo Sánchez [film], United States: Haxan Films.
Cloverfield (2008), directed by Matt Reeves [film], United States: Bad Robot Productions.
Dear Daughter (1996), directed by Louis Lentin [documentary], Dublin: Irish Film Board.
The Devil's Doorway (2018), directed by Aislinn Clarke [film], Ireland: 23ten.
The Devil's Woods (2015), directed by Anthony White [film], Dublin: Whitewashed Films.
The Exorcist (1973), directed by William Friedkin [film], United States: Hoya Productions.
The Hole in the Ground (2019), directed by Lee Cronin [film], Dublin: Savage Productions.
The Magdalene Sisters (2002), edited by Peter Mullan [film], Scotland: Scottish Screen.
Paranormal Activity (2007), directed by Oren Peli [film], United States: Blumhouse Productions.
Sex in a Cold Climate (1998), directed by Steve Humphries [documentary], Ireland: Testimony Films.
Without Name (2016), directed by Lorcan Finnegan [film], Ireland: Lovely Productions.

Part Three

History and horror in televisual storyworlds

7

Lace collars and cowboy cravats: Gothic time-travelling with *Penny Dreadful* and *The Nevers*

Stephanie Green

Introduction: A haunted past

One 'can hardly help noticing', Zagarrio (2015: 22) observes, how the American screen industry 'constantly loots literature'. *The Nevers* (2021) and *Penny Dreadful* (2014–16) are two series that wrest characters, styles and settings from popular fiction and films with historical settings to create stories that are simultaneously new and old. Time-travel fantasy *The Nevers* starts out by recruiting the late nineteenth century's obsession with science and belief through larger-than-life stock characters – including a host of unruly 'New Women' drawn from British periodicals of the 1890s (Richardson and Willis 2019 [2002]) – ultimately confounding late-Victorian story settings and conventions with a futuristic sci-fi narrative of transformative return. *Penny Dreadful* brings together the incipient decadence and industrial anxiety of *fin de siècle* literary London with the 'Wild West' landscapes of early twentieth-century America to create a panoply of Gothic sensationalism. Both series provide settings and stories that foreground the historical imagination as a rich visual and textual haunting, amid intimations of apocalyptic threat, through which the audience is immersed in a perpetually unfolding, although seemingly anachronistic, narration. In these instances, the use of the past reflects the ways in which our mediated culture emphasizes 'iconic correspondences', as Sobchack (1997: 5) suggests: a 'calling up of and provocation to, historical consciousness' from which we seek to make meaning for our own worlds and times (1997: 13). *The Nevers* and *Penny Dreadful* both reflect this shifting engagement with tropes and ideas of times past, moving well beyond looting to embrace and extend the possibilities of form and genre.

This chapter considers how *The Nevers* and *Penny Dreadful* use historical motifs and tropes, including costume and design elements, to situate their characters in imagined worlds that are at once both strange and familiar, creating stories whereby the past is in conversation with the future, not only as tropic readaptation, but also as resistance to the theme of apocalyptic determinism that runs through both series. Marcia Landy (2015: ix–xxii) discusses the concept of counter-history as a way to think differently about visual media and its engagements with history, a decentring that encompasses alternate perspectives and techniques such as temporal and narrative discontinuity. Landy (2015: x) argues for thinking counter-historically as a means of relocating the historical in the cinematic realm of 'invention, artifice, theatricality and conjecture' to allow for embodied thought and emotion. She draws on the Deleuzian notion of 'becoming' to invoke the impetus of 'acting counter to the past and therefore on the present, for the benefit, let us hope, of a future' (Deleuze and Guattari 1987, quoted in Landy 2015: 125), in ways that resist temporal and ideological determinism. This idea has resonance for the characters of *The Nevers* and *Penny Dreadful*, faced with devastating communal threats – from disease, corruption and oppression to imminent military and environmental annihilation. The series discussed here are not works of history, of course, but by evoking familiar stories of the past they allow audiences to experience an idea of human history, expressed performatively, resisting a compulsion towards intense chronological destruction – even to redress the imperative of a future past already 'written'.

The Nevers and *Penny Dreadful* are among a profusion of historically infused fantasy adaptations from the oeuvre of nineteenth-century British Gothic fiction generated in recent years, featuring famous characters such as Frankenstein, Dracula, Dorian Gray and Jekyll/Hyde and other stock fiction personae, which repeatedly reappear in through numerous 'retellings, reimaginings, remakes, and reboots' (Manea 2016: 42). Along with the settings and tropes that identify them, such characters are now embedded in the Western contemporary screen narrative milieu, even when detached from the formal housing of their original stories. Although its first season was widely reviewed and welcomed by fans of the Gothic/sci-fi genre known as steampunk,[1] *The Nevers* was short-lived, partly due to Covid-19 pandemic, and has received little scholarly engagement to date. *The Nevers* does, however, possess a wealth of intriguing referentiality woven through a back-from-the-future rescue narrative, with an intriguing mid-season shift from fantasy spectacle to futurist horror. *Penny Dreadful*, by contrast, has attracted a lively response from scholars since its first season release. Its retwisting of famous supernatural characters, stories and settings from historical popular fiction exploits the hybridity of 'pulp' fictional genres, to allow for 'a new kind of story invention' (Albertsen 2017) within a self-contained transmedia world of potentially unlimited possibility. Attention has been given, for example, to its uses of repetition (Braid 2017; Lee and King 2015), identities and archetypes (Anyiwo 2018), recursive adaptation (Green 2021) and even cultural contamination (Albertsen 2017). It has been examined as an adapted vision of the Gothic metropolis (Loutitt 2016), for its shifting gender politics (Kohlke 2018; Posada 2020), its literary influences (Farizova 2020) and much more.

While they operate differently in terms of narrative in a number of ways, what *The Nevers* and *Penny Dreadful* have in common is how they conjure an imagined experience of the historical constructed partly through a process of literary 'memefication' (Lee and King 2015). Adapting characters from Gothic novels such as *Frankenstein: or, The Modern Prometheus* (Shelley 1980 [1818]), *Dracula* (Stoker 1997 [1897]) and *The Strange Case of Dr Jekyll and Mr Hyde* (Stevenson 1930), *The Nevers* and *Penny Dreadful* set out to explore the trauma, excitement and uncertainty of a potentially radical late-Victorian and post-millennial identity. Stock characters from Victorian sensation novels and American adventure Westerns are also part of the mix, 'breaking down the barrier between the past and present, transforming classic texts into contemporary cultural iconography' (Lee and King 2015), inviting viewers to enter these reimagined narrative realms with frightening histories that seems very like one that Western culture already knows. In both series, a sense of history is expressed partly as a tension across shifting timescapes. While both series reference the Victorian British *fin de siècle*, they are temporally and geographically situated in the zone of the imagination, adjacent to yet not bound by specific time periods, where past, present and future are linked by a pull towards global catastrophe, which a group of characters band together to resist or break. As Bruno Latour (1993: 330–1) points out, while acknowledging the importance of the historical, the future is not absolutely determined by a 'stultified compulsion' towards humanity's demise. There is scope, these two series suggest – for human and non-human recovery and repair.

Sourcing the sense of wonder

The readaptation of story elements from historical fiction is useful to consider in various ways, showing how new narratives work with the past to create stories that already seem familiar, while at the same time responding, as Park-

Finch (2017) observes, to their social, historical and media contexts. The repetition of elements within Gothic-inspired adaptations might be regarded as a form of hauntology (Derrida 2006) – the seductive return of our spooky preoccupations – or as a rhetoric of collective recall, converging associations and meanings through a process that turns fiction 'into a media of cultural memory' (Erll 2008). Manea (2016:48) argues that reappearing characters and stories from classic Gothic fiction across contemporary mediascapes can be seen as an example of remediation, merging established personae in ways that reform and reinscribe their original sources. In the context of rapid transmedia proliferation (Jenkins 2017), the tropes of Gothic repetition might even be considered as a type of 'creepypasta' – a digital auto-evolution of horror tropes, figures, memes and legends (Cooley and Milligan 2018).

Another way to think about the recycling of originary texts is how they draw on ideas of the past in conversation with the future, speaking to narrative continuities of human hope, anxiety and even terror in terms of reciprocity, rather than as apocalyptic imperative. Of particular interest here is the way *The Nevers* and *Penny Dreadful* rework allusions to urban history, literature culture and design to produce strange and marvellous happenings: 'a sense of wonder' (Stephan 2016: 4). A fantastic vision of the metropolis of London as a site of counter-historical becoming forms the spatial foundation for both series. In *Penny Dreadful* this is represented by allusions to Gustave Doré's hallucinatory nineteenth-century engravings (Gupta 2014) – shadowy bridges, alleys, archways, vaults, factories and hovels housing the destitute and working poor (Cooke n.d.). This idea of London is founded on the horrors of colonialism and domestic urban poverty, and constantly reimagined as an historically layered 'urban jungle' (McLaughlin 2000: 1–26), ideologically subsumed under 'the constant threat of deliberate and indifferent destruction' (Williams 1973: 302). The city is repeatedly represented in Gothic text and screen narrative as host to darkling forces of human and supernatural kinds, most obviously in key source texts, such as *Dracula* and *The Picture of Dorian Gray* (Wilde 2003 [1890]). Television drama series *The Nevers* and *Penny Dreadful* draw on the illusory power of this forged metropolis to produce the accoutrements of an interior decay propagated by outside alien threats, and to convey the instability of a world that is constantly in conflict with itself, as the centre that cannot hold to history, captured in W. B. Yeats' (1989 [1920]: 158) poetic figure of the spinning gyre as the moment of crisis in which temporal linearity appears to collapse.[2] It is this quality that most strongly performs the distinctive but overlapping engagement in these two series with the intimations of destructive impulse and a powerful struggle with the prospect of a future horror which their characters strive to prevent.

Penny Dreadful series costume designer Gabriella Pescucci turned directly to Doré's illustrations, in particular his 1872 work 'Over London-By Rail', to help create the show's dark atmosphere, its looming architecture evoking the sense 'of a giant dystopic machine' (Gupta 2014). Pescucci incorporated this complex mechanistic quality at a fine level of detail in her set and costume designs, including the designs for the intricate lace high collars worn throughout the series by Vanessa Ives. These spectacularly elaborate items reflect the imagined precision of a machine age in which the performances, measurements and strictures of the feminine were defined by body containment, most famously by means of the tight-laced corset – a constraint that is rejected by another key character in the series, the unashamedly vengeful Lily Frankenstein (2.6: 2.7). For Vanessa's evening costumes, Pescucci also drew from impressionist French painters – for instance, the elegant salon gowns of female portraiture depicted in the works of Édouard Manet, Pierre-August Renoir and Berthe Morisot. The actors' costumes used samples sourced from vintage clothes (Friedlander 2014). Decorative detail such as lace and netting on sleeves and jacket bindings copied nineteenth-century patterns (National Clothing Forum 2019). Not only historical sources were used. For example, Dorian Gray's costume was inspired by outfits worn by David Bowie and Mick Jagger (Davies 2014), which satirically or playfully adapted period fashion styles.

Book and magazine illustrations also influenced the look and feel of the series, including drawings by Aubrey Beardsley published in archetypal *fin de siècle* literary magazine *The Yellow Book* (1894) (Martin-Payre 2020: 16) and illustrations from 1930 edition of Stevenson's *Strange Case of Dr Jekyll and Mr Hyde* by S.G. Hulme Beaman. According to production designer Jonathan McKinstry, sets were modelled on actual sites, including London's Soho and Dublin's Natural History Museum (Ryan 2016). The result of this complex historical reimagining creates elements that Matthias Stephan (2016: 4) describes as necessary to the fantasy genre, using metaphor and metonym to produce strange and marvellous happenings. The historical verisimilitude of *Penny Dreadful* works partly to convey authenticity, at the same time drawing on the prolific memetic power of Victorian representation to recreate new realms of the fantastic.

Martin Dines (2018: 101) alludes to the ways that, as a genre, the penny dreadful novelette conveyed 'the sensuous pleasures of the disorderly city' as a cheap, showy fictional world that seems 'more real than real life'. Drawing on related genre elements, an ethos of decay masked by high society theatrics is apparent in Whedon's *The Nevers*, as London's narrow streets and passages lead to underground caverns filled with lurking alien terrors and strange waifs who find in each other the strength to confront the darkness. Produced by Sam Mendes and John Logan, three-season series *Penny Dreadful* also recruits this key element of the genre, with its fast-paced and melodramatic plot lines and musically charged cliff-hangers. A heavy sense of fear darkens London's stairwells, hallways and drawing rooms in *Penny Dreadful*, creating a profusive claustrophobia that portrays the old, decaying city, in the throes of remanufacture by the iron fist of industrialization, as tumescent with corruption and danger. The idea of London evoked in both these series is also acquired from lithographs, paintings and news reports. Just as importantly, as Chris Louttit (2016) suggests, the world of nineteenth-century London is recreated from countless post-hoc screen evocations of the old city eternally wrapped in coal-fuelled fog blanketing hidden excitements, mysteries and monsters, from early Sherlock Holmes films such as the film series featuring Basil Rathbone (1939–46) to Tim Burton's *Sweeney Todd* (2007).

A world of impossibilities

Something of an ontological dissonance occurs in *The Nevers*, where a London filled with Dickensian exaggerations and flourishes is contrasted with a 'new world' of another kind. This is a future where Earth has been irredeemably poisoned and human life can barely be sustained. Its only possibility of recovery lies with an alien figure, in the guise of Amalia True (Laura Donnelly), whose motives are initially obscure. First developed by Joss Whedon and completed by a team led by Phillipa Goslett, *The Nevers* has been described by critics as 'X-men with Victorian women' (Hopson 2021; Selcke 2021). It is centred around St Romaulda's Orphanage in late Victorian, London, a charitable foundation which protects 'The Touched' – individuals who are endangered due to their remarkable powers. According to Whedon, the title alludes to things that could not happen and people 'not of the natural order', who nevertheless exist in this particular storyworld (Yehl 2018). In other words, *The Nevers* is a tale of the fruition of impossibilities, people with magical powers, the opening of a gateway to worlds across time and space and the potential rewriting of the past to save the future. Whedon withdrew half way through production, to be replaced by Philippa Goslett – although, as Ben Travers (2021) points out, the story retains aspects of Whedon's style and tone. Like *Penny Dreadful*, *The Nevers* takes up familiar Victorian themes, such as scientific experimentation, monstrosity, emergent feminism and oppression masquerading as social reform. Also, like *Penny Dreadful*, it is not always clear which characters are the heroes and which the monsters.

The Nevers is propelled by a moment in 1896 when a passing alien spaceship from the future supposedly 'touches' some Londoners with light, giving them special powers (1.1): a back-from-the-future scenario that builds into the intimations of an inter-galactic war across time and space. Its personae are wrested from popular nineteenth-century literary and thespian sources and remade for this ramshackle world, such as Dickensian ruler of London low life, The Beggar King (Nick Frost), imperious philanthropist Lavinia Bidlow (Olivia Williams), impresario of *fin de siècle* decadence Hugo Swann (James Norton) and a host of unruly women cyclists. Its central character is the intriguing Amalia True, leader of the St Romaulda group, whom we later come to know as Zephyr Alexis Navine (1.6). She is supported by medico Horatio Cousens (Zackary Momoh) and electrical 'magician' Penance Adair (Ann Skelly), an experimental inventor of entertainingly weird contraptions and vehicles, magical machines that are part of the attempt to find a way back to a survivable future. Among the throng of the 'Touched' is also Maladie (Ann Manson), a damaged waif who dwells in London's dark places, bent on revenge and destruction, while in possession of Amalia's secret.

Heavy-handed in its use of Victorian accoutrements – from bustles and lorgnettes to looming monsters and underground dungeons – the series received mixed critical reception at the outset as confusing and overcrowded (Berman 2021). Indeed, the first few episodes of *The Nevers* might be described as a historical fantasy horror *mélange*, cluttered with crazy spectacle and exaggerated dramatization. However, in Episode 6 the series reveals its full generic promise, moving from 'steam-punky romp' – as *Guardian* reviewer Lucy Mangan (2021) puts it – to embrace sci-fi, as *fin de siècle* intimations of apocalypse are overtaken by the stark vision of a future where human life on Earth is all but destroyed. Amalia/Zephyr is revealed as an alien, a 'Galanthi', who has survived conflict on Earth and travelled back through time, propelling the wave of strange happenings in 1896 London.

Fantasy writer C.S. Pacat (2017) reflects that world-building can be seen as 'a performance in three acts', founded on the creation of a sense of authenticity and exposition. Detail is important for Pacat through three stages of story development, to create vividness and texture. Achieving believability through detail is vital in bringing together story and visual design elements. Attention to foundational elements, including detail, is evident in *The Nevers*, from its crumbling brickwork hovels to formal Victorian drawing room settings. Although the profusion of storylines, costumes and characters in *The Nevers* tended to overwhelm viewers (Mangan 2021), it did gain audience traction with the shift in generic scope and its presage of alien horrors to come.

A sense of the past

Propelled by a series of ghastly murders *Penny Dreadful* evokes the idea of a haunted past through stories of a world on the brink of a profound and disturbing transformation. The series recruits issues and anxieties such as spiritualism, sexuality, industrialization, female suffrage and scientific experimentation to evoke the transformative ethos of the age and its attendant threat of ultimate destruction. This is achieved through both story action and setting, from the shadowy streets and interiors of London, to the industrialized Gothic cave that houses Victor Frankenstein's new experiments in human re-production (1.1). The effect is to shift the viewer's sense of the past through the fictional technique of recursive adaptation, reworking new characters and stories from classic literature to create a magical world in which fictional characters live again through new settings and encounters, unconstrained by space and time.

The narrative arc of each season is generated through details and nuances drawn from frequently rehearsed ideas of the decadence and modernity of London at the *fin de siècle*. This is evident from the first episode of Season 1, when the chief hunters of the demimonde – Vanessa Ives (Eva Green) and Sir Malcolm (Timothy Dalton) – hunt down a vampire nest in the dark bowels of the city (1.1). Via werewolf character, Ethan Chandler (Josh Hartnett), the series expands to take in the grandiloquent dangers of an American desert wilderness (3.5–3.6), transporting viewers directly in time, via both the documented social and cultural traces of nineteenth- and early twentieth-century society and the familiar tropes of popular screen culture (Louttit 2016).

As Alison Lee and Frederick D. King (2015) argue, *Penny Dreadful* 'disrupts linearity and undermines notions of the authority and priority of an originating text' so the sources become 'memes that have come to redefine history as a myth of modernity'. The repetition and resurgence of such memes foreground a heightened recognition of visual and literary figures not merely as endlessly available narrative archetypes that recur through the overlapping storyworlds of the series but as a vehicle for reproducing popular culture. The originary texts themselves are like ghosts 'haunting' the series, proliferating an idea of the past within which the audience is immersed, *in medias res*, through a perpetual unfolding of visual and literary narration (Sobchack 1997: 5). This haunting calls up an impression of 'historical consciousness' that is at once chronologically and temporally situated – in the experimental milieu of late nineteenth-century London and the cinematic plains and deserts of early twentieth-century America – and yet anachronistic (Kohlke 2018). Both *The Nevers* and *Penny Dreadful* refuse actual temporality, however, instead occupying a space within a Gothic universe that audiences quickly recognize.

In *Penny Dreadful*, this world is populated by creatures that have long haunted the Gothic imagination: mad scientists and manufactured creatures, blood predators, witches, troubled detectives and supernaturally endowed Wild West gunslingers. As Monterrubio-Ibáñez (2020: 16) remarks, the series 'brings the mythical characters together, each of them providing the essential idiosyncrasy of his/her Evil and the epicentre of the syncretism that builds and complexifies throughout the 3 seasons'. Woven together, their stories produce a layer of emotional resonance, inflected through an endlessly adaptive figuration of the monster as hunter/saviour, persecutor/victim, destroyer/survivor. The monster is not only at home in the metropolis, however. As we follow Ethan's story, the shadowy underworld of London gives way to the exposure of the American 'Wild West', with its dry open spaces and seemingly unregulated threats. Ethan is forced to face the violence of his early life (2.10), his father's brutality and the massacre he caused as a cavalryman during the American Civil War, while pursued by Hecate, the youngest of the three witches (3.5). Thus, from the tearing compression of the city to the agoraphobia of a harsh new America, the evolving mythology of the monster allows the series to produce an 'ontology of otherness' imbued with a sense of loss.

Literary and cinematic transformations

World-building in *Penny Dreadful* and *The Nevers* does not just rest on the use of familiar historical allusions. It also draws heavily on much more recent examples of popular culture that recast representations of the past. That the inhabitants of these series are larger-than-life adaptations of well-known character archetypes reflects story elements already made familiar by a profusion of horror/fantasy dramas with neo-Victorian settings, such as *Dracula* (2013–14) and *Ripper Street* (2012–16). Their strategy of remediation also relies on setting and syncretic characterization as vital elements in their construction as evolving, multi-stranded narratives.

It is the literary allusiveness that is perhaps most immediately apparent in *Penny Dreadful*, though, in terms of producing a sense of historicity. The scenes and settings abound with references to literature of the period, high and low brow. As Ryan Britt (2015) remarks: 'Even when *Penny Dreadful* has a walking, breathing, living literary reference, it can't seem to help itself by making even more literary references.' The allusions themselves act a little like memes, but work more extensively to help create a complex edifice of story manufacture. Logan commented publicly that his literary influences for the show were extensive, including nineteenth-century poetry as well as Gothic fiction (Ulaby 2014). The writings of Romantic poet John Clare (1793–1864) are referenced, for instance, when Victor Frankenstein's first creature takes the poet's name, perhaps as an evocation of Clare's personal experience of heartbreak. Other Romantic writers are also mentioned, including William Wordsworth. Indeed, Nina Farizova (2020: 177) maintains that the series can even be regarded as an adaptation of Romantic poetry and thus as a neo-Romantic work. The series encompasses later literary references, however, to authenticate an imagined historical moment. Season 3, for instance, opens amid public mourning for Lord Alfred Tennyson (1809–92) as the pall of death over London casts Vanessa into despair. Unable to shake off the burden of memory, from this moment she becomes vulnerable to the predatory demon who first opened the chink into her world (1.5).

Story labyrinths

While *The Nevers* and *Penny Dreadful* draw key features from the classic novels of late-Victorian Gothic with which to weave their original narrative strands, they also generate a labyrinth of new storylines. In *The Nevers*, characters are loosely based on familiar personae, while in *Penny Dreadful* characters are directly adapted from novels such as Oscar Wilde's *The Picture of Dorian Gray* (2003 [1890]) and Mary Shelley's *Frankenstein* (1980 [1818]) and given new story treatments. These figures are intertwined, for example, when Dorian meets the mysterious Lily, Victor Frankenstein's exquisite female creation (1.4). In turn, she is dazzled by Dorian's beauty, his hunger for life and his collections of fine art and objects. The corresponding figure to Bram Stoker's archetypal vampire, Count Dracula (Christian Camargo), doesn't appear in *Penny Dreadful* until Season 3, but his arrival is presaged in Episode 1 of the first season, when Vanessa, Sir Malcolm and their friends attack the vampire lair. In both series, there is plenty of Dickensian atmosphere – deep shadows and portentous threats, obscure villains and impenetrable nightmares worthy of *Great Expectations* (Dickens 1861), *Bleak House* (Dickens 1852) and *Our Mutual Friend* (Dickens 1864). Equally influential, of course, are the historical 'penny dreadfuls' and their 'dime store' descendants, exaggerated stories that gained mass circulation during the nineteenth and early twentieth centuries. Cheap, often luridly illustrated, these vivid works sported titles such as *The Black Band, or, The Mysteries of Midnight* (Braddon 1877). Both *The Nevers* and *Penny Dreadful* incorporate a little of the haunted realism of Victorian sensation fiction, for example written by Wilkie Collins (1859–60) and Mary Braddon (1862), in the elusive spectres and damaged women whom we meet as the narratives unfold. We are even invited to pity the witches who are gripped in the patriarchal demon's thrall (2.9). In the case of Logan's *Penny Dreadful*, a plenitude of American adventure Westerns – such as those produced by prolific magazine writer W.C. Tuttle (1883–1969) and Zane Grey (1872–1939), whose books shaped the mythology of the American West, contribute to the flavour and ethos of key characters and episodes.

Logan acknowledges that the cinematic legacy of twentieth-century cinema has broadly shaped his imagination. The spatiality of the series, its shadowy atmospherics, looming shadows and impassioned surges of violence and desire, and the pathos of its victims and monsters all allude to the horror heritage of movies such as James Whale's *Frankenstein* (1931) and Terence Fisher's *Dracula* (1958). He remarked in an interview:

> I grew up loving horror, feeling an alienated kid, myself, I found great kinship with them, with those who are perceived as demons or monsters or outlaws. And they've always moved me more than anything, more than Frankenstein's creature scared me when I watched Boris Karloff or Christopher Lee, I was moved.
>
> (Huver 2015)

While it is the dynamics of horror that may be most strongly foregrounded here, key story elements also take place against the backdrop of an American Wild West imported from Hollywood cinema 'in the grand tradition of Sergio Leone and other Italian maestros of the Spaghetti Western' (Crow 2016), when sharpshooter Ethan Chandler is forced to face his past crimes.

In turn, *The Nevers*' embrace of futuristic sci-fi through the strange appearance of alien beings in 1896 offers a storyline that seems to draw as much from the movies of Ridley Scott as from the novels of Ray Bradbury, H.G. Wells and Lewis Carroll. From this heritage of popular narrative, these series spin archetypal tales of villains and heroes, accompanied by a host of newly invented characters – traitors, hopefuls, users and victims, magical and quotidian beings. Their stories portray a pantheon of personae in ontological disarray, a mash-up mythology of characters and plot lines constantly in motion as they are reused and reinvented. As Britt (2015) observes, 'part of the reason this literary mash-up works so well is because other main characters are not plucked from the pages of beloved books, but instead *feel* like they have been'.

Penny Dreadful, most notably, uses news topics, social issues and debates from the late nineteenth and early twentieth centuries to situate its historicity, but these are also inflected through twenty-first-century popular culture. Impelling the dramatic action of *Penny Dreadful*'s first episode, for instance, is a nod to London's 'Ripper' murder scares of the late 1880s, as a mother and daughter are ripped to pieces in their home (1.1). This fearful event sparks rumours of the 'Ripper's' return – although, as we learn, the truth is more mysterious and horrifying. Visceral knife attacks on young women in the Whitechapel area between 1888 and 1891 terrified Londoners (Curtis 2008; Eddleston 2001), part of a rising sense of moral anxiety linked to cultural, sexual and industrial changes (Flanders 2015; Matthews 2016; Walkowitz 1988). Gruesome stories of the crimes proliferated as fodder for scare-mongering appetites in newspapers and books, underpinning the whole genre of serial screen murder where females are victimized by a psychopathic killer (Conrich 2012: 161).

Such references to history play on the scare-mongering media legacy of serial murder mythology, contributing to a heightened feeling of traumatic transgression. In Episode 2 of *Penny Dreadful*, for example, the *mise-en-scène* displays familiar tropes of Gothic horror: a dark foggy street, a shivering street-girl on a lonely park bench: a leering lamp-lighter and the sudden attack by a powerful but unseen monster. As she waits, the young woman unwraps an apple from a piece of newspaper to reveal the printed headline: 'Jack-the-Ripper' (1.2).

Her fear holds her in thrall as the monster seizes her body just beyond view, a classic thriller flourish. While our hunters of the demimonde in *Penny Dreadful* track down and overcome their first target – the unnamed vampire – the figure of the 'Ripper' is never put to rest. 'He' remains intangible, a late-Victorian London legend spread by newspapers and social fever to produce an endless number of subsequent fictional 'simulacra' (Conrich 2012: 161–3). The historically situated serial killer trope is further adapted in *Penny Dreadful* at the end of Season 1, with the devastating scene caused by lycanthrope cowboy adventurer Ethan Chandler at the Mariner's Inn. Ethan has been pursued by detectives from the Pinkerton Agency for an earlier crime, which he committed in the United States in his werewolfish state. Gripped by the transformative power of the rising moon at the Mariner's Inn, he is again unable to resist turning, ripping apart the others around him (1.8). The public scandal and fury caused by the 'Ripper' scare echo through Season 2.

Similarly, in *The Nevers*, the fearsome resonance of the 'Ripper' is expressed through the unhinged character of Maladie, who is described by Inspector Frank Mundi (Ben Chaplin) as the worst murderer London has ever seen (1.5). Attired as a punk Lady Havisham with ragged hair and black-ringed eyes, Maladie represents a vicious, impulsive threat to ordinary Londoners and to the 'Touched', which seemingly cannot be contained. She is driven by a fury that stems as much from psychic illness as her alien-acquired power. Her persona is nevertheless inflected with pathos due to her victimization and abandonment. Maladie is the only one who recalls the moment London was overshadowed by the spacecraft as it emitted the beams of light that gave magical powers to the 'Touched' (1.1). When she is captured, treated brutally by the constabulary and sentenced to a public hanging, Amalia helps her to escape, repaying a debt she owes, but also releasing Maladie's destructive volatility (1.5). In practice, the idea of the counter-historical works here as a deliberate striving for something more than revisioning. It is nothing less than an attempt to shift the imbalance of power that, in the future, brings humanity to the edge of planetary annihilation. For the Galanthi, the world of the late-Victorian era figures as a point in time before the point of no return from which the ablated human world of the far distant future might be cast out.

If the 'Ripper' mythologies are among the sources for *The Nevers*, as for *Penny Dreadful*, the series is equally imbued with *fin de siècle* literary allusions – albeit less indirectly. The 'New Women' novels of the era may not be mentioned specifically in *The Nevers*, but the feminist themes and ideas expounded in them undoubtedly contribute to the ethos of the series, such as works by Olive Schreiner (1855–1920), Sarah Grand (1854–1943) and Florence Dixie (1857–1905). Chronological disruption, another popular theme of the era, is central to *The Nevers* and H.G. Wells' notion of a time travel device as portrayed in *The Time Machine* (1895) is another inevitable trope here. The atmosphere of danger and mystery in *The Nevers* and the chiaroscuro visualization of impending conflict with unknowable future forces is by turns frightful and comical in their exaggeration and theatricality. The result, however, is the creation of fresh, yet familiar storyworlds, haunted by the ghosts, strangers and monsters from realms that seem to be hurtling, all too like our own, towards an unfathomable transformation. Brent Linsley (2019: 196) observes that such fantasy narratives can help us to consider contemporary threats in terms of the unsustainability of Western capitalism, remaining mindful that promises of utopian solutions may further entrap humankind in a trajectory of ongoing wastage. Others, such as Schubart (2018: 77), approach fantasy stories as a vehicle for imagining new possibilities: the yet-unreal. *Penny Dreadful* and *The Nevers* offer a vision of possibility, orientated both towards past and present/future, in which the decisions and actions of characters may destroy or renew the worlds they inhabit.

Evolving stories: World without end

Through visual, literary and narrative design, *Penny Dreadful* and *The Nevers* use adaptations from historical and modern sources to create new stories with the potential to further adapt and change. In a variety of ways, they exemplify the 'looting' of literary and historical sources (Zagarrio 2015: 22) to build a screen drama storyworld and the 'memefication' of history that goes with it. The counter-historical here resides in a loosening of the tension-line of documentary and memory to allow for more inclusive understandings of the past through fantasy narrative, and attempting to acknowledge the embodied thought and emotion as part of historical account (Landy 2015: x). These fantasies provide radical and queer perspectives on the Victorian *fin*, the beauty and horror of its legacies for the post-industrial era strained by the haunted longevity of hope, desire and transformation.

As a story franchise, *Penny Dreadful* has spawned a graphic novel prequel sequence by Krysty Wilson-Cairns (2017), illustrated by Louis De Martinis and a new television iteration set in Los Angeles (Logan 2020). Promising as it is, however, *Penny Dreadful* never realized its early promise of reimagining the terms of representation in contemporary popular culture. While Victor Frankenstein's suffering slave of human creation, the Creature, John Clare (Rory Kinnear), makes peace with his past, little changes for the women of the series. When the series closed unexpectedly after Season 3, Marie-Louise Kohlke (2018: 10) contends, audiences were left with an encoded endorsement of 'spectacular sexualized violence'. Vanessa Ives dies voluntarily at the hand of Ethan Chandler, becoming a sacrifice to the imperative of gendered historical continuity and the promise of a future no longer bound to historical imperative lapses. Heroism and sacrifice are packaged in terms of a violent cliché of gendered romance and the figure of the female destroyer remains taboo (Di Biasio 2017). The dust of Dracula's thwarted apocalypse is left to settle and history itself becomes little more than a commodity. Only Lily Frankenstein slips away, like her progenitor, Mary Shelley's monster, into the unknown (Green 2022).

Embryonic and overabundant, *The Nevers* unashamedly sets out to exploit the popularity of neo-Victorian fantasy, but it is not just a history-infused melodrama. Adding time-travelling science fiction into the mix engages its viewers through generic adaptation. *The Nevers* emerging storyline follows the Galanthi's wild attempt to reverse the Earth's destruction by humans as she brings seemingly magic 'technologies' from the future to late Victorian London. Production was halted after six episodes, due to the Covid-19 pandemic and although a further six episodes were made, the series ended with the first season. Like *Penny Dreadful*, *The Nevers* can be seen as the fruit of neo-Victorian narrative reconstruction, producing a visual and literary vehicle for the kind of story production that is already familiar to readers and viewers, bringing to new life the popular fiction of the past through a simulacrum of history (Louttit 2016). Interesting partly for the ways in which they attempt to reimagine the possibilities of storying, they also reflect contemporary fears and hopes for a time when humans will at last come to terms with existence as cooperation, rewriting the past and the future as reciprocity rather than as destructive determinism.

Notes

1   The term 'Steampunk' emerged as a way of describing fantasy stories set in an imagined past, usually Victorian or Edwardian, powered by strange and often magical mechanical devices. Scholars have debated definitions of the term and, while it has been regarded as a 'fad', Steampunk's qualities continue to appeal.
2   I make a similar point in Green (2021: 272).

References

Adcock, J. (2012), 'Vampires of Paris', *Yesterday's Papers*, 18 January. Available online: https://john-adcock.blogspot.com/2012/01/vampires-of-paris.html (accessed 3 September 2021).

Albertsen, A.N.B. (2017), 'The Contaminant Cobweb: Complex Characters and Monstrous Mashup', *Refractory a Journal of Entertainment Media*, 28. Available online: http://refractory.unimelb.edu.au/tag/penny-dreadful (accessed 22 October 2019).

Anyiwo, U.M. (2018), 'A Monstrous Narrative: Unraveling Gender and Ethnic Archetypes in Showtime's *Penny Dreadful*', in *Gender Warriors: Reading Contemporary Urban Fantasy*, edited by U.M. Anyiwo and Amanda Hobson, 111–30, Leiden: Brill.

Berman, J. (2021), '*The Nevers* Is a Pale Imitation of Joss Whedon's Classics', *Time*, 9 April. Available online: https://time.com/5953452/the-nevers-review (accessed 3 June 2022).

Braddon, M.E. (1862), *Lady Audley's Secret*, London: William Tinsley.

Braddon, M.E. (1877), *The Black Band, or The Mysteries of Midnight*, 1 July 1861 to 23 June 1862 (weekly) in *Halfpenny Journal*, London: George Vickers.

Braid, B. (2017), 'The Frankenstein Meme: *Penny Dreadful* and *The Frankenstein Chronicles* as Adaptations', *Open Cultural Studies*. Available online: https://www.degruyter.com/document/doi/10.1515/culture-2017-0021/html?lang=en (accessed 14 August 2023).

Britt, R. (2015), 'How Penny Dreadful Adapts Multiple Books at Once', *Electric Lit: Reading into Everything*, 19 May. Available online: https://electricliterature.com/how-penny-dreadful-adapts-multiple-books-at-once (accessed 17 June 2021).

Collins, W. (1859–60), 'The Woman in White', serialised in *All the Year Round*, edited by Charles Dickens. London: Chapman and Hall.

Conrich, I. (2012), 'Mass Media/Mass Murder: Serial Killer Cinema and the Modern Violated Body', in *Criminal Visions: Media Representations of Crime and Justice*, edited by P. Mason, 156–71, London: Routledge.

Cooke, S. (n.d.), 'Gustave Doré, The Graphic, and Social Realism of the Seventies and Eighties', *The Victorian Web*. Available online: https://victorianweb.org/art/illustration/socialrealism/5.html (accessed 14 February 2023).

Cooley, K. and C.A. Milligan (2018), 'Haunted Objects, Networked Subjects: The Nightmarish Nostalgia of Creepypasta', *Horror Studies*, 9 (2): 193–211.

Crow, D. (2016), '*Penny Dreadful* Season Three', *DenofGeek*, 8 April. Available online: https://www.denofgeek.com/us/tv/penny-dreadful/248813/penny-dreadful-season-3-trailer-release-date-and-more (accessed 3 June 2022).

Curtis, L.P. (2008), *Jack the Ripper and the London Press*, New Haven, CT: Yale University Press.

Davies, M.L. (2014), 'Penny Dreadful Comic-Con Panel Recap', *Collider*, 25 July. Available online: https://collider.com/penny-dreadful-comic-con-panel-recap (accessed 10 June 2021).

Deleuze, G. and F. Guattari (1987 [1980]), *A Thousand Plateaus: Capitalism and Schizophrenia*, translated by B. Massumi, Minneapolis: University of Minnesota Press.

Derrida, J. (2006), *Spectres of Marx: The State of the Debt, the Work of Mourning and the New International*, London: Routledge.

Di Biasio, A. (2017), 'Contemporary Television Series and Literature: An Intense Transformative Embrace', *Fusion: Global Art Words and Music*, 8 August. Available online: http://www.fusionmagazine.org/contemporary-television-series-and-literature-an-intense-transformative-embrace (accessed 17 June 2021).

Dickens, C. (1852), *Bleak House*, London: Chapman and Sons.

Dickens, C. (1861), *Great Expectations*, London: Chapman and Sons.

Dickens, C. (1864), *Our Mutual Friend*, London: Chapman and Sons.

Dines, M. (2018), 'Designs for Living Rooms', in *Queering the Interior*, edited by Andrew Gorman-Murray and Matt Cook, 96–107, London: Bloomsbury.

Eddleston, J.J. (2001), *Jack the Ripper: An Encyclopedia*, Santa Barbara: ABC-CLIO.

Erll, A. (2008), 'Literature, Film, and the Mediality of Cultural Memory', in *Cultural Memory Studies: An International and Interdisciplinary Handbook*, edited by Astrid Erll and Ansgar Nünning, 389–99, Berlin: Walter de Gruyter.

Farizova, N. (2020), 'Romantic Poetry and the TV Series Form: The Rhyme of John Logan's Penny Dreadful', *Adaptation*, 13 (2): 176–93.

Flanders, J. (2015), *The Invention of Murder: How the Victorians Revelled in Death and Detection and Created Modern Crime*, London: Macmillan.

Friedlander, W. (2014), 'Q&A: Designer of *Penny Dreadful*'s Hauntingly Beautiful Costumes', *Variety*, 8 May. Available online: https://variety.com/2014/tv/news/penny-dreadful-eva-green-timothy-dalton-costumes-1201174825 (accessed 7 January 2023).

Green, S. (2021), 'Vampire Apocalypse and the Evolutionary Sublime: The "End of Days" in John Logan's *Penny Dreadful*', *Continuum: Journal of Media and Cultural Studies*, 35 (2): 270–81.

Green, S. (2022), 'The Killing Characters of *Penny Dreadful*', in *Serial Killers in Contemporary Television: Familiar Monsters in Post-9/11 Culture*, edited by B. Robinson and C. Daigle, Ch. 6, Toronto: Routledge.

Gupta, S.H. (2014), '*Penny Dreadful* Costume Designer Gabriella Pescucci on Her Dreadfully Delicious Designs', *IndieWire*, 28 June. Available online: https://www.indiewire.com/2014/06/penny-dreadful-costume-designer-gabriella-pescucci-on-her-dreadfully-delicious-designs-24778 (accessed 7 January 2023).

Hopson, T. (2021), *Punch Drunk Critics*, 2 February. Available online: https://punchdrunkcritics.com/2021/02/the-nevers-teaser-joss-whedons-upcoming-hbo-series-looks-like-a-victorian-era-x-men (accessed 7 January 2023).

Huver, S. (2015), '*Penny Dreadful* Creator John Logan on Season 2's Supernatural Secrets', *CBR*, 3 May. Available online: https://www.cbr.com/penny-dreadful-creator-john-logan-on-season-2s-supernatural-secrets (accessed 17 June 2021).

Jenkins, H. (2017), 'Transmedia Logics and Locations', in *The Rise of Transtexts: Challenges and Opportunities,* edited by Benjamin W.L. Derhy Kurtz and Mélanie Bourdaa, 220–40, New York & Abingdon: Routledge.

Kohlke, M.L. (2018), 'The Lures of Neo-Victorianism Presentism (with a Feminist Case Study of *Penny Dreadful*)', *Literature Compass*, 15 (7): 1–14. Available online: https://doi.org/10.1111/lic3.12463/ (accessed 28 December 2023).

Landy, M. (2015), *Cinema & Counter-History*, Bloomington, IN: Indiana University Press.

Latour, B. (1993), *We Have Never Been Modern*, Cambridge, MA: Harvard University Press.

Lee, A. and F.D. King (2015), 'From Text, to Myth, to Meme: *Penny Dreadful* and Adaptation', *Cahiers Victoriens et Èdouardiens*, 82: 1–10 (Autumn). Available online: https://journals.openedition.org/cve/2343 (accessed 17 June 2021).

Linsley, B. (2019), 'A Sense of Unending: Apocalypse and Post-Apocalypse in Novels of Late Capitalism', PhD thesis, University of Arkansas. Available online: https://scholarworks.uark.edu/etd/3341 (accessed 31 January 2023).

Louttit, C. (2016), 'Victorian London Redux: Adapting the Gothic Metropolis', *Critical Survey*, 28 (1): 2–14. Available online: https://doi.org/10.3167/cs.2016.280102 (accessed 28 December 2023).

McLaughlin, J. (2000), *Writing the Urban Jungle: Reading Empire in London from Doyle to Eliot*, Charlottesville, VA: University of Virginia Press.

Manea, D. (2016), 'A Wolfs Eye View of London: *Dracula, Penny Dreadful*, and the Logic of Repetition', *Critical Survey*, 28 (1): 40–50.

Mangan, L. (2021), '*The Nevers* Review: Not Even Magical Aliens Can Save This Cursed Mess', *The Guardian*, 18 May. Available online: https://www.theguardian.com/tv-and-radio/2021/may/17/the-nevers-review-not-even-magical-aliens-can-save-this-cursed-mess (accessed 17 June 2021).

Martin-Payre, C. (2020), '"One of Us": Dorian Gray, Untimeliness, and *Penny Dreadful*'s Contemporary Victoriana', *Polysèmes. Revue d'Ètudes Intertextuelles et Intermédiales*, 23 (2): 1–17. Available online: https://doi.org/10.4000/polysemes.7052 (accessed 28 December 2023).

Matthews, M. (2016), 'Penny Dreadfuls, Juvenile Crime, and Late-Victorian Moral Panic', *The Victorian Web*. Available online: http://www.victorianweb.org/genre/matthews1.html (accessed 3 September 2021).

Monterrubio-Ibáñez, L. (2020), '*Penny Dreadful* (2014–2016): Postmodern Mythology and Ontology of Otherness', *Communication & Society*, 3 (1): 15–28.

National Clothing Forum (2019), 'Movie Costumes of Vanessa Ives from *Penny Dreadful* Series: Her Day Dresses and Outerwear'. Available online: https://nationalclothing.org/622-movie-costumes-of-vanessa-ives-from-penny-dreadful-series-her-day-dresses-and-outerwear.html (accessed 3 January 2023).

Park-Finch, H. (2017), 'From *Madame Bovary* to *Ryan's Daughter*: Literary, Cultural, and Historical Palimpsests', *Adaptation*, 10 (1): 51–72.

Pacat, C.S. (2017), 'Fantasy Worldbuilding: The Power of Detail', *Writing Queensland*, 258 (September/November): 14–15.

Posada, T. (2020), 'Old Monsters, Old Curses: The New Hysterical Woman and *Penny Dreadful*', in *Neo-Victorian Madness: Rediagnosing Nineteenth-Century Mental Illness in Literature and Other Media*, edited by S.E. Maier and B. Ayres, 229–51, New York: Springer.

Richardson, A. and C. Willis (2019 [2002]), *The New Woman in Fiction and Fact: Fin-de-Siècle Feminisms*, London: Palgrave Macmillan.

Ryan, M. (2016), '*Penny Dreadful* Production Designer on His Emmy-Nominated Work', *Variety*. Available online: https://variety.com/2016/tv/features/penny-dreadful-jonathan-mckinstry-season-three-showtime-sets-emmy-production-design-1201839690 (accessed 5 January 2023).

Schubart, R. (2018), *Mastering Fear: Women, Emotions, and Contemporary Horror*, London: Bloomsbury.

Selcke, D. (2021), 'The First Episodes of *The Nevers* Were a "Grand and Ambitious Prologue"', *Fansided*, 29 May. Available online: https://winteriscoming.net/2021/05/28/first-episodes-the-nevers-grand-ambitious-prologue-laura-donnelly (accessed 3 June 2022).

Shelley, M. (1980 [1818]), *Frankenstein or the Modern Prometheus*, Oxford: Oxford University Press.

Sobchack, V. (1997), 'The Insistent Fringe: Moving Images and Historical Consciousness', *History and Theory*, 36 (4): 4–20.

Stephan, M. (2016), 'Do You Believe in Magic? The Potency of the Fantasy Genre', *Coolabah*, 18: 3–15.

Stevenson, R.L. (1930 [1886]), *The Strange Case of Dr Jekyll and Mr Hyde*, frontispiece and illustrations by S.G. Hulme Beaman, London: Bodley Head.

Stoker, B. (1997 [1897]), *Dracula*, New York: W.W. Norton.

Travers, B. (2021), '*The Nevers* Review: Joss Whedon's HBO Fantasy Series Is Messy, Maddening – and Kind of a Hoot', *Indiwire*. Available online: https://www.indiewire.com/2021/04/the-nevers-review-hbo-joss-whedon-series-1234628588 (accessed 3 June 2022).

Ulaby, N.R. (2014), 'Lurid Meets Literary in *Penny Dreadful*: An All-star Gothic Revue', *NPR*, 8 May. Available online: https://www.npr.org/2014/05/08/310706522/lurid-meets-literary-in-penny-dreadful-an-all-star-Gothic-revue (accessed 3 June 2022).

Walkowitz, J.R. (1988), 'Science and the Séance: Transgressions of Gender and Genre in Late Victorian London', *Representations*, 22 (2): 3–29.

Wilde, O. (2003 [1890]), *The Picture of Dorian Gray*, Harmondsworth: Penguin.

Williams, R. (1973), *The Country and the City*, Oxford: Oxford University Press.

Wilson-Cairns, K. (author) and L. De Martinis (illustrator) (2017–19). *Penny Dreadful*. Vols 1–3, London: Titan Comics.

Yamato, J. (2014), 'SXSW: Showtime's *Penny Dreadful* Debuts Juan Antonio Bayona-Helmed Premiere Episode', *Deadline*, 9 March. Available online: https://deadline.com/2014/03/sxsw-2014-showtime-penny-dreadful-first-episode-josh-hartnett-juan-antonio-bayona-696249 (accessed 3 September 2021).

Yeats, W.B. (1989 [1920]), 'The Second Coming', in *The Collected Poems of W.B. Yeats*, edited by Richard J Finneran, 187, New York: Springer.

Yehl, J. (2018), 'Joss Whedon Explains Title of His HBO Series *The Nevers*', *IGN*, 22 July. Available online: https://www.ign.com/articles/2018/07/21/joss-whedon-explains-title-of-his-hbo-series-the-nevers-comic-con-2018 (accessed 28 December 2023).

Zagarrio, V. (2015), '"The True Story That Inspired the Movie": Cinema, Literature and History in the Digital Age', *Rivista di Studi Americani*, 26: 19–38.

Films and television series

Dracula (1958), directed by Terence Fisher [film], United Kingdom: Hammer Film Productions.

Dracula (2013), created by Cole Haddon and Daniel Knauf [TV series], United Kingdom: Sky Living. United States: NBC.

Frankenstein (1931), directed by James Whale [film], United States: Universal Pictures.

Penny Dreadful (2014–16), directed by John Logan [TV series], United States and United Kingdom: Neal Street Productions and Showtime Networks.

Penny Dreadful: City of Angels (2020), directed by John Logan [TV series], United States: Desert Wolf Productions.

Ripper Street (2012–2016), created by Richard Warlow [TV series], United Kingdom: Tiger Aspect Productions.

Sherlock Holmes (1939–46), directed by Sidney Banfield and Roy William Neill [film series], United States: Twentieth-Century Fox and Universal Pictures.

Sweeney Todd: The Demon Barber of Fleet Street (2007), directed by Tim Burton, written by John Logan [film], United Kingdom and United States: Dream Works/Paramount.

The Nevers (2021), directed by Joss Whedon [TV series], United States: Phillipa Goslett, HBO.

8

Pretty ballads, bastard truths: History, memory and the past in *The Witcher*

Agnieszka Stasiewicz-Bieńkowska

Introduction

In 'The End's Beginning', the first episode of the Netflix show *The Witcher* (2019–), Queen Calanthe of Cintra (Jodhi May) casts her husband Eist (Björn Hlynur Haraldsson) a sharp look of reproach when he speaks about the looming war with Nilfgaard in the presence of their granddaughter, Cirilla (Freya Allan). Raised among the troubadours hailing Calanthe's triumphs, young Ciri appears undisturbed by the troubling news, and is eager to listen to war stories from the past. Her royal grandmother, however, displays no sense of pride at the memory of her conquests, remembering instead the violent death of thousands of her soldiers. When Ciri praises the ballad of Calanthe's victory in the Battle of Hochebuz, Eist explains with brutal honesty that, 'Pretty ballads hide bastard truths' (1.1).

The themes of history, memory and the haunting past permeate the universe of *The Witcher* (*Wiedźmin*), the internationally celebrated transmedial fantasy storyworld originating from the bestselling literary series by Andrzej Sapkowski. Infused with Slavic aesthetics and considered 'a tribute to the Polish language and to Polishness' (Blacha and Kubiński 2016; cf. Jaworowicz-Zimny 2020: 4–5), *The Witcher* phenomenon has proved intelligible in diverse cultural contexts, holding a fascination for readers, audiences and gamers worldwide. Sapkowski's six novels and two collections of short stories, which constitute the saga, have been translated into numerous languages, and have inspired the creation of the blockbuster video-games developed by the Polish studio CD Projekt RED. In June 2015, an English rendition of Sapkowski's short story collection *Ostatnie życzenie* (1993) – *The Last Wish* (2007) – was listed as the only translated book among the *New York Times*' fifteen best-selling paperbacks in the United States, along with such internationally acclaimed titles as George R.R. Martin's *Game of Thrones* (Drewniak 2020: 205). As Paulina Drewniak observes, translated books seldom reach the status of bestsellers in the US 'translation-resistant market' – a success 'as rare as unicorns, and equally sensational' in the light of the international hegemony of English-language fantasy fiction (2020: 205; cf. Drewniak 2016: 174). In 2019, *The Witcher* was adapted for the small screen in a television fantasy show produced by Lauren Schmidt Hissrich, swiftly becoming one of Netflix's most popular productions (Clark 2019; Parrotanalytics 2020). Ever since the premiere of the series, Sapkowski's books have repeatedly ranked high among the *New York Times* bestsellers.

The storyworld of *The Witcher* has captured the attention of numerous scholars across disciplines. Several Polish-language volumes centred on the phenomenon have been published in the new millennium, including literary analyses by Katarzyna Kaczor (2006) and Magdalena Roszczynialska (2009), and two edited collections investigating the series' diverse media iterations (Dudziński et al. 2015; Dudziński and Płoszaj 2016). *The Witcher*'s franchise has been examined from a variety of perspectives. Its polysemantic, culturally loaded language inspired a number of linguistic analyses, with scholars considering diverse translatory challenges of the novels and video-games. Various studies examined *The Witcher*'s intertextuality, with a particular emphasis on the reimagined literary, folk and fairy tale tropes (see Deszcz-Tryhubczak and Zarzycka 2012; Dobosiewicz 2013; Kostecka 2014; Roszczynialska 2009). Others critically engaged with the saga's Slavic inspirations (Majkowski 2018; Zaborowski 2015), looked into the *Witcher*-themed LARP events and tourism (Jaworowicz-Zimny 2020) and interrogated it through the lenses of postcolonialism, 'race', otherness and monstrosity (e.g. Błaszczkowska and Jakubiak 2015; Cieśliński 2015; Majkowski 2013; Roszczynialska 2009). With the international interest in *The Witcher* rising rapidly, further studies have emerged, including those centred on the new performances of masculinity and the series' resistance against the hegemonic representations of gender (see e.g. Cuklanz and Erol 2021; Matuszek 2017).

This chapter aims to contribute to a deeper understanding of *The Witcher* by focusing on the politics of memory and history, and by exploring the complex relationship between the past and the present in *The Witcher* novels and television show. The fascination with history and its myriad representations has previously been recognized as the foundation of Sapkowski's storyworld. Various scholars have pointed to multiple historical allegories and allusions in both the literary and the video-game series (e.g. Drewniak 2020; Uniłowski 2017). More importantly, the meditation on the nature of historiography and philosophy of history – as well as various meanings of historical processes and accounts – has been acknowledged as both the focal narrative concern and the organizing metaphor of Sapkowski's novels (Majkowski 2013; Roszczynialska 2009).

Centred on the eponymous hero Witcher Geralt of Rivia, a nomadic mutant and contract killer of monsters, and princess-warrior Cirilla, Geralt's foster daughter, *The Witcher* draws its fans into a web of sophisticated narratives, where the protagonists' adventures are woven into a history of violent conflicts and ruthless political games tearing up the saga's realms. In a universe resembling the realities of mediaeval Europe – a familiar aesthetics for the fantasy genre (e.g. Majkowski 2013; Sapkowski and Bereś 2019 [2005]) – the Empire of Nilfgaard and the Kingdoms of the North clash time and again in bloody combat, and frictions between human and non-human races frequently escalate into outbursts of violence.

Spinning the tales of invasions and conquests, wars and war traumas, and cultures slowly fading or brutally erased, *The Witcher* engages on multiple levels with the complexities of memory and history. In *Cultural Memory Studies*, Astrid Erll (2008: 2, 7) proposes that the seemingly competing categories of memory and history ought to be replaced with 'a notion of different modes of remembering in culture' – with history as yet another manifestation of cultural memory defined as 'the interplay of present and past in socio-cultural contexts'. While the dichotomic perception of memory and history has been subjected to scholarly criticism as artificial or counterproductive (Erll 2008; see also Domańska 2006: 15–17), I find some elements of this concept useful for my analysis. In *The Witcher*, institutionalized history is often depicted as 'an instrument of oppression and identified with state, imperialism ... and anthropocentrism' (Domańska 2006: 15, quotation in English after Rybicka 2012: 128). Memory, in turn, is frequently represented as a space for the stories silenced by history, one that challenges hegemonic historical accounts and articulates a longing for historical justice. The boundaries between history and memory in *The Witcher* are, however, fluid and permeable, and both are narrated as involved with the discourses of power, and a vast reservoir of anxiety and trauma.

The Witcher's preoccupation with uncertainties and horrors of memory and history bears a mark of the Gothic approach to the past. While the series does not represent the Gothic genre as such, it frequently relies on the Gothic repertoire of mysterious ancestries, usurped power, the spectacle of graveyards and ruins, repressed histories and the present haunted by the violence of yesteryear. Drawing on Andrzej Sapkowski's literary series and Lauren Schmidt Hissrich's television show, this chapter employs the Gothic paradigm of the past in order to explore how individual and collective relationships with memory and history are represented and problematized in *The Witcher*'s storyworld. Focusing on the themes of conveying, (re)imagining and instrumentalizing the past, it investigates *The Witcher*'s interrogative approach to the discourses of ideology and power that are at play in the processes of constructing history. The chapter further examines the trope of the past as a haunting spectre that lingers in the places of memory and loss, exploring the constant irresolution between remembrance and oblivion as a key narrative tension of the saga.

The songs we sing about our triumphs: Writing and rewriting history

When celebrated bard Jaskier (Joey Batey) meets Geralt of Rivia (Henry Cavill) in the second episode of *The Witcher* television series, he promises to efface the witcher's ill-famed role in the massacre of Blaviken from human cultural memory. Jaskier harbours no doubts that his ballads possess the power to remove Geralt's stigma as 'the butcher', as 'All the North would be too busy singing the tales of Geralt of Rivia, the-the White Wolf or-or something' (1.2). Composing a poem about their violent encounter with elven freedom fighters, Jaskier voices no concern about factual accuracy, declaring the romanticized, confabulated version of events a more secure path to 'make history' (1.21.2). Informed about the human betrayal of elves, the bard still refuses to amend the lyrics. Historical truth and justice surrenders to political agenda, popular tastes and personal gain, and elves remain narrated as invaders and fiends, defeated by the brave witcher, 'a friend of humanity' (1.2).

In her study of time and the notion of historical veracity in the nineteenth-century vampire texts, Stephanie Green (2017: 94) accentuates the Gothic rejection of the 'unified and reliable story of the past'. The Gothic narrative, Green argues, at once depends on the authenticating power of historical records and accounts, and is revealing of their ambiguous, illusory character. In *The Witcher*, both individual and collective pasts are related from a rich variety of perspectives, with a plethora of fictive historical sources – chronicles, memoirs, manuscripts, ballads, textbooks and more – producing multiple historical narratives. *The Witcher*'s universe is outfitted with an extensive historiography that seemingly operates to establish the credibility of events (Roszczynialska 2009: 59, 78). However, as argued by Majkowski (2013) and Roszczynialska (2009) in their respective analyses of Sapkowski's polyphonic narration of the Battle of Brenna, any means of describing past events in *The Witcher* is ultimately revealed as inadequate and fragmentary. From a florid chronicle of a venerable historian to a seemingly objective succinct description in a military textbook, the accounts of the past are subjected to fabrication, mythologization and blatant propaganda, disfigured in accordance with political interests and interpreted through a historian's personal worldview – their authenticity questionable and impartiality feigned (Majkowski 2013: 373, 386–94; Roszczynialska 2009: 82–91; cf. Uniłowski 2017: 523).

In *The Witcher*, the processes of creating history – by selecting and constructing various aspects and versions of the past – are depicted in no uncertain terms as deeply entangled in the discourses of ideology and power. The nightmares of history become filtered, aestheticized and translated into seductive narratives of heroism and adventure, moulded into a shared romantic mythology of the past. In the Art Gallery of Glory, where young adepts of wizardry are to study the history of magic, humans arrive onto the Continent as haloed saints, harnessing the Power and taming tumultuous sea waters. Yet the grand landing is swiftly revealed as likely to have been marked by 'hanging over the side [of the ship], vomiting bile' rather than by glorious deeds (Sapkowski 2013: 133–4). More importantly, the visual accounts of the subsequent massacre of elves are conspicuous by their absence, purged from historical accounts 'so as not to spoil a beautiful legend' (Sapkowski 2013: 135–6).

Institutionalized versions of history in *The Witcher* are left with little epistemic authority and are stripped of their status of the objective key to the past, as the saga unmasks their constructedness and refracting power. Historical 'truths' are recognized as murky and conjoined with legends, and the radical practices of exclusion as inherent to hegemonic discourses of history. The question of *which* – or, more accurately, *whose* – historical account will ultimately prevail is repeatedly narrated as a matter of cardinal importance, representing history as susceptible of appropriation and manipulation. The shouts of triumph over the North's victory in the war have yet to die down when the Northern leaders already begin contemplating what ought to fill the pages of future history books. Reducing historical accounts to 'scribblings', useful only as far as they are translatable into instruments of control, they intend to rewrite the collective war effort of diverse races – humans, dwarves, elves and more – into 'the chronicles of humanity' (Sapkowski 2017b: 445). The aspects of the past that are deemed to be of value are carefully chosen and adapted to replace those not serving the anthropocentric political agendas. Consequently, historians' future works are to be sanitized of any content that could blur the boundaries between the human 'us' and non-human 'suspicious elements' (2017b: 444–5).

With multiple competing iterations of history, historical 'truth' in *The Witcher* often becomes construed as a point of reference by which to navigate the borders of selfhood and otherness. Belonging and the capacity to recognize friend from foe are shown to be dependent upon the internalization – or at least the knowledge – of a 'correct' account of the past. Mysterious sorcerer Rience inadvertently reveals his allegiance to Nilfgaard when he refers to the fall of Cintra as a 'battle' and a 'conquest of the town' (Sapkowski 2017a: 46). 'I've never heard anyone describe those events like that', explains one of the Nordlings. 'For *us*, it has always been a massacre. The Massacre of Cintra. No one refers to it by any other name' (Sapkowski 2017a: 46, author's emphasis). Years after the decisive Battle of Brenna, Nilfgaardian textbooks explain the shattering defeat of Nilfgaard with sabotage and conspiracy of various 'subversive elements' and 'base traitors' (Sapkowski 2017b: 321). A cadet who presumes to point out the tactical mistakes of Nilfgaardians is chastised for referring to sources 'of doubtful quality', and sternly reminded that the desired outcome of the final exam depends on remembering the 'authentic' account of the past (Sapkowski 2017b: 321). The latter notion, however, is repeatedly punctured in *The Witcher*, where the idea of historical authenticity is replaced by a historical narrative established and accepted within a given context.

Referring to the Proustian conception of history, Maria Beville (2014: 56) speaks of the past as 'an inaccessible ideal ... that is conjured in the living present as a spectre of itself inevitably deferred from its ontological origins'. Seen through the lens of the Gothic, Beville (2014: 58) argues, the past reveals itself as volatile and unstable, rendering the historical 'truth' evasive and impossible to reach (cf. Uniłowski 2017: 523). In *The Witcher*, history is represented as incoherent and fragile, vulnerable to change and constantly subjected to silencing and reinvention. Priceless manuscripts that were to revive the past to the posterity become lost, stolen or incinerated without being read (Sapkowski 2016: 108–10; Sapkowski 2017b: 453). Cities are drained of their history upon the removal of their original names, and only few remember that the urban grandeur of the North has been built upon ancient metropolises of the exiled elves (2.2; Sapkowski 2017a: 193–4). Toponymy becomes an instrument of power and a terrain of symbolic violence, where the act of renaming completes the conquest through 'confiscat[ing] memory and genealogy of the place' (Rybicka 2012: 137). As explained by Istredd (Royce Pierreson), a wizard-historian, elves had inhabited the Continent long before humans, and were mercilessly slaughtered once they had shared their magical arcana. Central to the scene is – yet again – the process of reimagining and silencing the past. As soon as the wizard utters his first words, the soundtrack begins to play an eerie, wistful song, tellingly entitled 'Rewriting History' (1.2). 'Rewriting history with the stories we tell … the songs we sing about our own triumphs, it's what we do', Istredd concludes (1.2). The elven roots of the Northern cities, as well as of the magic academy Aretuza, were consigned to oblivion in order to portray the human race as the Continent's pioneer settlers and the original wielders of Power.

The repressed past, however, rarely truly surrenders, lingering in the places and objects of memory and trauma. It returns as a nightmare that casts a long shadow over the future and always lies in wait to pounce upon the present.

Among bones, tombs and ruins: The past as a haunting spectre

In *The Witcher*, individuals, races and nations alike are routinely constructed as captives of their pasts – a state that reflects the Gothic belief in the haunting power of bygone days and deeds. For Princess Cirilla, the terrors of the past are literalized through the figure of a black-armoured Nilfgaardian knight ordered to find and seize her during the siege of Cintra. An epitome of the Gothic phantom-like monster that stalks their victim through reality and dream, the dark knight embodies the carnage of Ciri's people and her desperate flight through the blazing city, the memory of his voice paralyzing the heroine long after the battle: 'the knight shouted loudly. Cintra was in that cry. The night, slaughter, blood and conflagration were in that cry' (Sapkowski 2013: 189; cf. 93–4; Sapkowski 2017a: 110; 2.1; 2.2). These terrors are rarely truly put to rest – as Ciri talks about the massacre, she foregrounds the continuity of her traumatic experience: 'I was frightened … I'm still frightened. It's not ended, it will never end' (BE 110).

In *The Witcher*'s storyworld, a number of fictive historical events – the genocide of elves, the Massacre of Cintra and the Battle of Sodden – recur within the plot, revealing the past as a vast reservoir of nightmares. In the study of the horror genre's engagement with historical narratives, Adam Lowenstein (2005: 1) speaks of traumatic historical moments as 'wounds in the fabric of culture and history that bleed through conventional confines of time and space'. 'Some wounds cannot be healed', echoes Geralt of Rivia, discussing the Battle of Sodden with sorceress Triss Merigold (Anna Shaffer) (2.4). A Sodden veteran, Triss is tormented by flashbacks and visions of the Sodden Hill where she fought to defend the North against Nilfgaard. Mistakenly identified as one of the fallen, and commemorated along with thirteen other mages on the obelisk raised on the battlefield, Triss returns to the horrors of Sodden through memories, nightmares and magical trance. Addressing her as the 'Fourteenth' – a warrioress 'already dead', if for the time being able to elude her gruesome destiny (Sapkowski 2017a: 111) – the corpses and spectres of the Hill speak of the places of historical trauma as eventually inescapable, and construe the past as a predator pursuing its prey: 'The day will come when the Hill will claim you. The mass grave, and the obelisk on which your name is engraved will claim you' (Sapkowski 2017a: 65; cf. 108–12; Sapkowski 2013: 402; 2.4).

The themes of memory and the haunting power of the past are frequently tied to physical locations – places of longing, mourning and loss. With its characters living, fighting and seeking sanctuary or redemption among ruined castles, graveyards, memorials or bone-strewn dungeons, the storyworld of *The Witcher* is pervaded with spatial and material tropes of the Gothic paradigm. These places of the yesteryear can literally become a birthplace of monsters: the enigmatic dark monoliths – described as repositories of the Continent's history – reveal themselves as gateways for ancient savage beasts (2.3). More often, however, these are the places of historical trauma that continue to encroach on, inspire and trouble the present. In *The Witcher*, these tropes often find their locus in the sites of ruin.

In their contemplation of ruins as cultural signifier, Mitsi et al. (2019: 6) foreground the borderline status and contradictory meanings inherent to the cultural imagination of ruins, evinced through their complex relationship with space and time:

Ruins evoke the grandeur and inevitable decay of cultures and civilizations in the distant past, while constituting the main vehicle of reconstructing that past in the present. It is in the nature of the ruin to always oscillate between the before and after, standing, both temporally and spatially, at a liminal point of in-between-ness. Ruins ... point to something magnificent and glorious ... which was gradually or suddenly lost.

A central locale of the Gothic imagination, ruins are often construed as spaces 'beyond reason, law and civilized authority ... stimulat[ing] irrational fancies and fears' (Botting 2014: 4). Often hidden in desolate wilderness, they are liminal terrains placed outside of the borders of human society. In *The Witcher*, the weather-beaten remains of the sacred elven palace Shaerrawedd are entombed in the 'wild forest', covered in moss, tree roots and ivy (Sapkowski 2017a: 193–6). A cragged, labyrinthine path through the mountains leads to the stronghold of Kaer Morhen – once a magnificent castle and a training centre for witchers, today a crumbling shelter for the few remaining. Geralt and Ciri enter Kaer Morhen in darkness amidst gale, greeted by cracked walls, dimly lit corridors, an old bridge sinking into precipice and 'mounds of skulls baring their broken teeth and staring into nothingness through the black holes of their eye sockets' (2017a: 49; 56–9, 63; 2.2). While in *The Witcher*'s onscreen adaptation deadly monsters secretly inhabit the walls and the dwellers of the stronghold (2.2; 2.8), the literary Kaer Morhen is narrated as safe haven for the witchers and Ciri. Yet, both on page and screen, the spectacle of bones and ruins evokes the images of the threatening past – the carnage of the witchers slaughtered by bloodthirsty fanatics who destroyed the might of Kaer Morhen long before Ciri was born (2.1; 2.2; Sapkowski 2017a: 63). While Ciri's guardians refuse to speak to her about the attack, the witcher-princess hears the voices of the fallen amidst the scattered bones. She communicates their desire to be buried – and thus remembered and recognized as persons rather than a macabre history lesson, a symbol or a warning (2017a: 64). Sorceress Triss, in turn, reassures herself that all wounds of history eventually vanish along with the bones turning into ash (2017a: 64). The witchers, however, choose to leave the skeletons exposed as an eternal memento of the unspeakable horrors of the past, and keep the location of their home secret, haunted by trauma passed down the generations (2.2; 2017a: 63).

Materialized in skeletons and ruins, the past in *The Witcher* is difficult to exorcize, seeping and erupting into the present. The confiscated story of the elven annihilation is safeguarded in neatly arranged skulls and bones in the clandestine spaces of Aretuza (1.2) and the ruins of the decaying Shaerrawedd palace. Shaerrawedd is construed as a spatial anchor to the memory of the massacred elven freedom fighters who were led centuries ago into an uprising against humans by elven warrioress Aelirenn. With no hope for victory or a swift return, the elves had destroyed Shaerrawedd and other architectural wonders before retreating into wilderness, choosing to lose them 'to history [rather] than humans' (2.2; Sapkowski 2017a: 193–6).

While the elven nation reveres Shaerrawedd as a memorial to the fallen and a bygone elven glory, the deteriorating palace is soon revealed to be more than just a symbol of the lost past. The ruins of Shaerrawedd become a site of 'reanimation [and] provocation, opening old wounds, and stimulating the transmission of values' that would otherwise have remained silenced – manifesting the power that Elżbieta Rybicka (2012: 133) finds present in the literary depictions of places of memory. The story of the uprising lives on among elves, and the spectre of beautiful Aelirenn will be symbolically raised by a new generation of fighters.

In 'American Ruins and the Ghost Town Syndrome', Martin Procházka (2014: 29) construes ruins as a space of 'spiritual significance', capable of producing a connection to the past that resembles religious devotion. As such, the ruins of Shaerrawedd are marked by excess of memory, and young elves approach them as they would a shrine – to gaze upon the white marble block depicting Aelirenn. Translating historical trauma into collective identity, the sight inspires them to yet again fight and die for the lost palace and the past it represents (Sapkowski 2017a: 203–4). While Shaerrawedd is absent from *The Witcher*'s TV adaptation until Season 3, the elves there return to plundered Cintra – now restored to its stolen elven name Xintrea – to rebuild their civilization (2.2). Infusing minds with heroic, glorious imaginings of the past, these places of memory become a site of power, channelling the past into the present, only to resurrect the tragedies and nightmares of history. The archetypical fantastic conception of history as a force of illumination and rescue – as sense and 'salvation encrypted in the past' (Majkowski 2013: 343–6) – gives way to the Gothic horrors of the past awakened, as the elven race is yet again betrayed, persecuted and displaced.

For Geralt and Ciri, the visit to the hidden palace provides an opportunity for reflection on remembering and making sense of the past. As the Witcher explains the Shaerrawedd's importance for elven identity, he reveals the ruins as a space of deep ambivalence. In his story, temporality, mourning and obliteration embodied by the lost palace are intertwined with the narratives of permanence and timeless existence. Geralt questions the romanticized history of elven struggle for freedom, linking it with the ultimate ruin of their race. In an act of confrontation between the past and the present/future, the symbolism of the palace's cracked marbles is juxtaposed against the stories of continuity and survival embodied in the bush of Aelirenn's roses, which are ever-blooming among the Shaerrawedd's debris (Sapkowski 2017a: 196–7).

Along with the places and objects of memory and loss, the traumas and darkness of the past speak to the present through people's hearts and minds. A flash-forward scene in the saga's fourth volume, where a team of modern-day scientists discovers a manuscript from the Witcher's era, initially functions to bring to the fore the distance between enlightened present and barbaric past. Yet the document that holds the promise to shed light on what is now known as 'Dark Ages' ultimately proves to have been excavated in the times just as full of darkness. '[A] victory of science' announced by the jubilant scientists is promptly negated by the ignorance of three criminals who thrust the manuscript into a fire. Set in the wild space of a night-time forest, the scene evokes the Gothic notion of darkness – 'an absence of light', of rationality, understanding and scientific knowledge (Bottlng 2014: 2), and brings in the superstition, illiteracy and corruption that were to be confined to the 'Dark Ages'. While the scientists carefully prepare for the opening of the priceless tube, the thieves throw it on the ground and bust it open with their boots (Sapkowski 2016: 108–10). Upon discovering that the 'treasure' contains writing rather than gold, the men are seized by panic:

> "Letters?" Kamil Ronstetter roared, paling in horror. "Written letters? What a bitch!"
>
> "Writing, meaning spells!" Billy Goat jabbered, his teeth chattering in terror. "Don't touch it, son-of-a-sodding-bitch! You might catch something from it!"
>
> Zdyb didn't need telling twice, throwing the page onto the fire and nervously wiping his trembling hands on his britches … The priceless writing from the Dark Ages burned with a tall, bright flame … And then the flame went out and *darkness* covered the earth.
>
> (Sapkowski 2016: 110, author's emphasis)

In *A Geography of Victorian Gothic Fiction*, Robert Mighall (2003: 9) construes 'the conflict between the civilized and the barbaric, the modern and the archaic, the progressive and the reactionary' as an essence of the Gothic imagination. In *The Witcher*, the ignorant thieves stand in marked contrast to the scientists, conjuring images of savagery and dragging the reader right back into the Dark

Ages. The boundary between the irrational past and the enlightened present proves illusory. The discourse of modern-day progress and civilization that was to distance the present from the anachronistic past becomes unsettled through the revelation of the moral and intellectual darkness that continues to prevail, shattering the confidence in the modern reliance on reason, and incising deep fractures in the supposedly rational modern social order.

Conclusion

The modes of remembering the past – the ways stories of the past are conveyed, (re)imagined, invented and used – are a central narrative concern of *The Witcher* storyworld. Considering such themes as the construction of historical meanings and accounts, and the notion of the yesteryear as a force haunting the present, this chapter employs the Gothic paradigm of the past to explore some of the ways in which *The Witcher* represents and reflects upon the complexities, uncertainties and horrors of memory and history.

Tapping into the Gothic imagery of violent pasts, *The Witcher* offers a vision of history that is dark, unreliable and threatening. A signature trope of the Gothic (see e.g. Botting 2014: 52), the stories of the past, present and future interweave and the narrative shifts abruptly among various spatio-temporal realities, fragmenting the temporal continuum with flashbacks and flash-forwards. History is represented as unstable and entangled in discourses of power, which problematizes the process of producing historical knowledge and invites a critical consideration of historical truth. As the saga brings to the fore the mechanisms of silencing, rewriting and instrumentalizing the past, it flays the gilded coating of romanticized historical accounts in order to reveal the horrors that lurk underneath.

In *The Witcher*, the darkness and threats of the days bygone rarely remain safely stored in the past; instead, they escape into the present through places and objects of cultural memory and historical significance. While articulating discontinuity, loss and dislocation, these places and objects grant voices to the spectres of the past and bear testimony to history – or histories – that would otherwise have been obliterated. As the legacies of historical trauma, ruined castles and unburied bones intrude upon the present with an uncanny ability to dissolve the boundaries of time, ripping open historical wounds and affecting the fates of new generations. While some pasts appear to have been lost forever – there will be no repopulating Kaer Morhen with youngster Witchers (2.6) and humans will not disappear from the elven lands – other pasts continue to tear through the fabric of today, their nightmares revived and relived.

In the storyworld of *The Witcher*, it is memory and history rather than monster-infested wilderness or swamps that are a cradle of horror, a site of most savage conflicts and a source of trepidation. In the final volume of Sapkowski's series, refugees from the war with Nilfgaard gather around a nightly campfire amidst the haunted woods. Their conversation on war and historical justice is repeatedly interrupted by ferocious growls of the beasts inhabiting the forest. The men, however, appear unperturbed, immune to the horrors of the monster, which fade against their experience of the ultimate horrors of history (Sapkowski 2017b: 453). Within the universe colonized by myriad lethal creatures – strigas, ghouls or succubi – it is memory and history, and the traumas they produce, that often become the truest of monsters, introducing a dimension of terror, uncertainty and darkness unrivalled by any of the Witcher's supernatural opponents.

References

Beville, M. (2014), 'Gothic Memory and the Contested Past: Framing Terror', in *The Gothic and the Everyday: Living Gothic*, edited by L. Piatti-Farnell and M. Beville, 52–68, London: Palgrave Macmillan.

Blacha, M. and P. Piotr Kubiński (2016), 'Creating *The Witcher*'s World: An Interview with Marcin Blacha of CD Projekt Red', *Culture.pl*, 22 December. Available online: https://culture.pl/en/article/creating-the-witchers-world-an-interview-with-marcin-blacha-of-cd-projekt-red (accessed 1 June 2021).

Błaszkowska, M. and M. Jakubiak (2015), 'Inni, obcy, potworni. Wokół zagadnień obcości i inności w cyklu wiedźmińskim', in *Wiedźmin: bohater masowej wyobraźni*, edited by R. Dudziński, A. Flamma, K. Kowalczyk and J. Płoszaj, 69–81, Wrocław: Stowarzyszenie Badaczy Popkultury i Edukacji Popkulturowej 'Trickster'.

Botting, F. (2014), *Gothic*, 2nd ed., London: Routledge.

Cieśliński, Sz. (2015), 'Mutant, odmieniec, wiedźmin. O problematyce rasizmu w wiedźmińskim cyklu Andrzeja Sapkowskiego', in *Wiedźmin: bohater masowej wyobraźni*, edited by R. Dudziński, A. Flamma, K. Kowalczyk and J. Płoszaj, 51–67, Wrocław: Stowarzyszenie Badaczy Popkultury i Edukacji Popkulturowej 'Trickster'.

Clark, T. (2019), 'Netflix's *The Witcher* Dethroned *The Mandalorian* as the Biggest TV Series in the World', *Insider*, 30 December. Available online: https://www.businessinsider.com/witcher-passed-mandalorian-as-biggest-tv-show-in-the-world-2019-12?IR=T (accessed 27 January 2022).

Cuklanz, L. and A. Erol (2021), 'The Shifting Image of Hegemonic Masculinity in Contemporary US Television Series', *International Journal of Communication*, 15: 545–62.

Deszcz-Tryhubczak, J. and A. Zarzycka (2012), 'On Alien Alders: The "Erl-King" Inspirations in Andrzej Sapkowski's Witcher Saga', in *Collision of Realities: Establishing Research on the Fantastic in Europe*, edited by L. Shmeink and A. Böger, 187–204, Berlin: De Gruyter.

Dobosiewicz, J. (2013), 'Baśń odarta z otuchy, czyli Sapkowskiego zabawy z Grimmami', in *Grimm: potęga dwóch braci. Kulturowe konteksty Kinder – und Hausmärchen*, edied by W. Kostecka, 201–11, Warszawa: ASPRA-JR.

Domańska, E. (2006), *Historie niekonwencjonalne. Refleksja o przeszłości w nowej humanistyce*, Poznań: Wydawnictwo Poznańskie.

Drewniak, P. (2016), 'Are We There Yet? A Snapshot in the Haphazard History of *Wiedźmin*'s English Translations', in *Wiedźmin: polski fenomen popkultury*, edited by R. Dudziński and J. Płoszaj, 171–87, Wrocław: Stowarzyszenie Badaczy Popkultury i Edukacji Popkulturowej 'Trickster'.

Drewniak, P. (2020), 'Literary Translation and Digital Culture: The Transmedial Breakthrough of Poland's *The Witcher*', in *Translating the Literatures of Small European Nations*, edited by R. Chitnis, J. Stougaard-Nielsen, R. Atkin and Z. Milutinovic, 205–26, Liverpool: Liverpool University Press.

Dudziński, R. and J. Płoszaj (eds) (2016), *Wiedźmin: polski fenomen popkultury*, Wrocław: Stowarzyszenie Badaczy Popkultury i Edukacji Popkulturowej 'Trickster'.

Dudziński, R., A. Flamma, K. Kowalczyk and J. Płoszaj (eds) (2015), *Wiedźmin: bohater masowej wyobraźni*, Wrocław: Stowarzyszenie Badaczy Popkultury i Edukacji Popkulturowej 'Trickster'.

Erll, A. (2008), 'Cultural Memory Studies: An Introduction', in *Cultural Memory Studies: An International and Interdisciplinary Handbook*, edited by A. Erll and A. Nünning, 1–15, New York: De Gruyter.

Green, S. (2017), 'Time and the Vampire: The Idea of the Past in *Carmilla* and *Dracula*', in *Hospitality, Rape and Consent in Vampire Popular Culture: Letting the Wrong One In*, edited by D. Baker, S. Green and A. Stasiewicz-Bieńkowska, 89–105, Cham: Palgrave Macmillan.

Jaworowicz-Zimny, A. (2020), '*The Witcher* Novels and Games-Inspired Tourism in Poland', in *Contents Tourism and Pop Culture Fandom: Transnational Tourist Experience*, edited by T. Yamamura and P. Seaton, 46–61, Bristol: Channel View Publications.

Kaczor, K. (2006), *Geralt, czarownice i wampir. Recycling kulturowy Andrzeja Sapkowskiego*, Gdańsk: słowo/obraz terytoria.

Kostecka, W. (2014), *Baśń postmodernistyczna: przeobrażenia gatunku. Intertekstualne gry z tradycją literacką*, Warszawa: SBP.

Lowenstein, A. (2005), *Shocking Representation: Historical Trauma, National Cinema, and the Modern Horror Film*, New York: Columbia University Press.

Majkowski, T.Z. (2013), *W cieniu białego drzewa. Powieść fantasy w XX wieku*, Kraków: Wydawnictwo Uniwersytetu Jagiellońskiego.

Majkowski, T.Z. (2018), 'Geralt of Poland: *The Witcher 3* between Epistemic Disobedience and Imperial Nostalgia', *Open Library of Humanities*, 4 (1): 6.

Matuszek, D. (2017), '*The Witcher*, or the End of Masculinity (as We Know It)', *Kinephanos* (July): 127–46.

Mighall, R. (2003), *A Geography of Victorian Gothic Fiction: Mapping History's Nightmares*, Oxford: Oxford University Press.

Mitsi, E., A. Despotopoulou, S. Dimakopoulou and E. Aretoulakis (2019), 'Introduction,' in *Ruins in the Literary and Cultural Imagination*, edited by E. Mitsi, A., 1–22, Despotopoulou, S. Dimakopoulou and E. Aretoulakis, Cham: Palgrave Macmillan.

ParrotAnalytics (2020), 'United States TV Audience Demand for *The Witcher*'. Available online: https://tv.parrotanalytics.com/US/the-witcher-netflix (accessed 27 January 2020).

Procházka, M. (2014), 'American Ruins and the Ghost Town Syndrome', in *A Companion to American Gothic*, edited by C.L. Crow, 29–40, Hoboken, NJ: Wiley Blackwell.

Roszczynialska, M. (2009), *Sztuka Fantasy Andrzeja Sapkowskiego. Problemy poetyki*, Kraków: Wydawnictwo Naukowe University Press.

Rybicka, E. (2012), 'Place, Memory, Literature (from the Perspective of Geopoetics)', translated by Jan Pytalski, *Teksty Drugie*, 2: 126–39.

Sapkowski, A. (2013), *The Time of Contempt*, translated by David French, New York: Orbit.

Sapkowski, A. (2016), *The Tower of the Swallow*, translated by David French, London: Gollancz.

Sapkowski, A. (2017a), *Blood of Elves*, translated by Danusia Stok, New York: Orbit.

Sapkowski, A. (2017b), *The Lady of the Lake*, translated by David French, London: Gollancz.

Sapkowski, A. and S. Bereś (2019 [2005]), *Historia i fantastyka*, Warszawa: Supernova.

Uniłowski, K. (2017), 'Historia jako parodia. Saga o Wiedźminie Andrzeja Sapkowskiego', in *Narracje fantastyczne*, edited by K. Olkusz and K.M. Maj, 519–33, Kraków: Ośrodek Badawczy Facta Ficta.

The Witcher (@witchergame) (2020), Twitter, May 28. Available online: https://twitter.com/witchergame/status/1266057420557766657/photo/1 (accessed 5 January 2022).

Zaborowski, P. (2015), 'Mitologia słowiańska w cyklu o wiedźminie', in *Wiedźmin: bohater masowej wyobraźni*, edited by R. Dudziński, A. Flamma, K. Kowalczyk and J. Płoszaj, 21–31, Wrocław: Stowarzyszenie Badaczy Popkultury i Edukacji Popkulturowej 'Trickster'.

Episodes of *The Witcher*

'The End's Beginning' (2019), *The Witcher*, season 1, episode 1, Netflix, 20 December.
'Four Marks' (2019), *The Witcher*, season 1, episode 2, Netflix, 20 December.
'A Grain of Truth' (2021), *The Witcher*, season 2, episode 1, Netflix, 17 December.
'Kaer Morhen' (2021), *The Witcher*, season 2, episode 2, Netflix, 17 December.
'What Is Lost' (2021), *The Witcher*, season 2, episode 3, Netflix, 17 December.
'Redanian Intelligence' (2021), *The Witcher*, season 2, episode 4, Netflix, 17 December.
'Dear Friend' (2021), *The Witcher*, season 2, episode 6, Netflix, 17 December.
'Family' (2021), *The Witcher*, season 2, episode 8, Netflix, 17 December.

9

'Brings back some memories': Spectres of history in *Twin Peaks: The Return*

Martin Fradley and John A. Riley

'I am dead ... yet I live': Ghost modernism and the return of *Twin Peaks*

Originally titled *Northwest Passage* and pre-sold as a televisual milestone long before its pilot episode first aired, David Lynch and Mark Frost's *Twin Peaks* (1990–91) remains perhaps the most revered cult TV artefact of the last thirty-five years. Much to the frustration of viewers anticipating a sentimental reprise of the original series' memorably idiosyncratic pleasures, however, *Twin Peaks: The Return* (2017) taunted the show's morbidly devout fandom with yawning tonal and aesthetic divergences between the sprightly *Twin Peaks* of the early 1990s and the reflexively depressive *longeurs* of the 2017 (re)incarnation. A torpid and often bewilderingly capricious televisual phantasmagoria, *Twin Peaks*' belated third season provided an inimitably oneiric eighteen-hour meditation on historical recurrence, Gothic temporality and the closed futurity of nostalgia.

Rejecting misty-eyed nostalgia for the era of Francis Fukayama's 'end of history', *The Return* instead placed the uncanny spectre of mid-century American history at its epicentre. Most strikingly, *The Return*'s pivotal eighth episode featured a protracted and disturbingly lysergic depiction of mid-1940s atomic testing, the nuclear sublime here reconfigured as the traumatic geopolitical double of the thematic cornerstone of *Twin Peaks*' dense mythology – the incestuous rape and murder of Laura Palmer (Sheryl Lee). Beyond the series itself, commercial paratexts *The Secret History of Twin Peaks* (2016) and *Twin Peaks: The Final Dossier* (2017) also recontextualized the already expansive mythology of *Twin Peaks* within over 200 years of US social, cultural and political history. Thus, even while each episode opened with the aural catnip of Angelo

Badalamenti's melancholy theme – 'the musical approximation of a lovelorn sigh' (Norelli 2017: 1) – *The Return* insistently critiqued the historically situated self-approbation of its beloved antecedent. As we have discussed elsewhere, *The Return* arrived during the first year of Donald J. Trump's fractious presidency – a serendipitous sense of timing, given the way both Trumpism *and* the third season of *Twin Peaks* illustrated in different ways the Gothic flipside of end-of-history triumphalism (Fradley and Riley 2019a). Rather than a self-satisfied reboot of earlier pleasures, *The Return* is best understood as both revisionist interrogation of the ideological complacency of *Twin Peaks'* 1990s incarnation *and* a surreal refraction of a deeply amnesiac twenty-first-century political culture.

Thus, after a 25-year pregnant pause, *Twin Peaks* re-emerged into a social universe still reeling from the financial crisis of 2007–8. Whereas the largely apolitical *Twin Peaks* of 1990–91 remained hermetically sealed from the contemporaneous realities of the early 1990s recession and the Gulf War, *The Return* acknowledged its place in a 'post-truth' culture structured by an unholy trinity of neoliberal capitalism, post-modern (a)sociality and the debased ideological static of social media. Symptomatically, *The Return* is haunted by what Stuart Jeffries (2021) dubs 'ghost modernism': spectral moments of ideological clarity amidst the chaos of a post-modern relativism, which *Twin Peaks* has long been understood to emblematize (Reeves 1995). In his book *Everything, All the Time, Everywhere: How We Became Postmodern*, Jeffries argues that the would-be 'playful' irony of post-modernism is little more than an insidious consumerist apologia for fundamentalist market logics:

> Post-modernism is a movement that disdained the modernist vision. Its enthusiasts saw it as a giddy, fun, libidinous carnival after the communal prison, a riot of colour and quotation that replaced modernism's acres of brutalising concrete. But post-modernism is more than cultural handmaiden to neoliberalism … It is at the same time both alibi for and indictment of the neoliberal order. Worse yet, its very indictments can serve as alibis.
>
> (Jeffries 2021: 3–4)

For Jeffries, the liberationist rhetoric that accompanied the fall of the Berlin Wall in 1989 and the subsequent fragmentation of the Soviet Union – the geopolitical context in which *Twin Peaks* first emerged – has proved to be little more than ideological sleight of hand. In its wake, the individual citizen-consumer emerges as the core unit of liberal democracies while a hegemonic post-modern libertarianism became realized in the corporate hegemony of Amazon, Netflix, Facebook and Twitter.

Jeffries' political discontent is clearly echoed in Linnie Blake's (2015) acerbic critique of Frost and Lynch's Gothic soap opera. Beginning with a nostalgic anecdote about her youthful encounters with Special Agent Dale Cooper (Kyle MacLachlan) et al., Blake revisits the earlier series with a quarter century of embittered hindsight.[1] Rather than an affirmation of sentimental memories, however, Blake finds in *Twin Peaks* a seductively interpellative inculcation into the brave new world being carved out by the radical energies of neoliberal capitalism:

> Watching *Twin Peaks* again ... a great deal has become apparent to me that was simply not "there" at the time ... I am less seduced by its bedazzling epistemological indeterminacy, generic hybridity, and often-absurdist pastiche of available styles. Mostly, I have come to question the ideological function of such representational practices – and this has led me to explore the links between postmodernism's rejection of the certitudes of the Enlightenment and the social malaise of the new millennium ... As an avowedly postmodern text from the period in which neoliberalism came to dominate global economics, *Twin Peaks* offers us a superb exemplification of the relation between postmodern representational practice and the coming into being of our own horrific world.
>
> (2015: 230)

Thus, as *Twin Peaks* wowed global audiences with its hip post-modern sensibility, that same seductive aesthetic served to mask the facile relativism, post-materialist complacency and brute socio-economic Darwinism of the period that birthed it. What is interesting about Blake's influential piece, however, is how closely *The Return* seems to affirm its critique of the horrors of post-millennial 'social malaise'. Indeed, the revisionism of *The Return* explicitly reimagines the town of Twin Peaks as a post-industrial dystopia, the busy sawmill so elegiacally rendered in the 1990–91 opening credit sequence now a burned-out metonym for the disenfranchised precariat who haunt the margins of the third series.[2]

Moreover, Mathew Ellis and Tyler Theus (2019: 34) point out that whereas the celebratory post-modernism of the original *Twin Peaks* 'treats the past as a collection of so many reified tropes able to be mined for empty aesthetic purposes', the mournfully reflexive *mea culpa* of *The Return* instead treats its original historical moment 'as something the meaning of which has to be continually worked through in the present'. Long-time Lynch scholar Martha Nochimson (2019: 238) concurs, arguing that *The Return* is as much a cultural landmark as its celebrated predecessor, a 'modernist epic story for television' that rejects neoliberal hegemony in favour of a clear-sighted rebuttal of the social and ontological chaos spawned by post-modern capitalism. As such, we argue that much of *The Return* can – and, indeed, *should* – be understood as a revisionist critique of the insidious political complacency Blake identifies as a hallmark of the original series. Resisting any comfortingly nostalgic respite from the sociopolitical realities of the twenty-first century, the hauntological 'ghost modernism' of *The Return* leads inexorably towards the final episode's harrowing evocation of the nightmarish *mise-en-abyme* at the heart of contemporary American culture.

'Viva Las Vegas': Gothic Americana in *The Return*

One of the most significant ways in which the third season of *Twin Peaks* marked itself out from preceding instalments was through its expansion of dramatic locales. Whereas the *Twin Peaks* of the early 1990s remained almost entirely hermetically sealed within the fictional confines of a small logging town in northern Washington State, *The Return* mapped its plot over a more spacious range of geographic locations, including New York, South Dakota, Washington, DC, Texas, Western Montana and New Mexico. However, by far the most significant of these regional dislocations was to Las Vegas, which ultimately rivals Twin Peaks itself as *The Return*'s central locus. Interpreted by Jean Baudrillard (2010 [1988]) as *the* prototypical post-modern city, the relocation of large parts of the series to the desert playground of Las Vegas is telling. As a carnivalesque celebration of consumerist pleasure, architectural kitsch and temporally entropic themepark history, Las Vegas typifies the libidinal economy of post-modern capitalism, wherein simulation and artifice are imbued with faux-emancipatory promise.

As Stuart Jeffries (2021: 113–14) points out, the wilfully amnesiac allure of Las Vegas encapsulates post-modern capitalism, an artificial pleasure garden in the desert that serves as 'a popular, commercial, fun retort to the patrician, mostly socialist and utterly funless architecture of modernism'. Taking up this theme of seductive artificiality, Justus Nieland (2012) positions a celebrated line of dialogue from the opening minutes of *Twin Peaks* (1:1) as thematically synoptic of the director's ambivalent post-war ontology. Spoken by Pete Martell (Jack Nance), the traumatized words – 'she's dead ... wrapped in plastic' – refer to the corpse of homecoming queen Laura Palmer, who is enshrouded in synthetic sheeting:

> Wrapped in plastic of the most everyday sort, beached as the unforeseen waste of a presumably more natural environment, Laura's embalmed body is rather like the synthetic environment of *Twin Peaks* itself: in its reanimations of absence,

in its uncanny blurring of the quotidian and the strange, and in its perverse contaminations of the 'nature' of small-town American 'culture' ... [W]e might take plastic *even more seriously* as the prime matter of Lynch's filmmaking ... This means understanding plastic not as a static substance – reified and hard, unchanging and resistant to history – but rather as pervaded by a mysterious dynamism.

(Nieland 2012: 1–2; emphasis in original)

As perhaps the *ur*-material of mid-century optimism and post-war material culture, plastic has become the Gothicized residue of utopian 1950s sincerity: a utilitarian symbol of modernist futurity laden with apocalyptic ecological portent. In Nieland's (2012) view, plastic is a 'fretful' substance that, like the Gothicism of *Twin Peaks*, marries domestic kitsch with uncanny dread. Not coincidentally, Lynch frames his own ambivalent fascination with the euphoric optimism of the 1950s in similar terms:

It was a fantastic decade in a lot of ways ... The future was bright. Little did we know we were laying the groundwork for a disastrous future. All the problems were there but it was somehow glossed over. And then the gloss broke, or rotted, and it all came oozing out ... Plastics were coming in, weird studies of chemicals and co-polymers and a lot of medical experiments, the atomic bomb and, a lot of, you know, testing. It was like the world was so huge you could dump a bunch of stuff and it's not gonna matter, right? It just kinda got out of control.

(Lynch, quoted in Rodley 2005: 4–5)

This materialist ambivalence is refracted in *The Return*, both through the bizarre 'plasticity' of the Las Vegas setting – which often serves as a brightly lit metropolitan double to the downtrodden town of Twin Peaks – and embodied by Dougie Jones (MacLachlan), a Vegas resident and one of Dale Cooper's numerous supernaturally manufactured *doppelgängers*. An amnesiac, largely monosyllabic idiot-savant seemingly capable of little more than basic bodily functions, Dougie is a grotesque inversion of Dale Cooper's caffeine-infused post-modern preppiness. Rather than mere fan-baiting, however, Dougie's near-catatonic adventures in the atemporal funhouse of Las Vegas become a fractured metaphor for the damage wrought by decades of neoliberal hegemony. Where the earlier incarnation of *Twin Peaks* celebrated Cooper as a playfully decentred post-modern subject, Dougie's amnesiac meanderings 'come to stand in for the difficulty of grounding oneself within the flows of global neoliberal capitalism', the character's rote verbal mimesis and infantile pleasure in instinctively remembered signifiers – coffee, case files, police badges – reconfigured as late-capitalist symptoms of 'a larger inability to position oneself within one's own history' (Ellis and Theus 2019: 31).[3]

This interweaving of ontological and temporal dislocation is most obviously rendered in Dougie's fixation on the statue of a cowboy that resides outside the offices of his employer, 'Lucky 7' Insurance (3:5–6). With his gun permanently drawn, this totemic revenant of North American expansionism points to *Twin Peaks'* long-term fascination with frontier mythology and its enduring legacy (Carroll 1993). Repeatedly asked to 'move on' by a security guard – the pop-psychotherapeutic phrasing is telling – Dougie mimetically copies the cowboy's stance in one of *The Return*'s innumerable examples of historical repetition. Like Dougie's fixation on other symbols of national authority and masculine prowess – police badges, the anachronistic poster of boxer 'Battling Bud' in his employer's office – the sequence is unsettling in its suggestion of a deeply atavisitic ideological *mise-en-abyme*. Beneath the broad comedy-of-amnesia, then, Dougie's ontological dislocation leaves him grimly mesmerized by exhausted remnants of national mythologies and the white supremacist ego-idealism of the Old West.

This point is reiterated in a later episode where Dougie becomes transfixed by an American flag drooping pitifully in the corner of a room while a meretricious rendition of patriotic anthem 'America the Beautiful' (1910) plays in Dougie's fugue-like imagination (3:9). Like the statue of the cowboy, these overlapping symbols begin as displaced Vegas kitsch – what could be more antonymic to rugged frontiersmanship than corporate insurance offices? – but become imbued with uncanny resonance through their repetition. Like so many of the Vegas sequences in *The Return*, this quietly tragi-comic scene finds its disturbingly Gothic flipside elsewhere when Cooper violently confronts a group of real-life cowboys in a bland Texas diner (3:18). Like the bizarre Twin Peaks-set scene where a young boy unthinkingly mimics the camo-clad machismo of his gun-toting father (3:11), the introjective national fantasies of regenerative violence are here reconfigured as an unending absurdist nightmare.

Thus, as *The Return* depicts the intrusion of quotidian socio-economic realities upon the town of Twin Peaks, so too is the infectious jazz-inflected *joie de vivre* of the original series displaced to post-modern Las Vegas. This form of textually disassociative splitting serves to open up a series of dialectical relationships, not only between hyperreal Las Vegas and the post-industrial realities of present-day Twin Peaks, but also between the fractured social worlds of *The Return* and the enraptured fantasmatic insularity of *Twin Peaks* in 1990–91. While much of the carnivalesque comedy and playful tonal register of the earlier *Twin Peaks* are relocated wholesale to Las Vegas, *The Return* also offers innumerable thematic parallels between the two locales, particularly around the core themes of economic precarity and capitalist exploitation. This is underscored by a range of characterizations that act as trans-geographical doublings. For example, the Fusco brothers – a comedic trio of Las Vegas detectives – find their earnest counterparts in Twin Peaks' triad of Sheriff Frank Truman (Robert Forster), Deputy Chief Hawk (Michael Horse) and Deputy Briggs (Dana Ashbrook). Similarly, Anthony Sinclair (Tom Sizemore) – the corrupt employee at 'Lucky 7' Insurance – is echoed by unscrupulous cop Chad Broxford (John Pirruccello) in Twin Peaks.

Elsewhere, while the 1990–91 double act of brothers Ben and Jerry Horne (Richard Beymer and David Patrick Kelly) spends the bulk of *The Return* either mournfully regretful (Ben) or hopelessly stoned (Jerry), their fraternal bonhomie is reprised via inseparable mobster-siblings Bradley and Rodney Mitchum (Jim Belushi and Robert Knepper). The same is true of their favoured environments. Once a joyously carnivalesque space, the Horne's Great Northern Hotel now feels more akin to a looming prison while the Mitchum's domestic spaces and Silver Mustang casino replace the Great Northern as key sites of absurdist comedy. While each of these reversals offers a disassociative tonal splitting between Twin Peaks and Las Vegas, the two at times bleed into one other. Twin Peaks' Roadhouse bar and the Mitchum's Vegas casino, for example, are both leisure spaces underpinned by latent violence and socio-economic disenfranchisement. In turn, while neoliberalism's human detritus ('Lady Slot-Addict', 'Drugged-out Mother') are configured as by-products of the tawdry glamour of the Vegas Strip, these anonymous economic derelicts are mirrored by the post-industrial precariat of Twin Peaks as exemplified by impoverished couple Becky and Steve Burnett (Amanda Seyfried and Caleb Landry Jones).

This overt class-consciousness is one of the key distinctions between *The Return* and the middle-class normativity of the original *Twin Peaks*. Indeed, from Mr C.'s hillbilly associates (3:1) and the spectral vagrants at the series' margins through to the disenfranchised working poor like Ella (Sky Ferreira) lurching precariously between Twin Peaks' low-pay burger joints (3:9), the spectre of socio-economic deprivation insistently haunts *The Return*. To this end, the reified hyperfemininity of Candie, Mandie and Sandie (Amy Shiels, Andréa Leal and Giselle DaMier) offers a useful synopsis of *The Return*'s latent class critique. An absurdist triad of plasticized automatons employed by the

Mitchums, Candie et al. combine blank obedience with photogenic vacuity. With their pink costumes deliberately evoking the burlesque outfits worn by sex workers at One-Eyed Jacks in the 1990–91 cycle, the trio form part of *The Return*'s lengthy continuum of exploited labourers freakishly dehumanized by the impossible demands of late capitalism.

In one intriguing episode, however, Candie evinces class consciousness when she 'accidentally' hits her employer (Rodney Mitchum) while attempting to swat a fly (3:10). Played out as broad slapstick comedy, but clearly coded as an (unconscious) attempt to break free from an exploitative cycle of anomie and contractually obligated boredom, this fleetingly violent insurrection leaves Candie distraught due to the ever-present threat of unemployment. Despite her apparent remorse, through the remainder of the episode Candie repeatedly expresses passive-aggressive dissent towards her employers, ignoring barked instructions and slowing her menial labours to a defiantly torpid pace. If Las Vegas is a hyperreal parody of the mythos of capitalist meritocracy, Candie's wilful dissidence is the spectre of historical materialism writ large within the consumerist perpetual present of the Vegas Strip. This tantalizing glimpse of insurrectionist portent is all-too-fleeting, however. With the bathetic return of Cooper's authoritarian FBI Agent, *The Return* stages a gleefully absurdist parody of ideological recuperation (3:16). As Cooper orders yet another manufactured facsimile to replace Dougie before climbing into the Mitchums' stretch limousine with a newly deferential Candie, viewers' long-term libidinal investment in the beloved Special Agent is reflexively unveiled as just as hollowed-out and illusory as the plasticity of Las Vegas itself.

'The absurd mystery of the strange forces of existence': Paratextual history as Lovecraftian phantasmagoria

Seven months prior to the return of *Twin Peaks* in May 2017, series co-creator Mark Frost published *The Secret History of Twin Peaks*, a historically sprawling epistolary tome consisting of a vast archive of letters, newspaper clippings and other documents compiled by Major Garland Briggs (Don S. Davis) and subsequently annotated by FBI agent Tammy Preston (Chrysta Bell). Shortly after *The Return* had completed its run in the summer of 2017, Frost released another novel, *Twin Peaks: The Final Dossier*, with notably sharper focus. The dossier comprises Preston's notes on several major *Twin Peaks* characters, detailing their lives since the end of the series' original run.

Critical writing on *The Return* often involves situating the revived series as part of a much wider – and notably unruly – cult phenomenon. If we consider, as most fans do, the canonical 'text' of *Twin Peaks* to consist of the three television seasons and the prequel film *Twin Peaks: Fire Walk with Me* (1992), then *The Secret History* and *The Final Dossier* can be understood as literary *paratexts*: material(s) that surround the main text and provide a series of contextual prisms through which to (re)interpret it. As Jonathan Gray (2010: 6) argues:

> Paratexts are not simply add-ons, spinoffs, and also-rans: they create texts, they manage them, and they fill them with many of the meanings that we associate with them. Just as we ask paramedics to save lives rather than leave the job to others, and just as a parasite feeds off, lives in, and can affect the running of its host's body, a paratext constructs, lives in, and can affect the running of the text.

In their respective monographs on the *Twin Peaks*, both Lindsay Hallam (2018) and Julie Grossman and Will Scheibel (2020) point to the gleeful amorphousness of *Twin Peaks*' brand of intermedial storytelling. Through its employment of paratextual materials such as the best-selling *The Secret Diary of Laura Palmer* (Lynch 1990), the cultural phenomenon of *Twin Peaks* repeatedly demonstrates the work of textual continuation to question where, and even *whether*, popular texts begin and end. For Grossman and Scheibel (2020: 89), as a result of the contribution of its paratextual ancillaries, *Twin Peaks* 'is thoroughly committed to a world-building aesthetics that emphasizes the singularity of a fictional universe but also its openness to expansion and its belief in the values of blurred textual boundaries and fluid notions of identity'.

In his analysis both of Frost's tie-in novels, Donald McCarthy (2019) surmises that the novels have a number of aims. He argues in *The Secret History*: 'In essence, Frost is telling the reader that while the *Twin Peaks* they know and love might not be exactly how they remembered it, the horror at its heart is still potent' (2019: 173). As preparation for the shock of *The Return*'s tonal and stylistic changes, 'Frost seemed to be teaching the readers of *The Secret History* to get used to a new, very ambiguous, and narrative shifting form of storytelling' (McCarthy 2019: 174–5). Focusing on various jarring discontinuities – Norma Jennings' (Peggy Lipton) mother, we are told in *The Final Dossier*, died in the mid-1980s, although she actually appears in the original series set in 1989 – McCarthy shows how these details couple with the layering of yet more mystery, which only answers questions with still more questions. Although McCarthy mentions the appearance of various real-life figures in the novels, he elides the thematic role of history from his analysis.

Following on from McCarthy, we can see that *The Secret History* does the contextual work of reframing *Twin Peaks* prior to the airing of the first episode of the third season, but does so by incorporating the series into a sweeping alternative history that goes back almost as far as the founding of the United States itself. The malevolent supernatural forces are revealed as being historical phenomena, involved somehow in key events throughout American history. After introducing the framing device of the contemporary FBI coming into possession of the dossier, *The Secret History* addresses the historical ellipsis created by the quarter of a century since the original series ended, but with characteristic perversity: beginning with the territorial era serves both to decentre the late 1980s/early 1990s as *Twin Peaks*' dominant time period and also – like *The Return* more broadly – to reframe the narrative as occurring outside of the environs of Twin Peaks itself.

Beginning just after the Louisiana Purchase (1803) and the decision to map the newly acquired territory, *The Secret History* links *Twin Peaks* with one of American history's founding moments. It also links *Twin Peaks* inextricably to American imperialism: the real purpose of the Lewis and Clark expedition (1804–6) was to establish a presence in the new territory before Britain and other European powers could gain a foothold. Later, during the 1940s and 1950s, *The Secret History*'s paradigm shifts from Native American mysticism to the science fiction themes that had seeped into popular culture during that time. *The Secret History* retrospectively turns Douglas Milford (Tony Jay) – a relatively minor character from the unloved latter stages of *Twin Peaks*' doomed second series – into a key historical player and long-time publisher of *The Twin Peaks Gazette*. Milford is revealed to have been a witness to another real historical event: the incident at Roswell, New Mexico in July 1947. Officially merely the recovery of US Air Force balloon debris, this event has inextricably become linked to conspiracy theories and UFO lore – another key happening in North American counter-history, in which Cold War paranoia and mistrust of government comingled. As Kathryn S. Olmsted (2009) argues, the UFO rumours began to cover up a secret espionage programme involving long-distance sound detection. But as Major Briggs comments in *The Secret History*, with as much resonance for misinformation campaigns as for UFOlogy, 'The point about the whole subject is this: once you open the top on this thing, the genie won't get back in the bottle' (Frost 2016: 122). In the novel, Milford's witness to a crash at Roswell becomes the starting point of his long involvement with extraterrestrial affairs, something only alluded to towards the end of *Twin Peaks*' original run (2:20).

Meanwhile, trailer park manager Carl Rodd (Harry Dean Stanton) understands this conspiracism in more earthly terms, which resonate with the alt-right leanings of *The Return*'s Dr Jacoby/Dr Amp (Russ Tamblyn): 'I don't know if it's the Knights of Columbus, the Knights Templar, the Illuminati or the Tri-Lateral Commission – it don't matter, they're all the same bunch in different costumes anyway, always have been' (Frost 2016: 307). Like *The Secret History* more broadly, Carl's musings about power and paranoia in the post-war United States can be understood as a form of cognitive mapping through which citizens attempt to make sense of the ontological chaos of post-modern capitalism (Knight 2000). Indeed, *The Secret History* itself begins with a telling quasi-Jungian preamble by Major Briggs, who notes that enduring mythologies and belief in the supernatural 'provide meaning in the face of a remorseless, indifferent universe' (Frost 2016: 7). This idea that the malevolent forces in *Twin Peaks* have always been there – and are constantly being narratively reframed but never truly understood in essence – is subsequently corroborated by Milford: 'This is the mother of all "others", and were we ever able to set our eyes on its ultimate nature we would find it as foreign, incomprehensible and indifferent to us as ours would be to bacterial microbes swimming in a drop of water' (Frost 2016: 357). It is in this sense that the two novels can be considered a *phantasmagoria*. They reframe *Twin Peaks* not as a soap opera with elements of murder mystery, but as a series of spectral visitations, with the paradigm shifting constantly from native American spirits to aliens to Masonic conspiracies to horrors unleashed by atomic technology – an interlinked, paranoid phantasmagoria of a piece with the works of Robert Anton Wilson and Robert Shea and H.P. Lovecraft.

There are significant similarities between *Twin Peaks* and Lovecraft, who seems to have been an influence on Frost's novels in particular. In the 1920s and 1930s, Lovecraft published a prolific number of short stories, largely set in a fictionalized version of his native New England, in which humanity fears its own insignificance in the face of the Great Old Ones, a pantheon of ancient deities indifferent to humans and their affairs, and terrifying on an existential level to behold. Moreover, as Lovecraft (2017 [1937]: 10) explained, his brand of cosmic horror explores the symbiotic relationship between temporality and cosmic dread:

> I choose weird stories because they suit my inclination best – one of my strongest wishes and most persistent wishes being to achieve, momentarily, the illusion of some strange suspension or violation of the galling limitations of time, space, and natural law … The reason why *time* plays a great part in so many of my tales

is that this element looms up in my mind as the most profoundly dramatic and grimly terrible things in the universe. *Conflict with time* seems to me the most potent and fruitful theme in all human expression.

This expressive mode, a feeling of unsettling temporal malevolence, is increasingly revealed and expressed in *Twin Peaks*, reaching its apex in Mark Frost's novels. In this context, the highly abstract, experimental eighth episode of *The Return* is neither an anomaly nor the indulgence of an ageing auteur whose primary medium was once experimental film. It is a deliberate strategy of *The Return* to evoke historical spectres as a way to expressionistically interrogate the American present.

'Gotta light?': Atomic testing and experimental TV

On 25 June 2017, Showtime telecast perhaps the most audacious and divisive segment of the whole *Twin Peaks* franchise (3:8). After briefly furthering the storyline of Ray (Balthazar Getty) and Mr C. (MacLachlan), in which Ray betrays and shoots Mr C. and ghostly vagrants begin to resurrect his body, there is a musical interlude from Nine Inch Nails. An incongruous title card announces an abruptly elliptical change of time and place: '16 July 1945, White Sands, New Mexico, 5:29 AM (MWT)'. Although this overdetermined historical specificity may not be immediately significant to the viewer, this is the year and place of the United States' first atomic bomb test. Unlike Mark Frost's novels, this is one of the few times that the television series refers unambiguously to a real-life historical event – and a pivotal one at that.

We see the atomic mushroom cloud erupt and the camera seems to enter it, giving us what Ashlee Joyce calls 'an impossible perspective on nuclear war' (2019: 26). Much of the remainder of the episode is taken up with lysergic imagery, soundtracked by ambient noise and by Krzystof Penderecki's harrowing avant-garde composition 'Threnody for the Victims of Hiroshima' (1961). Still in New Mexico – this time in 1956 – an abject creature crawls from the atomic test site. The same spectres who tore at Mr C.'s body reappear. They terrorize the populace, hijack a local radio station and play music that causes its listeners to fall asleep. As a young girl sleeps, the creature crawls into her mouth and nestles inside her.

With this audacious monochrome episode, largely devoid of dialogue and of conventional narrative, but laced with contemporaneous Frankfurt School portent, *The Return* reconfigures the mid-century American utopia as a nightmarish primal scene. This is a reworking of a common Lynchian trope, previously most clearly expressed in the opening sequence of *Blue Velvet* (1986). In this iconic sequence, Bobby Vinton's song 'Blue Velvet' (1963) accompanies idealized images of suburban America, but these gradually give way to grating industrial noise and the abject beetles that lurk beneath the surface of a lush green lawn. These images seem to express a Manichean outlook; an intensely dualistic worldview in which numerous deities are interlocked in an ongoing struggle between light and darkness.[4] *Twin Peaks* has, as we have shown, frequently been considered emblematic of post-modern relativism. Perhaps one of the series' greatest textual ironies is that it asks viewers to take pleasure from its many intertextual references and reflexive in-jokes at the same time it asks audiences to suspend their disbelief and emotionally invest in a dualistic battle between good and evil.

Images such as those that introduce *Blue Velvet* or that pervade episode 3:8 can also be read as sublimated, less-literal versions of Lovecraft's cosmicism. Anthropocentric notions of good are precarious compared to an evil that is nonetheless indifferent to human affairs. We suggest, though, that despite the use of supernatural trappings, the chaotic forces unleashed are not tentacled monsters, but rather a metaphorical erasure – not the erasure of an age of American innocence, but the annihilation of modernist grand narratives. This is in contrast to Ashlee Joyce's (2019) analysis. For her, the impossible perspective of the atomic explosion sequence is in no way eschatological:

> The conservatism of [*Twin Peaks*'] seasons one and two is buried beneath a superficial layer of aesthetic subversion that is offered up to an audience whose identity as consumers subsumes their politics. *The Return* is ultimately more political than the original, wearing its nuclear anxieties on its sleeve, although it cannot escape conservative elements of its own. The idea of the bomb as the source of evil and a corrupting force marking the destruction of innocence is a conservative, ethnocentric idea, ignoring such large-scale global atrocities as slavery, genocide, and colonialism.
>
> (Joyce 2019: 28–9)

Joyce's modishly banal brand of algorithmic critique arguably tells us much more about contemporary critical orthodoxies than it does about *Twin Peaks*. Indeed, it hardly seems worth labouring the point that Lynch himself is a politically ambiguous product of the US film industry with a distinctly America-centric point of view, and personal views that consist of a mass of New

Age contradictions. The massive scale of the atrocities notwithstanding, the possibility of total destruction on an existential level is what marks out nuclear destruction as different. Japanese viewers affected by the bombs detonated at Hiroshima and Nagasaki, or Kazakh civilians affected by the Soviet Union's own nuclear testing at Semipalatinsk might well find the images in 3:8 resonant, despite the Americocentric focus of the series as a whole. Moreover, *The Return* alludes to this directly through the enigmatic Naido (portrayed by Japanese actress Nae Yukki), eyeless as if maimed or mutated from atomic radiation.

Even before the episode cuts to the atomic testing, the episode foregrounds the ongoing trauma of *Twin Peaks* in a particularly visceral way, lingering on the spectral woodsmen retrieving an orb containing Bob's spirit (Frank Silva) from Mr C's prone body. As Raechel Dumas (2019: 330) explains:

> This scene essentially distils the violence that drives the original series into a highly abstracted and deeply frenetic vision that, like trauma itself, is cognitively unintelligible yet powerfully affective. In doing so, it also maps these traumatic scars onto the physical body. The viewer is confronted not only with an agitated open wound, but also with the possibility of a completely hollowed-out identity.

Though the shift from the Mr C. storyline to the sublime hallucinatory abstractions of the atomic test is jarring, this moment sets up the eviscerating nature of the atomic blast: cognitively unintelligible yet powerfully affective, and capable of annihilating more than just individual human beings to the point of totally annihilating humanity.

The abrupt temporal break from the present day to the 1940s and then the 1950s, followed by the return to a monochrome, tactile visual style more associated with Lynch's first feature, *Eraserhead* (1978), made this sequence an outlier even within this highly experimental series. However, this is more than experimentation for its own sake. As Dumas (2019: 338) notes, 'Through its abstracted meditation on the nuclear bomb, the episode confronts the viewer with an event whose annihilative power has been widely identified as "unrepresentable," while distilling this unspeakable violence into raw intensity.' Furthermore, the relevance of these events to the multitude of storylines that constitute the rest of *The Return* is unclear – that is, without reference to the paratextual insights of *The Final Dossier*. In the relevant passage, baffled by the paradox of whether Laura Palmer was killed in 1989 or simply disappeared, Tammy Preston begins to research Sarah (Grace Zabriskie), Laura's mother and only living relative. Tammy finds that Sarah was in New Mexico in the 1950s, fell unconscious as a result of the woodsmen's hijack of the radio station and was rushed to the emergency room as a result (Frost 2017: 131–6).

Of course, the *Twin Peaks* series was unlikely to ever explain the relationship of these 1940s and 1950s-set scenes to the main thrust of the action. But even without paratextual knowledge, one thing *is* clear: most viewers and commentators 'link this very real, very physical, historical first atomic explosion with the birth of evil, or an evil, into the world' (Marshall and Loydell 2021: 122). *Twin Peaks* had already placed incestuous sexual atrocity at the heart of the American Century through Leland Palmer's (Ray Wise) abuse and murder of Laura. But with *The Return*'s pivotal eighth episode, the series directly links themes of abuse (the violation of the girl who is revealed to be Laura's mother by the frog moth) to the birth of atomic weaponry and the ushering in of the nuclear age. Paratextually informed viewers who realize that this is Sarah Palmer will see the foreshadowing of her daughter's abuse in this moment. This abuse, committed in a domestic bedroom, is not only cyclical but, in Frost and Lynch's Manichean universe, *perpetual*.[5]

With the positioning of nuclear destruction at the heart of *Twin Peaks*, and its link to a cyclical, perpetuated familial abuse, we finally have an explanation-of-sorts for the series' relentless refusal of coherent narrative resolution. It is the possibility of total nuclear annihilation that forestalls explanation or recuperative narrative closure. As David L. Pike (2021: 11) explains, his exploration of how bunkers figured in Cold War culture:

> What the mid-1940s posited for the Cold War decades was an event (or constellation of events) from which it was impossible to draw any kind of positive experience or insight, and about which, moreover, the very attempt to do so was in itself a morally compromised position, a betrayal.

Pike's words characterize the fatalistic worldview revealed by Part 8 of *The Return* and, by extension, the rest of the series. By the final episode, it is no longer even clear whether Laura was murdered or disappeared, nor is it clear whether Laura and Carrie Page (also played by Sheryl Lee) are the same person, or if Cooper has somehow strayed into an alternative timeline. For *Twin Peaks*, the atomic destruction unleashed at White Sands throws everything into question. Granted, Mark Frost's novels return back as far as the Louisiana Purchase, but *The Return* positions the development of the atomic bomb as the series' foundational event. The very real annihilation of the bomb is not only the ethical abyss at the series' epicentre: in its annihilation of the epistemological certitude of modernity, it is also the primal scene of post-modernism.

Conclusion: 'The past dictates the future'

When we first began writing about *The Return* in autumn of 2017, the ideologically entropic Trump presidency was in full swing. For all its characteristic ambiguity, *The Return*'s protracted fever dream seemed to capture the fractious absurdity of the period more acutely than any other contemporaneous pop-cultural text. Among the many things that *The Return* obliquely refracted about that time was the troubling return of age-old political revenants and an unsettling sense of historical repetition. Just as the harrowing scream that concludes *The Return* testifies to the irresolution of trauma, the hypervisiblity of unresolved social conflicts during Trump's first years in office created an unmistakable aura of cultural and political stasis. As the historical repressed returned, the orthodox (neo)liberal worldview was exposed as uncannily Cooper-esque in its mixture of bewildered amnesia and right-side-of-history hubris. As such, the unmistakably fatalistic ambience of *The Return* is as emblematic of its cultural moment as the hallowed 1990–91 series, the twenty-first-century incarnation of *Twin Peaks* transmogrifying into 'an often harrowing meditation on the fractious relationship between a mis-remembered past, a nightmarish present, and a seemingly impossible future' (Fradley and Riley 2019a: 208).

The Return, then, is endlessly haunted by the ghosts of the twentieth century. The violent 'return' of history in the 2000s – marked all too clearly as we write by the Russian Federation's military invasion of Ukraine and the concomitant threat of thermonuclear remobilization – has been underscored by the catastrophic failure of a trinity of ideological projects. Indeed, in the unholy conjunction of ossified neoliberal ideology, hollowed-out post-modern relativism and the warped utopianism of an increasingly feral digital 'revolution', we find the uncanny cul-de-sac at the (in)conclusion of *Twin Peaks*. As Raechel Dumas (2019) so convincingly argues, *The Return*'s thematic emphasis on a continuous cycle of historical repetition bespeaks a traumatic cultural legacy, which increasingly entropic liberal democracies seem unwilling – or simply *unable* – to work through. Recalling Linnie Blake's (2015) righteous political ire, then, should we not understand Agent Cooper's overarching narrative trajectory – a decades-long necrophile rescue fantasy in pursuit of an impossibly lost object – as a grimly appropriate metaphor for the atrophied psychogenic fugue of twenty-first-century global politics? Ceding to the ever-gnomic Giant/Fireman (Carel Struycken), in *The Return*'s unrelenting Möbius strip of Gothicized historical reprise, the horror 'is in our house now'.

Just as it always has been.

Notes

1   Beyond Blake's (2015) disillusioned memories of *Twin Peaks*, 'nostalgia' as a key reflexive theme in *The Return* has already been extensively dealt with elsewhere; as such, we largely sideline it here. For further reading on this topic, see Anderson (2019), DiPaolo (2019), Fradley and Riley (2019a) and Hassler-Forest (2020).
2   For more on *The Return*'s depiction of neoliberal dystopia and socio-economic deprivation, see Fradley and Riley (2019a).
3   Grossman and Scheibel (2020) examine the stylized performances of actors Kyle MacLachlan, Ray Wise (Leland Palmer) and Sheryl Lee, linking their articulation of fractured (post)modernist selfhood with the intermedial storytelling of *Twin Peaks* more broadly.
4   Lynch and Frost's interests in older forms of religion and cosmology are underscored when malevolent supernatural entity Judy/'Jou-dei' is belatedly revealed to be a much earlier form of deity or wandering demon from Sumerian mythology dating back to at least 3000 BCE (Frost 2017: 121–2).
5   *The Final Dossier* all but confirms that the young girl is a pubescent Sarah Palmer (see Frost 2017: 133–7). In turn, Dumas (2019: 341) argues that in late adulthood the traumatized maternal figure of Sarah becomes 'a vessel for the depravity of atomic violence'.

References

Anderson, D.L. (2019), '"There Is No Return": *Twin Peaks* and the Horror of Pleasure', in *Make America Hate Again: Trump-Era Horror and the Politics of Fear*, edited by V. McCollum, 177–94, London: Routledge.

Baudrillard, J. (2010 [1988]), *America*, London: Verso.

Blake, L. (2015), 'Trapped in the Hysterical Sublime: *Twin Peaks*, Postmodernism, and the Neoliberal Now', in *Return to Twin Peaks: New Approaches to Materiality, Theory, and Genre on Television*, edited by J.A. Weinstock and C. Spooner, 229–44, London: Palgrave Macmillan.

Carroll, M. (1993), 'Agent Cooper's Errand in the Wilderness: *Twin Peaks* and American Mythology', *Literature/Film Quarterly*, 21 (4): 287–95.

DiPaolo, A. (2019), 'Is It Future or Is It Past? The Politics and Use of Nostalgia in *Twin Peaks*', in *The Politics of Twin Peaks*, edited by A. Di Paolo and J. Gilles, 35–52, Lanham, MD: Lexington Books.

Dumas, R. (2019), 'It Is Happening Again: Traumatic Memory, Affective Renewal, and Deferred Resolution, in *Twin Peaks: The Return*', *Quarterly Review of Film and Video*, 36 (4): 327–43.

Ellis, M. and T. Theus (2019), 'It Is Happening Again? *Twin Peaks* and "*The Return*" of History', in *Critical Essays on Twin Peaks: The Return*, edited by A. Sanna, 23–36, London: Palgrave Macmillan.

Fradley, M. and J.A. Riley (2019a), '"I Don't Understand How This Keeps Happening … Over and Over Again": Trumpism, Uncanny Repetition, and *Twin Peaks: The Return*', in *Make America Hate Again: Trump-Era Horror and the Politics of Fear*, edited by V. McCollum, 195–210, London: Routledge.

Fradley, M. and J.A. Riley (2019b), '"Dirty Bearded Men in a Room!": *Twin Peaks: The Return* and the Politics of Lynchian Comedy', in *The Politics of Twin Peaks*, edited by A. DiPaolo and J. Gillies, 69–92, Lanham, MD: Lexington Books.

Frost, M. (2016), *The Secret History of Twin Peaks*, London: Macmillan.

Frost, M. (2017), *Twin Peaks: The Final Dossier*, London: Macmillan.

Gray, J. (2010), *Show Sold Separately: Promos, Spoilers, and Other Media Paratexts*, New York: New York University Press.

Grossman, J. and W. Scheibel (2020), *Twin Peaks*, Detroit, MI: Wayne State University Press.

Hallam, L. (2018), *Twin Peaks: Fire Walk with Me*, Leighton Buzzard: Auteur Publishing.

Hassler-Forest, D. (2020), '"When You Get There, You Will Already Be There": *Stranger Things, Twin Peaks* and the Nostalgia Industry', *Science Fiction Film and Television*, 13 (2): 175–97.

Jeffries, S. (2021), *Everything, All the Time, Everywhere: How We Became Post-Modern*, London: Verso.

Joshi, S.T. (1995), *Miscellaneous Writings*, Sauk City, WI: Arkham House.

Joyce, A. (2019), 'The Nuclear Anxiety of *Twin Peaks: The Return*', in *The Politics of Twin Peaks*, edited by A. DiPaolo and J. Gillies, 13–34, Lanham, MD: Lexington Books.

Knight, P. (2000), *Conspiracy Culture: From Kennedy to the X-Files*, London: Routledge.

Lovecraft, H.P. (2017 [1937]), 'Notes on Writing Weird Fiction', in *The Great Old Ones: The Complete Works of H.P. Lovecraft*, 10–11, Scotts Valley, CA: CreateSpace.

Lynch, J. (1990), *The Secret Diary of Laura Palmer*, New York: Pocket Books.

McCarthy, D. (2019), 'How Mark Frost's *Twin Peaks* Books Clarify and Confound the Nature of Reality', in *Critical Essays on Twin Peaks: The Return*, edited by A. Sanna, 169–81, London: Palgrave Macmillan.

Marshall, K. and R. Loydell (2021), 'Sound Design, Music, and the Birth of Evil in *Twin Peaks: The Return*', in *Music in Twin Peaks: Listen to the Sounds*, edited by R. Wissner and K. Reed, 121–34, New York: Routledge.

Nieland, J. (2012), *David Lynch*, Urbana, IL: University of Illinois Press.

Nochimson, M.P. (2019), *Television Rewired: The Rise of the Auteur Series*, Austin, TX: University of Texas Press.

Norelli, C.N. (2017), *Soundtrack from Twin Peaks*, London: Bloomsbury.

Olmsted, K. (2009), *Real Enemies: Conspiracy Theories and American Democracy, World War I to 9/11*, Oxford: Oxford University Press.

Pike, D. (2021), *Cold War Space and Culture in the 1960s and 1980s: The Bunkered Decades*, Oxford: Oxford University Press.

Reeves, J.L. (1995), 'Postmodernism and Television: Speaking of *Twin Peaks*', in *Full of Secrets: Critical Approaches to Twin Peaks*, edited by D. Lavery, 173–95, Detroit, MI: Wayne State University Press.

Rodley, C. (ed.) (2005), *Lynch on Lynch*, London: Faber & Faber.

Films and television series

Blue Velvet (1986), directed by David Lynch [film], United States: De Laurentiis Entertainment Group.

Eraserhead (1978), directed by David Lynch [film], United States: American Film Institute.

Twin Peaks (1990–91) [TV series], United States: ABC, 8 April 1990–10 June 1991.

Twin Peaks: Fire Walk with Me (1992), directed by David Lynch [film], United States: CIBY Pictures.

Twin Peaks: The Return (2017) [TV series], United States: Showtime, 21 May–3 September.

Part Four

Female monsters and revolting women

10

'We're Americans': Remembering the 'other America' in Jordan Peele's *Us*

Amanda Howell

Introduction

Before revealing any plot details for his second feature, in May 2018 Jordan Peele shared on Twitter a poster image: a Rorschach-style inkblot rendering of two women. It was our first glimpse at the film's *doppelgänger* motif and Lupita Nyong'o's dual role as middle-class mother Adelaide Wilson and her monstrous double, Red. In *Monstrous Possibilities*, Lucy Baker and I (Howell and Baker 2022) observe the prevalence of the *doppelgänger* in contemporary horror entertainments featuring monstrous female protagonists, noting how it recalls the female Gothic's depiction of repressed subjectivities and their return. In *Us* (2019), Peele deploys this imagery of the double as well, but for a somewhat different purpose: to explore social patterns of repression and what he calls the 'societal monster'. He explains that we are our own worst enemy:

> not just as individuals but more importantly as a group, as a family, as a society, as a country, as a world. We are afraid of the shadowy, mysterious 'other' that's gonna come and kill us and take our jobs and do whatever, but what we're really afraid of is the thing we're suppressing: our sin, our guilt, our contribution to our own demise.
>
> (Peele, quoted in Rose 2019)

In contrast to the Hollywood tradition of evil twins and the familiar horror trope of good and evil mothers, but appropriate to Peele's sense of how we are 'our own worst enemy' the characters portrayed by Nyong'o will ultimately both be revealed to be at once victims, heroes and monsters.

The mysterious race of zombie-like, tunnel-dwelling government-created clones who rise up in a murderous rampage in *Us*, led by Adelaide Wilson's 'shadow' Red, could be interpreted in a number of ways in keeping with Peele's notion of the 'societal monster'. The reading in this chapter, guided by Peele's allusions in *Us* to US social history and films of the past, considers them as a monstrously hyperbolized image of America's poor – a literal underclass, alienated and alien. As such, the film's *doppelgänger* narrative both dramatizes and works to undermine the oppositional logics of poverty discourses governing America's understanding of itself in the contemporary period. As a corollary to foundational beliefs in rugged individualism, self-reliance and America as a meritocracy where hard work is rewarded as a reliable path to self-sufficiency and wealth, the poor have historically been viewed – and routinely politicized – as not just culpable for their poverty, but essentially different from the non-poor. Radically othered, they are rendered unworthy of the sort of social support that is commonplace in other similarly wealthy, industrialized countries (Katz 2013; Rank, Eppard and Bullock 2021). Allegorizing the discursive production of the poor-as-monstrous-other as the work of governmental mad science, *Us* depicts the subterranean race of *doppelgängers* Red calls 'the Tethered' as an abandoned experiment in social control that lives on in subterranean spaces aptly depicted as part-laboratory, part-schoolroom. Through them, Peele's film nightmarishly invokes – literalizes – the power of discourse as 'practices that systematically form the objects of which they speak' (Foucault 2002: 54). By contrast to the film's characterization of this oppressed and marginalized population, Peele depicts the Tethered's surface-dwelling twins – especially the Wilsons, an engagingly happy and secure African-American family – as the epitome of the American Dream, the embodiment of the mythic notion of upward social mobility that inspires contemporary America's neoliberalist ethic. Harking back to family-focused New Hollywood horror, and to Reaganite social and political histories, at the heart of Peele's historical allusionism – and his allegorical project – is the middle-class family as the aspirational fantasy that, over the course of the twentieth century, came to stand for America – for 'us'.

Central to the *doppelgänger* narrative of *Us* are iconic figures familiar from New Hollywood's family-focused horror: the lost and imperilled child and the good and heroic mother. As the locus of middle-class aspiration and embodiment of American futurity, and thus the 'telos of the social order' (Edelman 2004: 11), the figure of the child activates and organizes an array of political rhetorics, including those shaping America's relationship with its poor. For much of the film, we believe these two figures – the lost/imperilled child and the good/heroic mother – are in fact the same person at different stages of her life: Adelaide

Wilson. Seemingly traumatized by a mysterious episode at a funhouse hall of mirrors in childhood and then haunted by its memory in adulthood, she is driven by concern for her own children to increasingly embrace a more actively – even violently – heroic role. It is only at the film's conclusion that we discover there were, in fact, two children, and two histories of childhood trauma. While Addy of the opening sequence (Madison Curry) grew up to be the Tethered's leader Red, Adelaide Wilson is ultimately revealed to have been born of the Tethered, a changeling who forcibly substituted herself for her surface-dwelling twin during their funhouse encounter. It is a revelation that retrospectively remakes the film's narrative as its own dark double, troubling fundamental distinctions between self and other, the heroic and villainous, while making monstrous that aspiration towards upward mobility residing at the heart of the American Dream.

Allusion and allegory: Conjuring the past in *Us*

The opening shot of *Us* – with its pine-panelled retreat dominated by console television and leisure-time entertainments of VHS and Rubik's cube – appears, at first glance, to be yet another example of 1980s nostalgia along the lines of Netflix's retro horror fantasy, *Stranger Things* (2016–present). In *Stranger Things*, a childhood shaped by Reagan-era pop culture,[1] despite its darkness and monsters, is offered as a safe haven – an inviting pre-teen blanket-fort retreat, 'an anchoring in a fragmented world' (Stephan 2019: 27). As Kevin Wetmore (2018: 2) observes, 1980s nostalgia is one of the leitmotifs of twenty-first-century screen entertainment: 'Since the millennium and 9/11, American culture has called a "do over" and run straight back to the 80s.' *Us* echoes and indulges this nostalgic urge, especially through its allusions to films like *Poltergeist* (1982) in this image of a little girl transfixed by – absorbed in – television at the film's beginning and later through its engagingly Spielbergian depiction of the Wilson family in their confrontations with the uncanny. But the Reagan era is also depicted in *Us* as a site of trauma, being the historical point of origin for a monstrous uprising modelled, improbably enough, on the 1986 media event 'Hands Across America'. A kitschily forgettable fragment of the past, 'Hands Across America' – whose celebrity-studded spectacle of compassion was meant to draw attention to and raise $50 million for America's hungry and homeless during a period of resurgent poverty (US Census Bureau n.d.) – is reimagined as ground zero for a violent collision of past and present. When the film's vengeful race of subterranean *doppelgängers* rises to violently restage this vintage piece of social theatre, it brings into being what Adam Lowenstein (2005) calls an 'allegorical moment'. As Lowenstein (2005: 4) emphasizes, and Peele's film illustrates, 'Allegory', 'derived from the Greek *allos* ("other") and – *agorein* ("to speak publicly")', is the means to speak of that which has been consigned to silence, to represent what might otherwise be unrepresentable, and thus confront traumas of the past.

Noël Carroll (1982: 57) identifies allusionism as the core strategy by which New Hollywood directors established themselves as *auteurs*, revising popular genres 'so a personal vision shines through'. This is certainly the case with Peele as well, whose allusive practice like that of New Hollywood's *auteurs* before him generates a 'friction between the old and new' (1982: 57). While Peele's first feature *Get Out* referred back to the pervasive whiteness of New Hollywood's suburban horrors to critically engage with American histories and cultures of racism, *Us* alludes to its generic focus on the middle-class family to create an allegorical nightmare of privilege and privation through its *doppelgänger* narrative. The Spielbergian – or 'Spielburbian' (Williams 2014: 227) – Wilson family of *Us* both references and resists the pervasive whiteness of the middle-class designation (Reeves, Guynot and Krause 2018), exemplified by New Hollywood horror. In contrast to *Get Out* which depicts the white suburb as a space of terror and threat for Black men, the Wilsons enjoy the full entitlements of middle-class mobility and security. They have a summer house in a suburban bayside neighbourhood near Santa Cruz and call the police for aid without hesitation when it is invaded – in striking contrast to the terrifying prospect of police intervention at the climax of *Get Out*. What we see as the Wilsons' comfortable middle-classness is deliberate, part of Peele's personal project as an African-American filmmaker, 'to continue to present the spectrum of what we are and how we deserve to be represented' (quoted in Chang 2019). But it also echoes a familiar motif of New Hollywood horror with its disturbed burial grounds and gateways to hell, as the white sands and groomed gardens beneath the Wilsons' feet are not as solid as they seem, as made clear when the Tethered rise.

Peele says that his 'favourite horror images are the beautiful ones that are subverted' (quoted in Chang 2019). The Wilsons are 'beautiful' in their happy sense of security. Through them, *Us* harks back to the central role played by the middle-class family in New Hollywood horror as simultaneously the aspirational ideal of the American Dream and a site where horror can probe its vulnerabilities. Translating social and economic precarity into horror, the real-estate-value-bashing and home-wrecking spectres of *Amityville Horror* (1979) and *Poltergeist* referenced the insecurity wrought by America's record-breaking inflation and double-digit unemployment. In the decades since, the American economy has rebounded, but the middle class – an ambiguous designation despite its centrality to the country's definition of itself as a classless land of opportunity (Brooks 2012: 21, 122) – continues to dwindle in the widening gap between subsistence and high wage sectors (Temin 2017: 20–70). Ubiquitous within the American imaginary as a social identity embraced across a wide range of household incomes (Reeves, Guynot and Krause 2018), the middle class is nevertheless economically characterized by its fragility. Benjamin Bowser (2007: 1) describes the middle class as being 'a high-wire act, where actors rise and fall based on larger relationships between the wealthy and powerful and … the poor and powerless'. Translated into the language of body horror, such power negotiations between the middle class and the impoverished were allegorized as violent struggles to survive in New Hollywood films like *The Texas Chainsaw Massacre* (1974) and *The Hills Have Eyes* (1977). Similarly, the peacefully vacationing Wilsons are forced to defend themselves against the marginalized and monstrously othered Tethered who invade their home.

With their red boilersuits and scissors, the Tethered appear to be modelled on those monsters who stalked and slashed their way into middle-class suburban homes and dreams in *Halloween* (1978) and *Nightmare on Elm Street* (1984). But their uniformed sameness also calls to mind prisoners and manual labourers, the incarcerated and the working poor. Abandoned offspring of a government experiment in cloning, maddened by privation and isolation, they literalize the 'underclass' metaphor used in the Reagan era for those 'more or less stuck at the bottom, removed from the American Dream' ('The American Underclass' 1977: 14). This spatial metaphor was informed in turn by what Michael Harrington (2012 [1962]: 46) describes as a distinctive 'culture of poverty' separating the poor from the mainstream of America life. Harrington's *The Other America* describes Americans living below the poverty line amidst post-war prosperity (estimated at 22 per cent of the population) as dwelling in an 'invisible land' (2012 [1962]: 34), separated not just by the geography of regions like Appalachia, but by extreme cultural difference. Politicized by the Reagan administration in its treatment of poverty, this notion of a separate culture of the poor became the basis of conceptualizing poverty as a 'problem of persons' rather than of larger social and economic forces (Katz 2013: 3). Reagan-era exposés sensationalized, racialized and popularized the notion of an alien, othered American 'underclass', associating it with inner cities depopulated and deindustrialized after the Second World War, where poverty existed 'within a context of hopelessness' (Katz 1993: 21).

Press coverage such as the 1977 *Time* magazine article that sparked the 'underclass' debate (Katz 1993: 4) confounded categories of race and class by focusing on mostly Black inner-city populations, portraying the urban poor as 'more socially alien and more hostile than almost anyone had imagined' ('The American Underclass' 1977: 15). When later invoked by the Reagan administration's implicitly racist, explicitly populist, anti-welfare rhetoric, America's urban underclass appeared as that perpetually needful, dependent, perhaps even criminal minority of 'them' who burden and blunt the aspirations of the hardworking, middle-class majority of 'us' (Weiler 1992: 231–3). Most explicit in its racialization and demonization of welfare recipients was the Reaganite myth of the 'welfare queen' (Covert 2019). Derived from an older stereotype of the Black matriarch that pathologized and blamed female-headed households for their poverty (Moynihan 1965), the welfare queen was the greedy and selfish bad mother who defrauded the public of funds while raising her children into a culture of welfare reliance and criminality. Justified by these rhetorics, Reagan's government dismantled and defunded federal programmes created during Johnson's 'War on Poverty' and 'neo-liberalization of social welfare provisions accelerated' (Harris and Zakari 2015: 307). Consequently, despite economic growth, economic inequality increased in America from the 1980s onwards, a trend that continues into the present (Schaeffer 2020; Temin 2017). Well into the twenty-first century, the United States maintains one of the highest poverty rates in the world (Duffin 2020). And radically othered images of the poor have persisted into the present through, for instance, Trumpian rhetorics (Covert 2019), making the dark mirror imagery of the Tethered as an American underclass uncannily familiar.

When the Tethered invade the Wilson family's vacation home, their leader, Red, recounts for her captive audience a grim fairy tale about a girl and her 'shadow'. The girl grows into womanhood enjoying the comforts of the surface, while her shadow lives below in the Tethered's world of pain and privation. Red depicts the Tethered as hopeless victims of an inequitable system that even she, seemingly the only one with language, cannot explain or comprehend without recourse to divine mystery, her personal revelation that she was being 'tested by God'. As allegorical figures, the Tethered speak to and trouble anxieties about an intransigent, seemingly immutable culture of poverty that renders the enduringly poor 'alien' and 'hostile' ('The American Underclass' 1977: 14). Yet, when husband and father Gabe Wilson (Winston Duke) asks these mysterious home invaders, 'Who *are* you people?' Red replies with a smile, 'We're Americans'. This is Harrington's (2012 [1962]) 'other America' with a vengeance. Consequently, the Tethered's invasion is, in fact, an uprising – a rebellion. Crucially, while Red's account of her life below suggests that her terrifying children, Umbrae (Shahadi Wright Joseph) and Pluto (Evan Alex), were born monstrous, their otherness inbred, we learn otherwise when the missing fifteen minutes of the film's frame story is restored at the end. Through Adelaide Wilson's memory of her childhood, it is revealed in the film's final moments that she is not Addy of the opening sequence, but instead an offspring of the Tethered who forcibly substituted herself for Addy. With this flashback to what really happened in that seaside funhouse in the film's opening sequence, another narrative overlays the first retrospectively. And it provides a striking revelation: as nurture clearly trumped nature in Adelaide's socialization and transformation, Red's speculations regarding the Tethered's soullessness, and consequently the incomplete character of their humanity, are radically undermined. Only at this moment of revelation is the full horror of the Tethered's limited existence made clear. And ultimately, while the Tethered are represented in the guise of a monstrous 'them', in their actions they are instead a dark satire of and commentary on 'us'. Their bloody revolution, their conquest of the surface, even Adelaide's secret history of theft and subterfuge, all enact what is recognizable as a dark mirror of the middle-class credo for personal advancement that Adelaide herself shares with her daughter, Zora (Shahadi Wright Joseph): 'You can do *anything* you put your mind to.'

Imperilled children, good (m)others and hidden histories

Central to the allusionist system of *Us*, the image and idea of the child connect its narrative not just to films of the past but also to those social and political histories informing Peele's larger allegorical project. The 'perpetual horizon of every acknowledged politics' (Edelman 2004: 3), the child embodies middle-class aspirations, its hopes for the future, threatened when, in *Poltergeist* and *The Shining* (Kubrick 1980), the child is lost to and endangered by revenant histories. There are no ghosts in *Us*, but the Tethered are no less uncanny in their conjuring of a secret, buried past that threatens the security and coherence of the present. In the opening sequence of *Us*, in a glimpse between the vintage ad breaks, we see that the television's audience of one is a little girl, transfixed by the screen. Her reflection in its dark surface anticipates the numerous mirrors in the film, but also recalls that icon of suburban horror, Carol-Anne Freeling (Heather O'Rourke). In *Poltergeist*, threats to the Freeling children from a buried past strike at the heart of the presumed safety and security of suburbia and middle-class domesticity. Freedom from fear, as well as want, is the aspirational birthright of the middle class, as signalled by their family name. In *Us*, Addy is, like Carol-Anne, put in harm's way (if only indirectly) by her televisual fascination.

Inspired by the commercials we see her viewing with such intensity, she spends her 1986 birthday at the Santa Cruz boardwalk where she has that mysterious encounter in a funhouse hall of mirrors that sets the film's *doppelgänger* narrative in motion. The pre-credit sequence concludes with a close-up on her look of horror when she comes face to face with her mirror-self, her double, her shadow. This shot of her looking in the mirror, and her expression, recalls yet another endangered child and another iconic image from New Hollywood horror. As Danny Torrance (Danny Lloyd) looks into the bathroom mirror, telepathically connected to his father during his first visit to the Overlook Hotel in *The Shining*, he sees waves of blood flooding its lobby; his response is a similarly wide-eyed, open-mouthed look of complete horror. Danny, like Carol-Anne, is an uncanny child, positioned '"in-between" ... caught between the realms of the living and the dead, the present and the past ... associated with ghosts and a spectral realm that intrudes upon the temporal coherence of each film's "present" diegesis' (Balanzategui 2018: 18). Addy also mediates between one world and another, one time and another, poised as she is at the end of the pre-credit sequence on the threshold of the looking glass, later revealed to be a rabbit hole leading downwards and backwards to an alternative history of America – and the 'other America' of the Tethered. As such, Addy is the past of the Present Day, the 'embodiment of trauma' shaping the psyche of her adult self (Balanzategui 2018: 19). But she is also the medium through which a greater historical trauma is given allegorical shape when, in adulthood – as Red – she becomes the architect of the Tethered's bloody uprising, fashioning it from what she has lost. This mass uprising is her work of mourning, where she transforms her losses – of her world and herself – and her grief through a ritual performance of return. But it is also a violent act of defiance and liberation, a murderous confrontation calculated to compel an 'un-Tethering' on behalf of her community.

In addition to their uncanny character and their relation to spectral histories that disrupt and invade family life, Carol-Anne and Danny are both children who are saved and protected by self-sacrificing mothers – examples of what Sarah Arnold (2013) identifies as the archetypal 'Good Mother' of horror. There are, however, important differences between these films relevant to Peele's allusive project. *Poltergeist* – whose Spielbergian imagining of the family is mirrored in the Wilsons – is ultimately a reassuring film, despite its focus on monstrous violations of children and the comforts of middle-class home life. The heroic recovery of Carol-Anne from the ghosts of those whose burial ground is disturbed by suburban settlement ultimately works to solidify distinctions between the familiar 'us' and the monstrous 'them', confirming the security of the middle-class suburban dream and its nuclear family ideal (Gordon 2008: 112–27). By contrast, in *The Shining* internal and external forces converge to break down a family struggling to better its social and economic position by accepting the caretaking role at the Overlook, despite its tragic past. Stephen King's novel is very much focused on the trauma of a single family affected by economic precarity, domestic abuse and alcoholism. Stanley Kubrick's film, by contrast, emphasizes the way the nuclear family's dissolution is mirrored in and driven by the dark past of the Overlook, 'the deeper labyrinth of American history and the collective "ghosts" of its power ideologies' (Nolan 2011). Personified in the *doppelgänger* relation of Jack (Jack Nicholson) with his predecessor, Grady (Philip Stone), the unsettled ghosts of its history, its associated systems of power and abuse, express themselves in patriarchal violence that renews itself with each generation. In this schema, the familial security ultimately imagined by *Poltergeist* is impossible. The psychic vision of blood flooding the hotel that strikes Danny dumb is, we understand, from both the past and future of the Overlook, an image of the convergent horrors of history expressed in the visual language of generic excess – literally buckets of blood. The troubled past haunting the Freelings in *Poltergeist* is also represented through spectacular violence and terror. But, despite taking their house, the ghosts haunting the Freelings ultimately leave the family intact, apparently unmarked at the film's end (though living in a motel). Viewed through the generic lens of these earlier films, the Wilsons could not be more different from the Torrances, resembling as they do the Freelings in their companionate marriage and their affectionate, attentive parenting of lively, engaging offspring. Nevertheless, yet another allusion to *The Shining* following the credit sequence – a helicopter shot of the Wilsons' family car recalling the opening of Kubrick's film – hints at more ominous points of similitude. Like the Torrances, the Wilsons will be forced to confront, and will have their lives utterly transformed by, unquiet spectres of a buried American history.

In *Us*, as in *The Shining*, mysterious confrontations between past and present centre upon a child who is at once knowing yet unreadably opaque (Balanzategui 2018: 43–53). Adelaide Wilson's childhood memories from 1986 return to her in fragments on arrival at their summer home (Grandma's house), where she is prompted to recall her younger self and the time lost in the hall of mirrors at Santa Cruz boardwalk, as well as her troubling silence following this adventure. Like Danny, an uncanny figure who is at once psychically linked to his father and to the Overlook Hotel yet either doesn't consciously know or is unwilling to divulge what he sees (Balanzategui 2018: 43–53), the younger self of Adelaide's memory appears as an opaque, enigmatic figure. She is at once part of the past – familial memory – yet also resonant of secret knowledge that intrudes on the present. The nature of this is only revealed at the end: that she is a changeling, unable to speak, who has substituted herself for Addy, like a troll child in a fairy tale. Importantly, this changeling, this offspring of the 'other America' of the Tethered, is also an imperilled child. As confirmed by the tragically ugly ends of Red's monstrous children, Umbrae and Pluto, children of the Tethered inherit nothing but privation and social pathology – which for these two means an untimely and violent death. Unlike the middle-class child, they have no claim on the future.

Acknowledged by the sly smile she exchanges with her future self in the mirror at the film's conclusion – as Adelaide recalls the past while driving her family away from danger, miraculously complete, whole, undamaged, although surrounded by the bodies of the slaughtered – this changeling formulated her own solution to disenfranchisement. Refusing the historical lot of the Tethered, she saves herself, laying claim to the birthright of the middle-class child as the embodiment of futurity. Escaping from the underground, underclass 'them' to the surface-dwelling middle class 'us', she leaves behind another child, lost in her stead to monstrosity and marginalization. In this narrative scenario, we see dramatized the cruel zero-sum logic of America's social structure, where a shortfall in jobs is not balanced by social safety nets and where, as a consequence, 'one person's chances of doing well can be improved only at the expense of someone else' (Rank, Eppard and Bullock 2021: 167). As the 'winner' of this game, changeling Adelaide appears at once a villain and an all-American success story, a monster child and, in the present, a heroically good mother who has kept her family safe and well.

Considering this reframing of Reaganite horror's *fort/da* parables of children lost and found, threatened and protected, it is worth recollecting that both Addy (young Red) and the changeling (young Adelaide) are not just clones of one another; they were also both mothered (and, in the case of young Adelaide, evidently rehabilitated) by the same woman. Memorializing 'Grandma', prominently displayed in what was formerly her home, there is a painting of uncertain vintage in an exuberantly naïve style – a child's painting, perhaps. Suggestively positioned near a multigenerational photo of Adelaide and her mother with daughter Zora smiling in the foreground, it serves as commentary on her role as a mother. In the painting, a woman stands behind a young girl. Their proximity to the photo of three generations encourages us to read them as mother and daughter: both have natural hairdos and are clad in red capes like superheroes, their fists clenched and arms flexed upward in poses of strength, smiling broadly. Its familiar iconography of superheroism and Black Power comments on both Red's self-transformation into a revolutionary leader and likewise Adelaide's shift from a mostly passive to an actively heroic good mother who defies the patriarchally conscribed parameters of her role, as she refuses to be overshadowed 'by a more powerful agent: the father' (Arnold 2013: 37). When Adelaide contravenes husband Gabe's desire to stay in the luxuriously appointed home of the murdered Tylers, announcing, 'You don't get to make the decisions anymore', this marks a shift in the family. Hereafter, Gabe endorses her new leadership role, reassuring Zora when Adelaide leaves for her final showdown with Red: 'Mom knows what to do.' By revising the middle-class family of horror in this way, Peele valorizes the Black female head of household across multiple generations and sites, as an update on horror's stereotypical representation of the Good Mother. In relation to the larger allusive and allegorical project of *Us*, this also recalls and refutes one of the most contentious and tenacious of race-based poverty rhetorics in the post-Second World War period, whereby Black female heads of household were blamed for intransigent cultures of poverty. A theory proposed by the 1965 government report, *The Negro Family: The Case for National Action* (Moynihan), it 'turned black women's strengths and accomplishments into evidence that they had subverted the natural order of gender relations' (Katz 1993: 22). As previously mentioned, this stereotype of the domineering Black mother transmuted all too easily into her dark double in the Reagan era, the aggressively grasping and rapacious welfare queen who 'was blamed for perpetuating welfare dependency, transmitting a pathological lifestyle to children, and demoralizing black men' (Simien 2006: 72). As the messianic leader of an armed rebellion and the heroically protective middle-class mother, Red and Adelaide both allude to, but also subvert and critique, this historical representation, as each wields significant maternal authority for the purpose of empowering and defending those who depend on them. In this, and as adults shaped by their traumatic histories as lost and imperilled children, their similarities appear not just as a matter of DNA via the quasi-mystical bond of the Tethered, invoking *doppelgänger* tropes of the self and shadow-self, but also their shared childhood histories of good (m)othering.

Allusion, allegory and social protest: The Tethered and Hands Across America

Red, the revolutionary matriarch who names her mate Abraham after the one that schoolchildren of her generation were taught to call the 'Great Emancipator', is – like Peele himself – a dedicated allusionist. Explaining her masterwork – 'the untethering' – to her lookalike, Adelaide, she says it was not enough to kill their doubles who took sky and sun for granted; it was also necessary to 'make a statement' so the 'whole world would see, it's our time now'. As Red quotes *The Goonies* (1985), she draws attention to how she and the Tethered transform a faux social protest into a horrifically real one. Clearly a dark double for the director, Red finds her inspiration as Peele does in the popular culture of the 1980s. Her masterwork – though straightforward enough in terms of systematic slaughter – is presented to the film audience, and to those surface-dwellers who survive long enough to see it, as an exegetical challenge. As the red-clad Tethered stretch hand in hand across the transformed California landscape, it is clear that her bloody revolution is, as Ismail Xavier (2004: 343) puts it, 'a text ... that encourage[s] an allegorical reading'. Repurposing 'Hands Across America', itself a quirkily figurative fragment of social and media history, Red's tableau, its political theatre, transforms the generic verisimilitude of the *mise-en-scene* into something else, something othered, by its anti-illusionist intertextuality. An effectively unexpected means of taking her enemy off guard, it also requires a two-tiered reading, as grim material realities and performative politics of the past are projected through the scrim of theatricalized violence and defiant embodied display in the present, staged for the purpose of 'blasting open the continuum of history' (Benjamin 2007: 262). Red draws on the memory of the traumatic turning point of her childhood to radically remake and retake the world she lost. Peele, for his part, recalls a turning point in American socio-political history that transformed the nation's relationship with its poor to horrifically reimagine a return of the oppressed in an alternative, apocalyptic present.

But what of this historical fragment of the past? By 1986, despite economic recovery from the financial crisis of 1980–3, millions more Americans were experiencing poverty than even in the troubled 1970s, including a new, now all-too-familiar population of the working poor (Stricker 2007: 196). 'Hands Across America', the so-called 'Woodstock of the 1980s' (quoted in Lofland 1993: 75), aimed to raise public awareness of hunger and homelessness in America along with millions in funding by forming a 4,152-mile human chain from the Atlantic to the Pacific Ocean (Hunger Relief Act of 1986: 68–9). Despite taking the invisibility of the poor and their plight as its project, the poor themselves had a limited role to play in the event, unlike other Reagan-era demonstrations such as those by the Community for Creative Non Violence organized by homeless activists (Cress and Snow 1998: 76). The original promo for the event (Hands Across America 1986) confirms once again the iconic power of the child in political rhetoric, as its only images of the poor are children, with an emphasis on children of colour. Thus, at the same time 'Hands Across America' aimed to draw attention to the plight of the poor and homeless, it left their invisibility, otherness and exclusion largely in place. As 'an opportunity for celebrities … to indulge in a conspicuous display of compassion' (Reeves 1999: 56), it focused on 'mass changes in perception or consciousness' (Lofland 1993: 53) while avoiding any sort of anti-establishment conflict or confrontation. It was, as Richard Blow of *The New Republic* observed, 'an attempt to create an egalitarian society based not on equal distribution of wealth or property, but on spiritual equality – a sort of socialism of the mind' (Blow 1988: 25). Even President Reagan himself, very recently under fire for saying that the poor starved due to their ignorance (Clift 1986), was welcomed to participate in the 'feel-good event of the year' (Reeves 1999: 57).

Peele's version of the 1986 'Hands Across America' TV promo, which Addy watches in the pre-credit sequence is – like Red's choreography – another re-presentation of the past, a dark mirror or *doppelgänger* of this mass-mediated performance of collective caring. Staying close to the original with its ready-made emotional effects, it similarly relies on picture postcard imagery of 'America the Beautiful'. But it slyly abstracts its participants, representing them as an unsettling array of fractured fragments – eyes, hands, teeth[2] – just as America itself appears as a series of static, fragmentary, stereotyped images. And where, in the original, solemn children speak of their struggle with poverty, with hunger and homelessness, here, by contrast, the poor remain entirely faceless, mute: only a single, brief image of a homeless person digging through a New York garbage can is shown, their back to the camera. And, ominously, rather than starting its human chain in New York's Battery Park, with its stunning harbourside view of Lady Liberty, Peele features instead an image of the nearby World Trade Center, its twin towers shown at sunset, evoking a future-past catastrophe lying in wait for the United States, while highlighting the event's corporate character.

Prominently featured in Peele's commercial is the paper-doll imagery that inspires Red's design. Appropriately, this motif is taken not from the original marketing promo or plan for the 1986 event, but instead is inspired by a make-do response to the failure or shortfall of its aims: the numerous gaps in the human chain were filled with paper-dolls donated by school children for that purpose (Hassan 2016). From the snips we hear in the opening scene of *Us*, we know that industrious Addy is occupying herself in making these space-filling paper-dolls as she watches TV and plans for her birthday treat. Confirming texts 'that give us a sense of incompleteness or fragmentation (the sense that something is lacking) are more susceptible to allegorical readings than texts that seem clear and satisfactory in a first reading' (Xavier 2004: 343), the gaps and failures of 'Hands Across America' provoke both Red's and Peele's horrific re-visioning of the event. Both historically minded artists are invested in making these absences speak through horror, in making the invisible visible in their allegorical deployment of this Reaganite media event as the basis of protests against the othering and disenfranchisement of those forgotten Americans of *Us*.

Conclusion

Interrogating the pervasive assumption in America that 'poverty and welfare use' is 'an issue of them' rather than an 'issue of us', Mark Robert Rank, Lawrence M. Eppard and Heather E. Bullock (2021: 9) observe that the vast majority of Americans will experience poverty at some point in their lives. America's punitive lack of social support systems – the consequence of the structural assumption that the poor 'are somehow different from the typical or average American' (Rank, Eppard and Bullock 2021: 9) – has the effect of magnifying the impact of what might otherwise be transient episodes of economic precarity. The result is that rates of poverty are substantially higher in the United States than other industrialized nations and there is significant economic inequality. As Rank,

Eppard and Bullock (2021: 14) conclude, 'we have met the enemy, and they are us'. Peele's *Us* uses its horror, its monstrous *doppelgänger* invasion narrative, to allegorize the fear underlying the othering and alienation of the poor that shapes this system with its self-defeating inequities, while the film's work of historical allusion locates its point of origin in Reaganite transformations of the social.

In *Get Out*, Peele uses allusions to New Hollywood's suburban family-focused horror to undermine its 'whitopian' ideal (Means Coleman and Lawrence 2020), revealing the white supremacism lurking within a seemingly liberal, suburbanite community that, like monstrous white trash clans of 'backwoods' horror, lures and traps the unwary (Murphy 2020). *Us* similarly revisits and revises New Hollywood horror, but uses its tale of a comfortably middle-class African-American family attacked by its monstrous lookalikes to reflect allegorically on social divisions in America's putatively classless society, while highlighting the Reagan era as a traumatic turning point in its relationships with the poor. In its representation of the Tethered as a monstrous population living below the surface of the suburban American Dream, *Us* echoes the kooky, class-based fantasy of H.G. Wells' *Time Machine* (1895), with its murderous Morlocks. But it also uses the Tethered to critique Reagan-era denigration and demonization of the homeless and poor. When the Tethered rise to make their stand and claim their revenge, the funhouse mirror relationship between architect of this uprising, Red, and her twin, Adelaide Wilson, works to trouble those distinctions that other the Tethered. Through these figures and through the film's depiction of the Wilsons, *Us* redresses the enduring racialization of class categories in America – the whiteness of the middle class and the colouring of underclass cultures of poverty. Likewise, through its twinned anti-heroes, Red and Adelaide, it reframes and reclaims the denigrated category of the 'Black matriarch' – her departure from the patriarchal ideal appearing as at once monstrous but also shown as a type of heroism not accounted for by horror, nor indeed by popular culture more broadly. Ultimately, through the allusionist iconography of Red's uprising, her use (and Peele's use) of the paper-doll motif, *Us* emphasizes its engagement with the gaps and absences of history, its effort 'to show that which cannot otherwise be shown; to speak that which cannot otherwise be spoken' (Blake 2008: 5). At the same time, its quirkily allegorical horror uses a strategy of defamiliarization (Lowenstein 2005: 15) to spark a recognition of those categorized as 'them' by inherited rhetorics of poverty as being, in fact, 'us'.

Notes

1. There is no consensus on the periodization of 'the Reagan era'. This discussion regards it as spanning from the mid-1970s, when the former governor of California began a radio broadcasting career that made him the voice of a new conservatism and paved his way to a successful bid for the presidency in 1980, through/to his years as President, 1981–9.
2. Peele's fake ad quotes a frankly unsettling MTV 'Hands Across America' promo (1986) spot that commences with monstrous Dr Mabuse-style imagery of multiple superimposed eyes, followed by clusters of wriggling hands as it asks, 'What has 12 million eyes and over 50 million fingers?'

References

'The American Underclass: Destitute and Desperate in the Land of Plenty' (1977), *Time*, 110, 29 August, 14–27.
Arnold, S. (2013), *Maternal Horror: Film Melodrama and Motherhood*, London: Palgrave Macmillan.
Balanzategui, J. (2018), *The Uncanny Child in Transnational Cinema*, Amsterdam: Amsterdam University Press.
Benjamin, W. (2007), 'Thesis on the Philosophy of History', in *Illuminations: Essays and Reflections*, translated by H. Zohn, New York: Schocken Books.
Blake, L. (2008), *The Wounds of Nations: Horror Cinema, Historical Trauma and National Identity*, Manchester: Manchester University Press.
Blow, R. (1988), 'Moronic Convergence', *The New Republic*, 25 January, 24–7.
Bowser, B.P. (2007), *The Black Middle Class: Social Mobility – and Vulnerability*, Boulder, CO: Lynne Rienner.
Brooks, S. (2012), *American Exceptionalism in the Age of Obama*, New York: Routledge.
Carroll, N. (1982), 'The Future of Allusion: Hollywood in the Seventies (and Beyond)', *October*, 20: 51–81.
Chang, A. (2019), 'Jordan Peele Looked into the Mirror and Saw the Evil inside "Us"', *NPR*, 22 March. Available online: https://www.npr.org/2019/03/22/705875221/jordan-peele-looked-into-the-mirror-and-saw-the-evil-inside-us (accessed 5 June 2022).
Clift, E. (1986), 'Reagan Blames Hunger on "Lack of Knowledge"', *Los Angeles Times*, 22 May. Available online: https://www.latimes.com/archives/la-xpm-1986-05-22-mn-6950-story.html (accessed 5 June 2022).
Covert, B. (2019), 'The Myth of the Welfare Queen', *The New Republic*, 2 July. Available online: https://newrepublic.com/article/154404/myth-welfare-queen (accessed 5 June 2022).

Cress, D.M. and D.A. Snow (1998), 'Mobilization at the Margins: Organizing by the Homeless', in *Social Movements and American Political Institutions*, edited by A.N. Costain and A.S. McFarland, 73–98, Lanham, MD: Rowman & Littlefield.

Duffin, E. (2020), 'Poverty Rates in OECD Countries 2017', *Statista*, 17 January. Available online: https://www.statista.com/statistics/233910/poverty-rates-in-oecd-countries (accessed 5 June 2022).

Edelman, L. (2004), *No Future: Queer Theory and the Death Drive*, Durham, NC: Duke University Press.

Foucault, M. (2002), *Archaeology of Knowledge*, translated by A.M.S. Smith, New York: Routledge.

Gordon, A.M. (2008), *Empire of Dreams: The Science Fiction and Fantasy Films of Steven Spielberg*, Lanham, MD: Rowman and Littlefield.

'Hands Across America' (1986), YouTube. Available online: https://www.youtube.com/watch?v=WZorfXa5pBc (accessed 5 June 2022).

Harrington, M. (2012 [1962]), *The Other America: Poverty in the United States*, New York: Scribner.

Harris, D.A. and J. Zakari (2015), 'Neo-liberalism and Private Emergency Food Networks', in *The Routledge Handbook of Poverty in the United States*, edited by S.N. Haymes, M.V. de Haymes and R.J. Miller, 307–15, New York: Routledge.

Hassan, A. (2016), 'Your Wednesday Briefing', *The New York Times*, 25 May. Available online: https://archive.nytimes.com/www.nytimes.com/indexes/2016/05/25/nytnow/nytnow-email/index.html (accessed 10 June 2022).

Hills, M. (2005), *The Pleasures of Horror*, New York: Continuum.

Howell, A. and L. Baker (2022), *Monstrous Possibilities: The Female Monster in 21st Century Screen Horror*, New York: Palgrave Macmillan.

Hunger Relief Act of 1986: Joint Hearing before the Subcommittee on Domestic Marketing, Consumer Relations and Nutrition of the Committee on Agriculture [et al.] (1986), House of Representatives (on H.R. 4990) Ninety-ninth Congress, second session, 25 June. Available online: https://books.google.com.au/books?printsec=frontcover&vid=LCCN86603256&redir_esc=y#v=onepage&q&f=false (accessed 18 June).

@JordanPeele. [poster image] Us in Theaters March 2019, *Twitter*, 9 May 2018, 10:02 a.m. Available online: https://twitter.com/JordanPeele/status/994004752466767872?lang=en (accessed 10 January 2024).

Katz, M.B. (1993), 'Introduction: The Urban "Underclass" as a Metaphor of Social Transformation', in *The Underclass Debate: Views from History*, edited by M.B. Katz, 3–24, Princeton, NJ: Princeton University Press.

Katz, M.B. (2013), *The Undeserving Poor: America's Enduring Confrontation with Poverty*, Oxford: Oxford University Press.

Lofland, J. (1993), *Polite Protesters: The American Peace Movement of the 1980s*, Syracuse, NY: Syracuse University Press.

Lowenstein, A. (2005), *Shocking Representation: Historical Trauma, National Cinema, and the Modern Horror Film*, New York: Columbia University Press.

Means Coleman, R.R. and N. Lawrence (2020), 'A Peaceful Place Denied: Horror Film's "Whitopias"', in *Get Out: Political Horror*, edited by D. Keetley, 47–62, Columbus, OH: Ohio State University Press.

Moynihan, D.P. (1965), *The Negro Family: The Case for National Action*, No. 31–3, Washington, DC: US Government Printing Office.

MTV Hands Across America Promo (1986), YouTube. Available online: https://www.youtube.com/watch?v=cl9Rhd8yZZk (accessed 5 June 2022).

Murphy, B.M. (2020), 'Place, Space, and the Reconfiguation of "White Trash" Monstrosity', in *Get Out: Political Horror*, edited by D. Keetley, 72–86, Columbus, OH: Ohio State University Press.

Nolan, A. (2011), 'Seeing Is Digesting: Labyrinths of Historical Ruin in Stanley Kubrick's *The Shining*', *Cultural Critique*, 77: 180–204.

Rank, M.R., L.M. Eppard and H.E. Bullock (2021), *Poorly Understood: What America Gets Wrong about Poverty*, Oxford: Oxford University Press.

Reeves, J.L. (1999), 'Re-Covering the Homeless: Hindsights on the Joyce Brown story', in *Reading the Homeless: The Media's Image of Homeless Culture*, edited by E. Min, 45–64, Westport, CT: Greenwood Publishing Group.

Reeves, R.V., K. Guyot and E. Krause (2018), *Defining the Middle Class: Cash, Credentials, or Culture?*, Washington, DC: Brookings Institute.

Rose, S. (2019), 'This Is a Very Different Movie from *Get Out*', *The Guardian*, 5 June. Available online: https://www.theguardian.com/film/2019/mar/09/jordan-peele-on-us-this-is-a-very-different-movie-from-get-out (accessed 18 June 2022).

Schaeffer, K. (2020), '6 Facts about Economic Inequality in the US', *PEW Research Center*, 7 February. Available online: https://www.pewresearch.org/fact-tank/2020/02/07/6-facts-about-economic-inequality-in-the-u-s (accessed 5 June 2022).

Simien, E.M. (2006), *Black Feminist Voices in Politics*, Albany, NY: SUNY Press.

Stephan, M. (2019), 'Branding Netflix with Nostalgia: Totemic Nostalgia, Adaptation, and the Postmodern Turn', in *Netflix Nostalgia: Streaming the Past on Demand*, edited by K. Pallister, 25–40, Lanham, MD: Rowman & Littlefield.

Stricker, F. (2007), *Why America Lost the War on Poverty – and How to Win It*, Chapel Hill, NC: University of North Carolina Press.

Temin, P. (2017), *The Vanishing Middle Class: Prejudice and Power in a Dual Economy*, Cambridge, MA: MIT Press.

US Census Bureau (n.d.), 'Historical Poverty Tables: People and Families – 1959 to 2020'. Available online: https://www.census.gov/data/tables/time-series/demo/income-poverty/historical-poverty-people.html (accessed 5 June 2022).

Weiler, M. (1992), 'The Reagan Attack on Welfare', in *Reagan and Public Discourse in America*, edited by M. Weiler and W.B. Pearce, Tuscaloosa, 227–50, AL: University of Alabama Press.

Wells, H.G. (1895), *The Time Machine*, London: William Heinemann.

Wetmore, K.J. Jr (ed.) (2018), *Uncovering* Stranger Things: *Essays on Eighties Nostalgia, Cynicism and Innocence in the Series*, Jefferson, NC: McFarland.

Williams, T. (2014), *Hearths of Darkness: The Family in the American Horror Film*, Jackson, MS: University Press of Mississippi.

Xavier, I. (2004), 'Historical Allegory', in *A Companion to Film Theory*, edited by T. Miller and R. Stam, 333–62, New York: John Wiley & Sons.

Films and television series

Amityville Horror (1979), directed by Stuart Rosenberg [film], United States: Cinema 77, Professional Films.

Get Out (2017), directed by Jordan Peele [film], Los Angeles: Blumhouse and Monkey's Paw Production.

The Goonies (1985), directed by Richard Donner [film], United States: Amblin Entertainment.

Halloween (1978), directed by John Carpenter [film], United States: Compass International Pictures.

The Hills Have Eyes (1977), directed by Wes Craven [film], United States: Blood Relations Co.

Nightmare on Elm Street (1984), directed by Wes Craven [film], United States: New Line Cinema.

Poltergeist (1982), directed by Tobe Hooper [film], Los Angeles, CA: MGM Studios and Amblin Entertainment.

The Shining (1980), directed by Stanley Kubrick [film], Los Angeles and London: Producer Circle Company and Hawk Films.

Stranger Things (2016–), created by the Duffer Brothers [TV series], United States: 21 Laps Entertainment.

The Texas Chainsaw Massacre (1974), directed by Tobe Hooper [film], Texas: Vortex Production.

Us (2019), directed by Jordan Peele [film], Los Angeles: Blumhouse and Monkey's Paw Production.

11

'Cut them up': Lily Frankenstein, Valerie Solanas and the reanimation of radical feminism in *Penny Dreadful*

Anthea Taylor

Introduction

Penny Dreadful, a Showtime/Sky Atlantic co-production (2014–16) that continues to have an active fan base, is evidence of a heightened neo-Victorianism in recent popular culture (Primorac 2018). Drawing upon characters from the nineteenth-century novels invoked in its title, including Dorian Gray, Dracula, Dr Jekyll and Dr Frankenstein, the series is also populated with strong, independent women who seek to contest permissible Victorian femininities (manifested most clearly in the 'Angel in the House' figure). Although previous scholars have critically engaged with its key female protagonist, Vanessa Ives (Green 2021; Posada 2020; Schubart 2017), this chapter turns to one of the series' other minor literary characters to suggest the political possibilities of popular culture for thinking through, and troubling, the legacy of feminism in its more transgressive forms. In *Penny Dreadful*, Lily Frankenstein – the bride who never actually came to be in Mary Shelley's *Frankenstein* – mounts an explicit critique of the bonds of normative femininity, embodying a feminism that becomes increasingly more revolutionary as the series progresses. Her feminism is not that of the briefly depicted suffragettes but rather a form more aligned to twentieth-century radical varieties. Specifically, it bears an obvious intertextual debt to Valerie Solanas's (2004 [1967]) *SCUM Manifesto* and its parodic vision of a rage-fuelled eradication of men. In re-reading these texts – *Penny Dreadful* and the *SCUM Manifesto* – alongside each other in the more recent climate, wherein feminist anger is said to be 'all the rage' (Kay 2019: 591), it is clear that popular culture is central to discursive contestations over the meanings and histories of social movements, including modern feminism. Horror in particular is a genre amenable to feminist reimaginings, and to literalizing the 'horror' of negotiating gender and sexuality within the confines of patriarchal capitalism.

While critics have commonly dismissed *Penny Dreadful*'s depiction of the purportedly 'monstrous' Lily as ultimately antifeminist (Braid 2017; Griggs 2018; Kohlke 2018; Pedro 2021; Wright 2021), I conversely argue that she embodies a form of Solanas-inspired 'vigilante feminism' (D'Amore 2017), which urges a rethinking of feminist politics in all its temporalities.[1] In this chapter, problematizing these critiques of the series that fail to account for the generative capacities of anger, and anger as a specifically feminist affect, I demonstrate how Lily's feminism is most productively read in and through Solanas's text. In *Penny Dreadful*, the violence advocated in Solanas's manifesto is literalized as Lily accumulates a group of abused women and encourages them to seek revenge against their perpetrators. It seems, therefore, that Solanas's satirical exhortation for women to eradicate men – to 'cut them up' – underpins Lily's revolutionary feminist vision (Kouzas 2018). In this respect, radical feminism – like Brona/Lily herself – appears to be *reanimated*. Although many contemporary television series are accused of relegating feminism to the past, *Penny Dreadful* participates in an increasingly important and ongoing dialogue about the unfinished business of second-wave feminism (Eichorn 2015; Fraser 2013), including through its reworking of a historically much-derided – perhaps 'monstrous' – radical feminism.

Valerie Solanas, radical feminism and the generative rage of the *SCUM Manifesto*

As Jilly Boyce Kay (2019: 591) notes, over the past few years women's anger has become culturally legible in ways it has not been at other points in history (see also Banet-Weiser 2018; Chemaly 2018). Although *Penny Dreadful* pre-dates the #MeToo movement, with women refusing to be silenced and publicly calling for their abusers to be reprimanded (Boyle 2019; Fileborn and Loney-Howes 2019), alongside feminism's newfound 'luminosity' in media and popular culture (Gill 2016), the kinds of cultural and affective logics we have been witnessing over the past few years were germinating in this televisual text. For second-wave radical feminists, as well as for many in the present, anger is a 'radicalizing emotion that could shake women free of their attachments to the myths and illusions of political machismo, normative femininity, and the heterosexual contract' (Hesford 2015: 96). That is, it is politically generative, as *Penny Dreadful* posits (Kouzas 2018). More broadly, feminist critics such as Nancy Fraser (2013) and Kate Eichhorn (2015) have urged us to reconsider second-wave feminism as an unfinished project, arguing that its radicalism could function as an antidote to (neo)liberal feminism's limited entrepreneurial ethos and postfeminism's rhetoric of choice and disavowal of organized politics. As Eichhorn (2015: 254) emphasizes, second-wave feminism is best conceptualized 'not as a failed project but rather as the grounds for a feminist project not yet realized' – including in its more radical variants. Through Lily, as I demonstrate here, a form of radical feminism along with the anger that underpins tracts such as Solanas's and radical feminism more broadly (Kouzas 2018) is revived and offered up as an alternative to liberal forms that have been unsuccessful in redressing ongoing structural inequalities. That is, as decades of 'equality feminism' have made patently clear, it is only through more radical forms that women's liberation can be achieved.

As Breanne Fahs (2014) establishes, Valerie Solanas – like a number of radical feminists – has largely been relegated to the margins of feminist history. Originally self-published and distributed on the streets of New York in 1967, Solanas's *SCUM Manifesto* is a satirical piece of writing, a manifesto attacking the twin evils of patriarchy and capitalism. The *SCUM Manifesto* begins:

> 'Life' in this 'society' being, at best, an utter bore and no aspect of 'society' being at all relevant to women, there remains to civic-minded, responsible, thrill-seeking females only to *overthrow the government, eliminate the money system, institute complete automation and destroy the male sex.*
>
> (Solanas 2004 [1967]: 1, emphasis in original)

As an anti-reformist tract, it sees more possibility in the politics of destruction than reformation. Solanas, as Natalya Lusty (2009: 146) remarks, is 'less concerned with systematic critique … than with satirically highlighting the hypocrisy of these institutions and delivering ingenious solutions for "fucking up the system"'. The 'SCUM' of its title is said to be an acronym for the 'Society for Cutting up Men',[2] and it is this 'society' that seems to finally be brought into being by *Penny Dreadful*'s Lily Frankenstein (Kouzas 2018).

Solanas became a notorious figure after shooting pop artist Andy Warhol in 1968, her manifesto eclipsed by an act which seemed to suggest the actualization of her discursive feminist rage (Fahs 2014; Heller 2001; Lusty 2009). It is this incident that has led to some debate about whether the manifesto should be read satirically or as an incitement to violence. In terms of the latter, Amanda Third (2006: 109–10) argues that this 'angry and incendiary manifesto' prosecutes a form of '*terrorist feminism*', marked by 'a willingness to take the fight for women's liberation to its most terrifying and confronting limit' (emphasis in original). It is also, she suggests, a form that is consistent with much second-wave radical feminism, wherein 'it was not uncommon … to preach violence as a way of forcing an apocalyptic end to "patriarchy"' (Third 2006: 116). While Solanas's assault on Warhol may, for some, encourage a more literal reading of her writing – what Fahs (2008: 592) calls 'the overly reductive formulation of Warhol Shooting = *SCUM Manifesto* in practice' – I am persuaded by feminist scholars who instead underscore the text's parodic and satirical orientation, something we also clearly see in *Penny Dreadful*.

Along with Solanas (Fahs 2014), radical feminist thinkers such as Mary Daly (Monagle 2019), Shulamith Firestone (Margree 2018) and Germaine Greer (Taylor forthcoming) are being critically recuperated and their positioning within feminist intellectual history reimagined. In the case of Solanas, various feminist critics have sought to relocate her polemical text firmly within the history of the American second wave, especially in its more radical manifestations. For Alice Echols (1989: 104), 'Solanas's *SCUM Manifesto* was one of the earliest, wittiest, and most eccentric expressions of second wave feminism.' In a similar attempt to refigure the manifesto and its author's legacy, Dana Heller (2001: 187) argues that it is 'a radical document that should remind us of feminism's unacknowledged debt to the margins of the representable and the representative'. Solanas's manifesto was, as Mavis Haut (2007: 28) notes, marked by an 'unapologetic anger', and it is on these grounds that Lily's feminism most overtly resonates with hers. As Haut (2007: 28) continues, 'This anger reaches such extremes that it is no longer congruent with more specific concerns normally identified with feminism and, over the passing years, *Scum Manifesto* has never settled into the main corpus of feminism and continues to be perceived as an oddity or anomaly.' It is, then, a 'monstrous' text, existing on the margins of second-wave feminism. Like her writing, Solanas herself 'has been relegated to the "lunatic" fringe of radical feminism' (Hart 1997: 84), her pathologization serving to compromise or obscure the radical potentialities of her work for the present. Just as Solanas has largely existed on the edges of second-wave feminist history, so too the 'Bride of Frankenstein' (or, in *Penny Dreadful*'s rendering, Lily Frankenstein) has been a liminal figure, resurfacing from time to time in adaptations but never occupying centre stage. *Penny Dreadful* irrevocably alters both these cultural (mis)positionings.

Radical reanimation: From Brona Croft to Lily Frankenstein

In Mary Shelley's (1994 [1818]) *Frankenstein; or The Modern Prometheus*, scientist Victor Frankenstein brought into being a creature who has subsequently appeared in myriad and varied forms of film and television – as has his 'bride'. Although in the novel Frankenstein acceded to his creation's demands to fashion a mate for him, ultimately he 'tore to pieces the thing on which I was engaged' (1994 [1818]: 161). As narrator, Frankenstein reflects upon this destruction: 'The remains of the half-finished creature, whom I had destroyed, lay scattered on the floor, and I almost felt as if I had mangled the living flesh of a human being.' As Erica Hawley (2015: 218) argues, 'this section of the novel prompts the question: what could *she* have been? What sort of monster – what sort of woman – would this creature have been? What would she have looked like? What would she have thought of herself, her creator and her betrothed?' (emphasis in original). Remarking upon this figure's historical silence, Hawley (2015: 219) continues, 'she is never allowed to speak, or indeed to live; she is never given name or form'. Attempts to answer these questions in and through various cultural forms have seen 'the female monster become a cultural icon: readable, mythic, and imbued with meaning' (2015: 218), especially in film and television. (Two of the best known are James Whale's *The Bride of Frankenstein* [1935] and Kenneth Branagh's *Mary Shelley's Frankenstein* [1994].) *Penny Dreadful* is a recent attempt to give voice to 'the bride', which in itself is an important feminist gesture.

Rather than merely offering another iteration of Frankenstein's monster, it is the female creature that is recentred in this particular adaptation (Braid 2017: 238). As in Shelley's text, *Penny Dreadful*'s monster (aka John Clare) exhorts his creator to provide him with a 'companion': 'You will make me an immortal mate' (1.3). While initially reluctant to comply, Frankenstein sees his opportunity in the terminally ill Brona Croft. Formerly a sex worker from Belfast, Croft is one of the key characters in the Series 1 story arc, becoming romantically involved with Ethan Chandler (later revealed to be a vampire-hunting werewolf). While dying of tuberculosis, Brona is suffocated by Dr Frankenstein, ostensibly there to help ease her pain (1.8). Significantly, as Stephanie Green (2017) makes clear, 'Whereas his [Frankenstein's] first attempts at animation were stitched together from body parts, this new female creature is made from the body of a whole woman.' Using the electric charge from a thunderstorm, and with the help of his first creation, Dr Frankenstein successfully reanimates Brona (2.1).

Shortly after Frankenstein brings Brona back to life as Lily, he seeks to 'domesticate' and 'tame' her, consistent with Victorian gender ideologies, and they eventually begin a short-lived sexual relationship. Initially compliant, she is nevertheless puzzled at the myriad corporeal constraints women have to endure, and her feminist (re)awakening comes early in her renewed life. As Lily walks awkwardly in heels and feels suffocated by the corset, she questions the logic of women's dress and adornment:

> Lily: I can't breathe [of the corset] … I think I'm going to topple over [of the high heels]. Do all women wear corsets? … Seems, I don't know the word … cruel. So women wear corsets so they don't exert themselves? … what would be the danger if they did?
> Frankenstein: They'd take over the world. (2.4)

The corset, of course, is a familiar trope for the constrained Victorian woman, especially in neo-Victorian texts (Primorac 2018: 4). These comments pre-empt the political activism in which Frankenstein's second 'creation' comes to engage. Although Lily's initial brand of gender critique is more aligned with liberal feminism, it rapidly develops into its much more radical, anarchic form.

The 'snap', the monstrous feminist and vigilante politics

While Lily seems to have no memories of her traumatic past, in the tradition of the repressed they invariably return; one of the earliest signs of this comes when Lily as Frankenstein's daughter/lover, as in *The Bride of Frankenstein*, viciously rejects the monster for whom she was created. In the following scene, we see the beginnings of her own feminist 'manifesto', a kind of hyperbolic oratory characterizing her own, as well as Solanas's, speech acts:

> We flatter men with our pain, we bow before them, we make ourselves dolls for their amusement, we lose our dignity in corsets and high shoes, and gossip and the slavery of marriage – and our reward this service? The back of the hand, the face turned to the pillow, the bloody, aching cunt as you force us onto your beds

to take your fat, heaving bodies. You drag us into the alleys, cram yourself into our mouths for two bob [her Irish accent returns], when you're not beating us senseless ... Never again will I kneel to any man. Now they shall kneel to me.

(2.8, Lily to John Clare)

This impassioned monologue makes it clear how Lily's feminist consciousness has been fully raised, the personal irrevocably refigured as political as it so crucially was during feminism's second wave (and beyond). In Shelley's novel, the female monster appears as even more of an aberration than the original creature (Hawley 2015), a figure of abjection (Artt 2018; Braid 2017). With *Penny Dreadful*'s sympathetic rendering of John Clare as a poetry-consuming, sensitive soul who has been wronged by his creator, we may presume this positioning is reinscribed. However, as I will argue, Lily is also compassionately portrayed, with her abuse as Brona seen to justify her misandrist politics.

From midway through Season 2, Lily appears to be building towards what Sara Ahmed refers to as a 'feminist snap'. In Ahmed's (2017: 8) terms, 'a snap signals that a life one has been bearing is a life one is no longer willing to bear'. Multiple, quotidian enactments of gendered harassment, micro-aggressions, and literal and symbolic violence culminate in this feminist 'snap': 'Snapping, a moment when the pressure has built up and tipped over, can be the basis of feminist revolt, a revolt against what women are asked to put up with' (Ahmed 2017: 210). As with all 'feminist killjoys' (Ahmed 2004), Lily refuses to be compliant, silent or malleable – refusals made possible by her rebirth and accompanying supernatural strength. In a clear rendering of the *vagina dentata* (Griggs 2018: 31; see also Green 2017), Lily's first murder is performed while having sex with a stranger she met at a pub (2.7); she strangles him with her bare hands mid-coitus. As Barbara Creed (1993: 106) notes, 'The myth about woman as castrator clearly points to male fears and phantasies about the female genitals as a trap, a black hole which threatens to swallow them up and cut them into pieces.' The 'monstrous feminine', as Creed underscores, is defined in terms of her sexuality and the cultural fears it invokes, and these links between sex, power and death become even more pronounced as the series progresses.

After rescuing the young Justine from sexual slavery, Lily and the likewise immortal Dorian Gray – a queer character who becomes central to Lily's radicalization and pursuit of revenge – encourage her to violently slit the throat of one of her abusers. Afterwards, the three, covered from head to toe in blood and erotically charged by their protégé's first murder, participate in a *menage-a-trois* (3.3). Of course, the horror film 'abounds with images that play on the fear of castration and dismemberment' (Creed 1993: 107; see also Wright 2021), and *Penny Dreadful* utilizes such images to signal the ongoing threat posed by (radical) feminism, as well as queerness, to the recalcitrant patriarchal social order. Lily tells Justine she will help her recruit all the city's 'invisible women' as soldiers in their fight for 'freedom and liberty'. She thereby creates a community of damaged women, a sisterhood bonded in their gendered oppression. Given its basis in this abuse, it is a deeply affective politics. Lily becomes a kind of messianic and pedagogic figure, raising women's consciousness and empowering them to seek revenge, even offering detailed instructions on how to kill (3.6). It is not remarkable to suggest that 'rage and anger also have profound political utility', a presumption that underpins the *SCUM Manifesto* itself (Rowe and Chavez 2011: 282) as well as much contemporary feminist activism. Ahmed (2004: 173) notes that 'women's testimonies about pain ... are crucial not only to the formation of feminist subjects (a way of reading pain as structural rather than incidental violence), but to feminist collectives, which have mobilized around the injustice of that violence and the political and ethical demand for reparation and redress'. However, she cautions against 'ontologis[ing] women's pain as the automatic ground of politics' (2004: 174). Nevertheless, in *Penny Dreadful* it *is* through this shared pain and trauma that Lily's radical feminist collective is brought into being.

As in the *SCUM Manifesto*, this radicalism also manifests in Lily's explicit critique of the inadequacy of a reformist mode of feminist activism. For example, as the suffragettes pass with placards demanding the vote, she engages in this dialogue with one of her acolytes:

> Justine: They think as you do, the suffragettes.
> Lily: No, our enemies are the same but they seek equality.
> Justine: And we?
> Lily: Mastery. And they're all so awfully clamorous. All this marching around in public and waving placards. That's not it. How do you accomplish anything in this life? By craft? By stealth? By poison? By the throat quietly slit in the dead of the night? By the careful and silent accumulation of power.
> Justine: And when you have that power?
> Lily: Well, what do you do when you've assembled an army? You go to war. (3.3)

As Green (2017) argues, Lily here 'rejects the idealism of the late-Victorian suffrage campaigners seeking equality with men, to assert a claim for a different kind of female power – literally the creation of a super race of women warriors bent on destroying the male "grasp"' (see also Kouzas 2018: 67). For Braid (2017: 237), this wholesale dismissal of reformist tactics suggests that Lily's vision is 'not a feminist one'. However, Lily rejects only a certain *form* of feminism and seeks to replace it with a more revolutionary one, which has historically been derided because of its very radicality and cultural unintelligibility (Third 2006). For Lily, like Solanas, equality is seen to be what Germaine Greer (in Davey 2017) routinely dubs 'a profoundly conservative goal'. Instead, more radical tactics are required to achieve total liberation – a position with which I concur. As Solanas (2004 [1967]: 76) puts it in her manifesto, 'SCUM will not picket, demonstrate, march or strike to attempt to achieve its ends. Such tactics are for nice, genteel ladies who scrupulously take only such action as is guaranteed to be ineffective.' These are the 'ladies' Lily mocks, whose feminism is dismissed as patently inadequate. In contrast, her feminism will be fierce, violent and destructive – as patriarchy itself is exposed to be.

Lily's sisterhood of feminist vigilantes signals the effects (and affects) of the 'feminist snap' in its most extreme, collectivized form. For Lily and her damaged disciples, violence is integral to a viable feminist politics:

> We must be bloody or nothing else. And now you must prove your commitment to our great cause. Go now, every one of you, RISE UP, RISE UP [chanting as the suffagettes had]! Go into those dark streets you know so well … and find me a bad man … find him and bring me his right hand. Cut it off and hold it bleeding to your breast. Bring here, fling it on this table … Prove yourselves to me!'
>
> (3.7)

And they do. As Chrisanne Kouzas (2018: 67) notes, Lily, considerably empowered by her anger, 'assembles an army of sex workers, and with them carries out her misandrist plans to "destroy the male sex" á la Valerie Solanas'. In *Penny Dreadful*, then, Solanas's vision is literalized as Lily exhorts all her followers to bring her their perpetrators' severed hands. As they return, the dining table in Gray's mansion is piled high with the bloody hands of abusive men. Such dismemberment is in itself a form of symbolic castration; the removal of hands, too, invokes biblical imagery, wherein cutting off the hand is a gesture to impede sinning. It is also consistent with the hyperbole and excess at the heart of Solanas's writing (Haut 2007; Lusty 2009). As in Solanas's manifesto, which proposed a desire 'to cleanse society of men as its primary contaminant' (Fahs 2008: 593), Lily's sisterhood fully articulates the rage which is said to be illegible in postfeminist media culture (McRobbie 2009). While the #MeToo movement has been critiqued for its tendency to express 'trauma and rage but in an imprecise and insufficiently solidaristic way' (Kay 2021: 83), in *Penny Dreadful* this rage is harnessed in a collectivist project – albeit an ultimately unsustainable one.

At a more personal level, Lily's embrace of this newfound feminist subjectivity also represents an important form of self-making. As Green (2017) remarks, 'Remade by men, now Lily remakes herself' – a liberatory, agentic act which cannot be under-estimated. Emboldened by her immortality, and asserting that violence is necessary to emancipation, Lily tells her first disciple, Justine, that, 'Liberty is a bitch who must be bedded on a mattress of corpses' (3.3). While Lily is certainly not physically monstrous, she is coded monstrous in deeds, something critics suggest compromises the series' laudable critique of normative femininity (Wright 2021). However, the rage of Lily and her sisters – a response to years of sexual violence and abuse – is rendered sympathetically. In its depiction of their violent rampages, the series works to refigure femininity in significant ways. As Jack Halberstam (1993: 191) remarks:

> The depiction of women committing acts of violence against men does not simply use "male" tactics of aggression for other ends; in fact, female violence transforms the symbolic function of the feminine within popular narratives and it simultaneously challenges the hegemonic insistence upon the linking of might and right under the sign of masculinity. Women with guns [or, in this case, knives] confronting rapists has the potential to intervene in popular imaginings of violence and gender by resisting the moral imperative to not fight violence with violence.

While Lily's eradication of men is of course not a viable feminist strategy beyond *Penny Dreadful*'s diegetic world, such representations serve an important symbolic and political function: 'Imagined violence does not advocate lesbian or female aggression but it might complicate an assumed relationship between women and passivity or feminism and pacifism' (Halberstam 1993: 199). Furthermore, as the above implies, the Lily Frankenstein story arc can be seen as a form of rape revenge television (Read 2000). As in rape revenge narratives, the violence Lily advocates is not indiscriminate, but directed only towards those 'bad men' who have abused her and the other women in her sisterhood. Rikke Schubart (2007: 95) suggests that in rape revenge films, 'rape is the initiation rite that pushes women from being "soft" victims to becoming "hard" avengers'. Of course, Brona/Lily's reanimation is in itself a form of (re)violation, and it is this – coupled with her past trauma – that forms the basis of her political transformation. She recalls the sexual abuse she suffered as Brona, which provides the grounds for her murderous collective: 'I remember every man whoever used me, every filthy alley, every cruel bastard who hurt me and bent me to submission – all of Brona's shame and debasement, and everything she lost along the way' (3.6, to Dorian).

In response, Lily becomes, to rework Barbara Creed's (1993) term, the 'monstrous feminist', a monstrosity about which she is self-reflexive and through which she locates her power; she knows the limited ways her actions will become culturally legible, however. She anticipates attempts to discipline her feminist coterie, telling them: 'We are not women who crawl. We are not women who kneel. And for this we will be branded radicals. Revolutionists. Women who are strong, and refuse to be degraded, and choose to protect themselves, are called monsters. That is the world's crime, not ours' (3.6). These are astute observations about the ways in which the threat posed by feminists is managed via these discursive constructions of dissident women as aberrant and exemplars of a 'failed' womanhood. However, citing the series' reinscription of Victorian cultural anxieties *vis-à-vis* the 'New Woman' (Green 2017; Wright 2021) and its realization of 'the fear that the feminist will turn out to be a man-eater' (Braid 2017: 238), critics have argued that the representation of this violent, misandrist feminism serves to effectively undo the show's feminist potentialities. For example, Dina Pedro (2021: 210) notes that in depicting the 'feminist cause as radical and violent, the series shows misogynist and antifeminist undertones' (see also Griggs 2021). She suggests that in its representation of 'a tyrannical and aggressive form of feminism', *Penny Dreadful* 'reinforce[s] the same antifeminist discourse it appears to criticize' (Pedro 2021: 208). Chloe Buckley (2020: 374) also critiques the character of Lily for her failure to 'agitate for social or political change', something that overlooks the series' commentary on the inherent limits of those very reformist struggles (such as those pursued by the suffragettes). Rather than conceding that rage may function as a valuable heuristic device to reflect upon the inadequacy of structural remedies, Kohlke (2018: 9–10) similarly believes that *Penny Dreadful* reduces feminism to 'a misguided, misandrist, and megalomaniacal Gothic revenge fantasy'.

The series, of course, does not argue for a widespread actualization of Lily's murderous rape revenge tactics as a viable feminist response, but takes its cue from Solanas in its depiction of an extremist feminist reaction to a patriarchal order that is itself extreme in its symbolic and literal violence against women. However, for these critics, there is nothing generative about this representation of the violent liberatory tactics of Lily and her sisterhood, or what they may suggest about the inadequacy of existing structures or institutions to redress harms against girls and women. In contrast to these more pessimistic interpretations, Kouzas (2018) sees the series' value in making radical feminism intelligible for a broad audience. Specifically, she argues (2018: 69) that it demonstrates 'how the fantasy genre in particular, is a powerful medium for communicating politically marginalized ideas'. This reading of *Penny Dreadful* as performing a recuperative gesture when it comes to more radical forms of feminist politics is entirely persuasive, and I build upon it to further argue that Lily embodies a form of what Laura M. D'Amore (2017) identifies as 'vigilante feminism' – a moniker we could certainly apply to Solanas's brand of radical feminism.

In her study, which focuses on contemporary American fairy-tale revisions, D'Amore (2017: 387) suggests that vigilante feminism 'applies specifically to the performance of vigilantism by girls and women who have undertaken their own protection, and the protection of others, against violence – such as sexual assault, abduction, abuse, and trauma – because they have been otherwise failed in that manner'. She argues that the televisual female vigilante, through the reclamation of women's agency, is indebted to feminism, even if this is troublesome due to 'feminism's historical antiviolence stance' (D'Amore 2017: 390–1). As *Penny Dreadful* makes abundantly clear, 'vigilante feminists' responses to patriarchal violence are directly related to the violent world in which they exist' (D'Amore 2017: 391). In this respect, and like Halberstam's earlier work, D'Amore (2017: 402, 391) argues that popular culture's vigilante feminism is a 'powerful feminist fantasy' that acts as 'a response to violence against women, a corrective to a massive imbalance in power, and a life or death matter'. Like Solanas's unactionable manifesto, *Penny Dreadful* does not ultimately offer a viable or sustainable way of channelling feminist anger. However, in its representation of Lily's 'vigilante feminism', the series asks how women's rage might be harnessed for a revolutionary feminist politics. What strategies – discursive or otherwise – will create a world that is *otherwise* for oppressed and subordinated women?

Conclusion: Radical feminist futures?

Towards the end of the series, Frankenstein kidnaps Lily in an attempt to curtail her murderous sprees (3.7). He is aided by Dorian Gray, who betrays his lover after being relegated to the margins of the women-centred community she had created and becoming increasingly uncomfortable with her power. She is taken to Bedlam Hospital to be injected with truth serum, which Kohlke (2018: 10) argues will 'split off her monstrous self, restoring the docile "Angel of the House" to perfect obeisance'. Pessimistically, Kohlke (2018: 10) reads this as emblematic of attempts to manage and curtail feminism in the present: 'Implicitly, the scene invites viewers to revel with the male characters in the imminent vanquishing of the female monster'. Enslaved in the most literal fashion, tied to a chair by ankle chains, Frankenstein tells her that they will 'take away all [her] anger and pain' and 'make [her] into a proper [i.e. disempowered] woman' (3.7). Making overt her pathologization with a reference to getting her 'well', they plan to wipe her memory and strip her of her newfound power. While at Bedlam, Lily reveals to Frankenstein that as Brona she had a baby daughter, who tragically died of hypothermia and starvation while she was working; despite the pain, it is such memories she wishes to retain. Many critics argue that, through her presentation of 'herself as a mourning mother begging for empathy', Lily effectively 'abandon[s] her radical feminism' (Pedro 2021: 209; see also Kohlke 2018: 11). In these interpretations, Lily is successfully disciplined, 'tamed by her male creator who reasserts his dominance over her' (Griggs 2018: 31), and ultimately punished for her gendered transgressions and excessive feminism. In an alternative reading, however, perhaps Lily offers her creator the gendered performance he demands from her, in a strategic gesture to secure her release (3.8). She succeeds as Frankenstein abandons his plan and grants her freedom, ensuring she does not become – as she had feared – 'a non-person' (3.7). In this respect, she is *not* destroyed and the series leaves open the possibility of (another) resurrection of Lily as political agent. 'That Lily escapes like the archetypal Frankenstein's monster is a final reminder', Stephanie Green (2022a: 9) writes, 'of the shadowy promise that underlies all horror stories: the possibility of rebirth and return' (see also Green 2022b: 114).

After farewelling Dorian, Lily – the embodiment of radical feminism – simply departs the series, by implication leaving her revolutionary tendencies behind. However, through this lack of narrative closure, *Penny Dreadful* refuses to rule out the possibility of Lily's, and thus radical feminism's, re-emergence. In this chapter, I have argued that interpretations of Lily Frankenstein's depiction as merely exemplifying popular hostility towards more radical forms of feminism fail to concede the affective charge of the rage embodied by Lily, as well as the hyperbolic manifesto upon which it appears to be based and with which it productively stages an intertextual dialogue. The question prompted by Solanas's manifesto is also invoked by the series: 'Can the project of "man-hating" (something that is constantly – and publicly – rejected by most modern feminists) be useful, even on a theoretical level?' (Fahs 2008: 593). In *Penny Dreadful*, Lily is the traumatized woman with no recourse within existing political and legislative structures; she deploys the only tools at hand to reposition herself from object to subject, exposing the tensions between reformist feminism and its more radical variants.

Contra the expectations of previous critics, Gothic fantasy television series such as *Penny Dreadful* should not be critiqued for their failure to offer emulatable feminist tactics – just as Solanas's manifesto should not be read as a literal call to kill all men. As Lusty (2009: 144, 146) emphasizes, Solanas's reckoning with this traditionally masculinist genre was 'highly parodic', constituted by 'hyperbolic rhetoric' and 'provocatively satirical' prose. The series' misandry is similarly 'tongue-in-cheek' and 'used as a tool to make audiences question oppressive societal norms' (Kouzas 2018: 61). The kind of 'vigilante feminism' we may see operative within the manifesto's pages – and indeed within *Penny Dreadful* – must be read in terms of these tactical rhetorical manoeuvres, which seek to elicit certain affective responses from audiences. The series reflects upon different modes of feminist identification and activism in a way that invites a reconsideration of feminist temporalities and that works to undermine any linear model of feminist progress. Far from suggesting the work of feminism is done, *Penny Dreadful* asks us to rethink that work and how it may be performed, by whom and for what political and affective purposes? This question remains unanswered, both diegetically and extradiegetically, but is still urgent for audiences in the present.

Notes

1 Readings of the series as exemplifying the broader tendencies of postfeminist media culture have also been common (Buckley 2020; Pedro 2021; Primorac 2018); however, this chapter is focused on its overt engagement with radical feminism rather questions of feminism's disavowal.
2 However, some suggest that this acronym was not introduced by Solanas but was a marketing device by her publisher to capitalize on the shooting (Fahs 2008; Heller 2001: 168).

References

Ahmed, S. (2004), *The Cultural Politics of Emotion*, London: Routledge.

Ahmed, S. (2017), *Living a Feminist Life*, Durham: Duke University Press.

Artt, S. (2018), '"An Otherness That Cannot Be Sublimated": Shades of Frankenstein in *Penny Dreadful* and *Black Mirror*', *Science Fiction Film and Television*, 11 (2): 257–75.

Banet-Weiser, S. (2018), *Empowered: Popular Feminism and Popular Misogyny*, Durham, NC: Duke University Press.

Boyle, K. (2019), *#MeToo, Weinstein and Feminism*, London: Palgrave Macmillan.

Braid, B. (2017), 'The Frankenstein Meme: *Penny Dreadful* and *The Frankenstein Chronicles* as Adaptations', *Open Cultural Studies*, 1 (1): 232–43.

Buckley, C.G. (2020), 'A Tale of Two Women: The Female Grotesque in Showtime's *Penny Dreadful*', *Feminist Media Studies*, 20 (3): 361–80.

Chemaly, S. (2018), *Rage Becomes Her: The Power of Women's Anger*, New York: Simon & Schuster.

Creed, B. (1993), *The Monstrous Feminism*, London: Routledge.

D'Amore, L.M. (2017), 'Vigilante Feminism: Revising Trauma, Abduction, and Assault in American Fairy-Tale Revisions', *Marvels & Tales*, 31 (2): 386–405.

Davey, M. (2017), 'Equality Is a "Profoundly Conservative Goal" for Women, Germaine Greer Says', *The Guardian*, 8 March. Available online: www.theguardian.com/books/2017/mar/09/equality-is-a-profoundly-conservative-goal-for-women-germaine-greer-says (accessed 20 June 2023).

Dow, B. (1996), *Prime Time Feminism: Television, Media Culture, and the Women's Movement Since 1970*, Philadelphia: University of Pennsylvania Press.

Echols, A. (1989), *Daring to Be Bad: Radical Feminism in America, 1967–1975*, Minneapolis: University of Minnesota Press.

Eichorn, K. (2015), 'Feminism's There: On Post-ness and Nostalgia', *Feminist Theory*, 16 (3): 251–64.

Fahs, B. (2008), 'The Radical Possibilities of Valerie Solanas', *Feminist Studies* 34 (3): 591–617.

Fahs, B. (2014), *Valerie Solanas: The Defiant Life of the Woman Who Wrote SCUM*, New York: CUNY.

Fileborn, B. and R. Loney-Howes (2019), 'Introduction: Mapping the Emergence of #MeToo', in *#MeToo and the Politics of Social Change*, edited by B. Fileborne and R. Loney-Howes, 1–18, London: Palgrave Macmillan.

Fraser, N. (2013), *The Fortunes of Feminism*, London: Verso.

Gill, R. (2016), 'Postfeminism and the New Cultural Life of Feminism', *Diffractions*, 6. Available online: https://lisbonconsortium.files.wordpress.com/2012/12/rosalind-gill_postfeminism-and-the-new-cultural-life-of-feminism.pdf (accessed 14 August 2023).

Gorton, K. (2021), '"Don't Let the Bastards Grind You Down": Feminist Resilience/Resilient Feminism in *The Handmaid's Tale* (Hulu, 2017–)', *Critical Studies in Television*, 16 (3): 227–44.

Green, S. (2017), 'Lily Frankenstein: The Gothic New Woman in *Penny Dreadful*', *Refractory*. Available online: https://www.researchgate.net/profile/Stephanie-Green-4/publication/322632876_'Lily_Frankenstein_The_Gothic_New_Woman_in_Penny_Dreadful'/links/5be90b2da6fdcc3a8dcfe4e1/Lily-Frankenstein-The-Gothic-New-Woman-in-Penny-Dreadful.pdf (accessed 14 August 2023).

Green, S. (2021), 'Vampire Apocalypse and the Evolutionary Sublime: The "End of Days" in John Logan's *Penny Dreadful*', *Continuum*, 35 (2): 270–81.

Green, S. (2022a), 'Violence and the "Gothic New Woman" in *Penny Dreadful*', *Flinders University Languages Group Online Review*, 6 (3): 1–13.

Green, S. (2022b), 'The Killing Characters of *Penny Dreadful*', in *Serial Killers in Contemporary Television*, edited by C. Daigle, B. Robinson, 101–18, London: Routledge.

Griggs, Y. (2018), *Adaptable TV: Rewiring the Text*, London: Palgrave Macmillan.

Halberstam, J. (1993), 'Imagined Violence/Queer Violence: Representation, Rage, and Resistance', *Social Text*, 37: 187–201.

Hart, L. (1997), 'Killing Representation: Feminism and Violence at the Limit', *Psychoanalytic Review*, 84: 789–812.

Haut, M. (2007), 'A Salty Tongue: At the Margins of Satire, Comedy and Polemic in the Writing of Valerie Solanas', *Feminist Theory*, 8 (1): 27–41.

Hawley, E. (2015), 'The Bride and Her Afterlife: Female Frankenstein Monsters on Page and Screen', *Literature/Film Quarterly*, 43 (3): 218–31.

Heller, D. (2001), 'Shooting Solanas: Radical Feminist History and the Technology of Failure', *Feminist Studies*, 27 (1): 167–89.

Henderson, M. and A. Taylor (2019), *Postfeminism in Context*, London: Routledge.

Hesford, V. (2015), *Feeling Women's Liberation*, Durham, NC: Duke University Press.

Kay, J.B. (2019), 'Introduction: Anger, Media, and Feminism: The Gender Politics of Mediated Rage', *Feminist Media Studies*, 19 (4): 591–615.

Kay, J.B. (2021), 'Celebritised Anger: Theorising Feminist Rage, Voice, and Affective Injustice through Hannah Gadsby's *Nanette*', in *Gender and Australian Celebrity Culture*, edited by A. Taylor and J. McIntyre, 75–90, London: Routledge.

Kohlke, M. (2018), 'The Lures of Neo-Victorianism Presentism (with a Feminist Case Study of *Penny Dreadful*)', *Literature Compass*, 15 (7): 1–14.

Kouzas, C. (2018), 'Creating Space for Radical Feminism in Mainstream Television: Gender, Sexuality, and Power in *Penny Dreadful*', *Journal of Political Studies*, 20: 61–71.

Lusty, N. (2009), 'Valerie Solanas and the Limits of Speech', *Australian Literary Studies*, 24 (3–4): 144–54.

McRobbie, A. (2009), *The Aftermath of Feminism: Gender, Culture and Social Change*, London: Sage.

Margree, V. (2018), *Neglected or Misunderstood: The Radical Feminism of Shulamith Firestone*, London: Zero Books.

Monagle, C. (2019), 'Mary Daly's Gyn/Ecology: Mysticism, Difference, and Feminist History', *Signs*, 44 (2): 333–53.

Mulvey-Roberts, M. (2014), 'The Afterlives of the Bride of Frankenstein', in *Women and Gothic*, edited by M. Purves, 81–96. London: Cambridge Scholars Publishing.

Pedro, D. (2021), '"We're Going to Make You into a Proper Woman": Postfeminist Gender Performativity and the Supernatural in *Penny Dreadful* (2014–2016)', *Nordic Journal of English Studies*, 20 (1): 194–214.

Posada, T. (2020), 'Old Monsters, Old Curses: The New Hysterical Woman and *Penny Dreadful*', in *Neo-Victorian Madness: Rediagnosing Nineteenth-Century Mental Illness in Literature and Other Media*, edited by S.E. Meier and B. Ayres, 229–51. London, Palgrave Macmillan.

Primorac, A. (2018), *Neo-Victorianism on Screen: Postfeminism and Contemporary Adaptations of Victorian Women*, London: Palgrave Macmillan.

Read, J. (2000), *Feminism, Femininity, and the Rape Revenge Cycle*, Manchester: Manchester University Press.

Rowe, D.D. and K.R. Chávez (2011), 'Valerie Solanas and the Queer Performativity of Madness', *Cultural Studies <-> Critical Methodologies*, 11 (3): 274–84.

Schubart, R. (2007), *Super Bitches and Action Babes: The Female Hero in Popular Cinema, 1970–2006*, Jefferson, NC: Macfarland.

Schubart, R. (2017), 'The Journey: Vanessa Ives and Edgework as Self-Work', *Refractory: A Journal of Entertainment Media*, 28 (6): n.p. Available online: https://portal.findresearcher.sdu.dk/en/publications/the-journey-vanessa-ives-and-edgework-as-self-work (accessed 20 June 2023).

Solanas, V. (2004 [1967]), *The SCUM Manifesto*, London: Verso.

Shelley, M. (1994 [1818]), *Frankenstein; or The Modern Prometheus*, New York: Random House.

Taylor, A. (Forthcoming), *Germaine Greer: Celebrity, the Archive and Popular Feminism*, London: Routledge.

Third, A. (2006), '"Shooting from the Hip": Valerie Solanas, SCUM and the Apocalyptic Politics of Radical Feminism', *Hecate*, 32 (2): 104–32.

Wright, J. (2021), 'Unbridling the Bride: Feminism and Patriarchy in *Penny Dreadful*'s Frankenstein Narrative', *Journal of the Fantastic in the Arts*, 32 (10): 54–69.

Films and television series

The Bride of Frankenstein (1935), directed by James Whale [film], Universal City, CA: Universal Pictures.

Mary Shelley's Frankenstein (1994), directed by Kenneth Branagh [film], Culver City, CA: Tri Star Pictures.

Penny Dreadful (2014–16), directed by John Logan [TV series], UK and US: Neal Street Productions and Showtime Networks.

Part Five

Engaging the past through body horror

12

'Laden with human flesh': *Dying Breed* and Australia's engagement with its convict past

Clare Burnett

Introduction

'Few societies can have such a bleak beginning', remarks A. W. Baker of Australia's foundation as a British penal colony (1984: 32). The nation's relationship with its convict history has been volatile. At times, it has been conveniently ignored, at others employed as a cornerstone of a national identity, which 'accepted and even boasted of its convict foundations' (Hirst 2010: 59). One of the growing number of films re-examining Australia's relationship to its convict past, *Dying Breed* (2008), embraces the conventions of the backwoods horror movie, a 'landscape-specific subgenre' (Murphy 2020: 76) which includes US 'white trash' horror classics *Deliverance* (1972), *The Hills Have Eyes* (1977) and *The Texas Chainsaw Massacre* (1974), alongside Australia's own contribution, *Wolf Creek* (2006). *Dying Breed* features a group of young, middle-class tourists trapped in the sordid rural underbelly of Tasmania, threatened by forces specific to the locality – the 'cinematic cliché' of degenerate locals (Shelley 2012: 236). Here, the hillbillies or rednecks of US cinematic predecessors are recast as distinctively Australian, 'shaped by national mythologies and anxieties rooted in the post-colonial experience' (Ryan 2021: 98). The treatment of the rural poor within the American horror film has been extensively researched; by contrast, a focus on Australia's Gothicized landscape has restrained attempts to understand representations of its rural peoples within horror.

As manifestations of modern social, cultural and economic strains on rural communities in a largely metropolitan nation, *Dying Breed*'s locals can also be considered atavistic representations of Australia's dark and haunted history. Just as *The Hills Have Eyes* invokes the legend of Scottish cannibal Sawney Bean,

Dying Breed's monstrous family are the flesh-eating descendants of an infamous, real-life Tasmanian transportee and convict, Alexander Pearce, a 'man of horror and crime' according to contemporary Australian newspapers (Bonick 1857). Pearce was executed in Hobart in 1824 after absconding from the Van Diemen's Land penal colony twice, both times 'laden with the weight of human blood and believed to have banqueted on *human flesh*!' ('The Supreme Court of Van Diemen's Land' 1824). Pearce's story whetted appetites for sensation in the nineteenth century, feeding a fascination with cannibalism (Brown 2013). His legacy has maintained a stranglehold on the Australian imagination, influencing early writers such as Marcus Clarke, making appearances in early twentieth-century cinema (Stadler 2012) as well as its historical film dramas of the 2000s. But despite being one of the few horror films that engages with Australia's convict past, there has been little analysis of *Dying Breed* with its representations of Pearce and the convict mythology that surrounds him, an oversight this chapter will address.

Within a year of *Dying Breed*'s release, *Van Diemen's Land* (2009) and *The Last Confession of Alexander Pearce* (2009) appeared in cinemas, both focusing on Pearce within the sympathetic and realist confines of historical drama. But *Dying Breed* is significant for how, as a horror film, it exploits the dark histories with which modern Australia still grapples, situated as it is 'at the unpredictable and often painful juncture where past and present collide' (Lowenstein 2005: 9). Its sensationalized portrayal of the cannibal convict sets it apart from the realist depictions of historical drama films with similar subject matter and allows it to engage with fears about poverty, settlement, inheritance and isolation – enduring Australian anxieties that are not tied to a specific time or place. These fears are viewed through the history of the convict, a contested figure from the moment of Australia's origin as a modern nation – into which a chronicle of anxieties has been poured and whose impact on Australian culture 'has been swept under the carpet for years', according to *Dying Breed* director Jody Dwyer (Appleyard 2008). While Dwyer emphasizes histories that have been hidden and neglected, *Dying Breed* also itself perpetuates myths about early Australian history. For instance, it effectively erases the existence and experiences of Aboriginal Tasmanians, with the result that the Thylacine (or Tasmanian Tiger) – a figure of 'regret over the environmental impact of colonialism' (Rayner 2022: 122) – is the sole representative of pre-European Australia to appear in the film. However, despite its glaring omissions, the lurid excesses of its exploitation horror format and its questionable conceptualization of Tasmanian and Indigenous history,

Dying Breed nevertheless exposes and probes the painful convict legacy of Australia's founding, even as it rages against this traumatic past.

Convicts and cultural identity

In the late twentieth century, films such as *The Hills Have Eyes*, *The Blair Witch Project* (1999) and *Candyman* (1992) followed a long tradition within the horror genre that exploits legends to engage with and tell new stories about the past, often through the lens of the present. While 'realistic monsters' are nothing new in horror, it is less often that films directly repurpose a real-life 'bogeyman' such as Tasmania's Alexander Pearce, preferring instead a stand-in inspired by a real-life figure, whether it be Hannibal Lecter, Norman Bates or Leatherface. But Dwyer's aim in *Dying Breed* was to bring a specific rather than representative historical figure to life via popular entertainment (Appleyard 2008). Pearce's looming presence throughout Australia's history is symptomatic of the nation's ongoing fascination with the lawless and anti-authoritarian elements of its origins. This predilection resulted in the mythologization of outlaw bushrangers and a reframing of the convict 'as victim rather than agent of colonization' (Arrow and Findlay 2020: 3). Within *Dying Breed*, Pearce is both a victim of the imperial system and a perpetrator of the violence inherent in that historic system of subjugation. Thus, he represents a phase of contradiction in the process of cultural mediation which rewrote Australia's past 'from the point of view of the colonial subject, rather than from the point of view of the coloniser' (Turner 1993: 104). Emphasizing Pearce's role in these processes of history, *Dying Breed* disconcertingly opens as a historical drama, with a close-up of a quill writing the date and Pearce's name on parchment intercut with a confusingly violent chase sequence. At the sequence's conclusion this fictionalized Pearce (Peter Docker) rips out a British soldier's throat and offers the flesh to a passing thylacine. This prologue, followed by credits framed by blood-traced roots, locates the viewer in a moment of Australian history, mired in both the excessive violence and banal bureaucracy that engendered it. Conventionally, historical drama within the Australian film tradition has offered 'a peculiarly equivocal nationalism' (Turner 1989: 115), producing and reproducing Australian myths and images, and often locating them in the colonial past. However, as *Dying Breed*'s story unfolds, its juxtaposition of modern and historic interpretations of these myths disturbs and disrupts, seemingly in an attempt to dismantle these nationalistic conventions.

One of the destructive myths on which early Australia was built is that of *terra nullius* – that the land effectively belonged to no one and thus settlers could legally claim and exercise rights over that land. By the time *Dying Breed* was released, this myth had been exposed by landmark events such as the *Mabo* and *Wik* decisions in the 1980s and 1990s, which overturned the concept of *terra nullius* (Elder 2020). But this is not the only legal myth with which the nation has grappled. The arrival of convict settlers in the nineteenth century turned Australia into 'the dungeon of the world' (Turcotte 1998: 10). But the transportees were in fact relatively low-level British criminals sentenced to several years' transportation with a slim chance of returning home. Alexander Pearce himself was sentenced in 1819 in Ireland's County Monaghan to seven years' transportation for stealing six pairs of shoes (Byard and Maxwell-Stewart 2017). Legal boundaries then and now remain arbitrary and mutable but, as Katherine Biber (2005: 625) suggests, 'law always constructs an Other. It draws boundaries around itself. Everything within the boundary is within law's jurisdiction. Everything outside the boundary is lawless.' In this way, both Aboriginal peoples – who did not live within the social, cultural or political confines of the British imperial or subsequent federalized Australian system – and the convict – who was forcibly ejected from those categories – are seen as the Other. Pearce and his ilk represent in some ways 'the quintessential anti-authority figure, the Irish convict' (Hirst 2010: 60). In the absence of an active Indigenous presence in *Dying Breed*, the historic convict becomes uncomfortably associated with the nation's problematic beginnings, as well as the land itself. The Pearce clan, born from the horrors of the penal system – 'a tool of British imperialism' (Maxwell-Stewart and Quinlan 2022: 3) – believe they have right to the land and the bodies within it, for both sustenance and the continuation of their bloodline, mirroring and transmuting the nineteenth-century imperial justification for the subjugation of native peoples and the theft of land. Horrors were both inflicted upon and perpetrated by early convict settlers, who remained part of the imperial system while also being rejected and alienated by it. It is this victim/perpetrator dichotomy with which *Dying Breed* is engaged, differentiating itself from the 'convict as victim' trope of some historical dramas as part of the exercise it undertakes in problematizing Australian constructs of cultural identity. The lead police officer in the Pieman River region is seemingly an accomplice to the clan's violence – perhaps even a member himself – highlighting the mercurial loyalties and ambiguous boundaries of the law and its execution. This further adds to the feelings of isolation and hopelessness engendered in the film. There will be no recompense and no justice for the tourists stalked and murdered because there is no effective or impartial system of law and order to which they can appeal. The balance of power is decidedly in the hands of the Pearce family, in a vengeful inversion of their convict roots.

Dying Breed's invocation of the Alexander Pearce myth within the context of twenty-first-century horror highlights anxieties about Australian identity and self-perception, and the figure of the convict settler. A line of convoluted evolutionary development can be drawn between the convict, the bushranger and their relatively sanitized, modern reincarnations such as the 'larrikin', immortalized in the Ozploitation films of the 1970s and 1980s. These myths can be seen as 'ideologically dominant models of individual, collective and national identity' that were deployed across post-traumatic cultures, 'as a means of binding (hence isolating and concealing) the wounds of the past' (Blake 2008: 2). *Dying Breed*'s villainization of the Pearce family through its 'backwoods horror' narrative ensures they become mutated avatars of the 'pioneer' spirit and rugged individualism (Murphy 2013: 134) espoused within both US and Australian frontier and settler identities, but with the difference that they are descended from settlers who had no choice in their relocation.

Dying Breed uses body horror to violently stage a growing agitation over the glamourized figures of the bushranger and settler. For instance, one of the visitors to the backwoods town is Jack (*Wolf Creek*'s Nathan Phillips), a representative of the modern, urban-located larrikin figure that evolved from convict settler and bushranger legends. However, he is not characterized sympathetically through most of the film; purposely antagonizing the Pearce clan by slashing the tyres on their cars, he momentarily swings the pendulum of audience sympathy towards the hillbilly residents who are treated with disdain and disrespect by city-dwellers. While he attempts to retaliate against the cannibalistic family who killed his girlfriend, Rebecca (Melanie Vallejo), his efforts are ultimately futile and he is killed in an animal trap. This dimension of Australian identity is represented as shallow, focused on the pleasures of the body, as seen in Jack's pursuit of sexual relations with Rebecca and lack of empathy with Nina's ulterior motive for visiting the Tasmanian bush – to investigate the mysterious disappearance of her sister several years earlier. Jack and Matt (Leigh Whannell), Nina's cowardly and inconsequential partner, offer no acceptable alternatives to the Pearce clan. There are no heroes of the masculine variety to root for – which often cleaves the way for the 'final girl' as an emblem of hope (Clover 2015 [1992]). But even this is not to be. The surviving female visitor, Nina (Mirrah

Foulkes), is recaptured in the final scenes of *Dying Breed* and the cycle continues. The effect of the evisceration of these Australian cultural myths – the convict settler, the bushranger, the larrikin – leaves audiences with a problematic and disturbing sense that the foundational blocks of Australian cultural identity might be rotten at their core.

Due to their historical origins, these Australian identities are focused on the masculine. The Pearce clan is majority male. The mysterious Ethel (Elaine Hudson), whose role in and relationship with the family are ambiguous, and the child Katie (Sheridan Harvey) are the only female residents of the enclave. Neither is of reproductive age, so their uses to the Pearce men are limited. Horror and exploitation genres are replete with male-dominated communities centred around 'male violence against women' (Freeland 1995: 135). Likewise, a defining feature of early Australian history and culture is 'man's brutality to woman' (Phillips 1966: 74), particularly in convict settler communities where female convicts and freewomen were outnumbered by men (Alexander 2005). It is important to note, however, that it was Indigenous women who 'bore the brunt of patriarchal oppression' (Arrow and Findlay 2020: 6), with male colonists abducting, raping and killing Aboriginal women (Arrow and Findlay 2020: 5), bringing about the catastrophic decline in local Indigenous populations, especially in Tasmania. This gender-based violence was inevitably related to nationality, race and social status. In *Dying Breed*, Nina, played by an Australian actress but depicted as Irish, visits Australia for the first time with her boyfriend Matt. As a modern Irishwoman, she is directly contrasted with the Pearce family, which identifies itself as 'Irish, fifth generation' in a comparison that is almost laughable – one of the family members even does a poor imitation of an Irish jig, much to Nina's embarrassment. In Jennifer Kent's *The Nightingale* (2018), protagonist Clare's Irishness 'allows her to distance herself from the colonizers' (Arrow and Findlay 2020: 7), but in *Dying Breed*, nationality only emphasizes closeness with Pearce and his descendants. It also highlights the family's cultural ignorance and re-enforces the feeling that they are a community suspended in time with respect to their understanding of their own historical origins as well as their treatment of women. In *Dying Breed*, as in colonial Australia, this exploitation is partly sexual but also reproductive, reflecting a settler mythology that prioritizes the continuation of the colony. The young men of the Pearce clan, for instance, leer over the visiting women, and it becomes horrifically clear how they perceive the primary role of their female victims in flashbacks featuring Nina's sister. The ultimate goals of the violence they enact on the visitors are twofold: to consume and reproduce. Both activities are intended to ensure the continuation of the Pearce bloodline. As a sexually active couple, Jack and Rebecca are punished, not for the act of sex itself as a transgression, but because it does not result in reproduction that benefits the clan and ensures their continuation. The Pearce family have failed in the early settler mission of creating a self-sustaining community because they require constant, unwilling outside input to ensure their own continuation. They represent the horrific inversion of the 'familial harmony and orderly generational succession' (Hughes-d'Aeth 2019: 345) required and desired by settler colonies, located in abject territory and reliant on insular family and community units. Far from being part and parcel of an imagined rural idyll built by the individualistic and robust energies of settlers, this claustrophobic communal living is shown to breed insularity and stagnation, the jetsam that remains when the drive for colonization and settlement has been depleted and redirected elsewhere. Modernity does not reach this community in which generations live and die, and the only touchpoint with the outside world – the unwitting visitors who come across these enclaves – is treated with predatory suspicion.

Heredity and intergenerational criminality

The Pearce descendants wallow in poverty, surrounded by the detritus of civilization: rusting cars, worn-out tyres, discarded building materials and stray dogs. Shackles and photographs of manacled prisoners adorn the walls of the Trooper's Arms Hotel in the local township of Sarah – perhaps named for Pearce's real-life second escape from Sarah Island – in pride of place and as a memorial of their convict past. The outward chaos and decrepitude of the Pearce outpost – like that of another film about degenerate locals, the Australian horror comedy *The Cars That Ate Paris* (1974) – is a reflection of the corruption and disorder within. They are Tasmanian inbred stereotypes that 'exist at the edge of the world of credibility and reason' (Moran and Vieth 2006: 105), both geographically and metaphorically. Their convict past is represented as a 'poisoned inheritance' (Rayner 2022: 122), which corrupts and remains potent enough to create monsters in the present.

The Pearce descendants present an alternative history, one in which Australia never developed into an urbanized and relatively multicultural nation, highlighting the horror of a society unwilling to change or move on from its past. Their isolation allows the perpetuation of the original trauma of the convict experience and their insularity has promoted a belief in the superiority and infallibility of their bloodlines, used as justification for violence. They can be seen as an incarnation of the nineteenth-century scientific perception that acquired traits, which at the time included criminality, 'are preserved by heredity and passed on by descendants' (Rafter, Posick and Rocque 2016: 100). The logical conclusion if the Pearce family are avatars of this intergenerational criminality is that they will become capable of any transgression, even the unthinkable – whether that be inbreeding or cannibalism. The worst member of the family is portrayed as an inbred monster akin to those of *The Hills Have Eyes*. His physical deformity marks the nadir of this intergenerational process of devolution, in 'striking contrast with the obvious good health of [his] conventionally attractive middle-class victims' (Murphy 2020: 80). However, most of the Pearce clan look on the surface physically normal – save for their teeth – indicating that the introduction of genetic diversity through the rape of visiting women has countered any inbreeding. Some members of the clan have identified the obvious need to diversify the gene pool. Ethel kills a litter of inbred puppies in front of Nina and Katie, muttering, 'Parents were brother and sister. I tried to keep them apart. I warned them this would happen. It always does.'

An obsession with breeding and the preservation of the family line runs throughout the film, and becomes inextricably linked to anthropophagy, to the point where the practice has secured a sacred place in Pearce family traditions. Indeed, some of the most horrific scenes in *Dying Breed* are related to food and consumption, mouths and teeth. There is a bucket of bloody tissues in the town's 'Surgery' which is revealed via flashbacks to contain the teeth of victims, and the child Katie is ultimately shown to have sharpened teeth. Jack, Matt and Nina find the dismembered and hanging corpse of Rebecca being prepared for consumption, and the pies that are sold at the town's Pieman Bakery have some suspiciously crunchy additions. The cannibalism is also historicized – the 'Pieman' rhyme sung by Katie is a bastardized version of the eighteenth-century English nursery rhyme 'Simple Simon'. It is unclear when the link between Pearce and the 'Pieman' was first made. Although he was described in early twentieth-century newspaper accounts as a 'pieman in Hobart Town' (Anon 1916), historians have suggested there was no evidence that Pearce engaged in this profession (Stadler 2012). However, this association invokes the character of Sweeney Todd, who first appeared in 'The String of Pearls', a penny dreadful published in England in the 1840s (Haugtvedt 2016). Grafting the legend of a cannibalistic barber, whose accomplice baked his victims into pies, onto a real-life Tasmanian figure who himself became mythologized blurs the lines between real life, myth and fiction, also the tension between Australian culture and the imperial cultures that had preceded and informed it. Cannibalism during the time of the real Alexander Pearce was attributed to the 'uncivilized and primitive' Other, for the purpose of asserting white superiority over 'savage' natives, and thus justifying the colonization and subjugation of Indigenous peoples (Daniel 2003: 7). It is a powerful trope in colonial discourses, which 'disclose the fear of the native "Other"' (Biber 2005: 624), although of course there is no credible evidence to suggest Indigenous Australians practised the cannibalism ascribed to them by early colonists (Biber 2005: 625).

Tales of cannibalism among desperate and starving Europeans lost in the Outback or on the run were often framed in individualistic rather than communal terms – tarring only the desperate criminals with the brush of deviant behaviour rather than an entire peoples, allowing Europeans to dissociate from the practice by ensuring it remained within the cultural realm of the Other. Thus, the 'white cannibal' Pearce appeared to nineteenth-century audiences to have 'gone native' (Anon 1916). Despite attempts to distance themselves from it, cannibalism was nonetheless pervasive within narratives about the colonial period. As a result, it has been perceived as a projection of the European's own desire to consume and assimilate. Within the Pearce clan, cannibalism serves this purpose, incorporating outsiders in an attempt to keep 'its "tradition" and "culture" alive' (Bullock 2011: 74). Distinct from its US counterparts, the Pearce family's anthropophagy is a perverse inversion of the British imperial overlord's obsession with aristocratic blood and the purity of the bloodlines. But the 'failure of dynastic ambition' is also a common theme in settler narratives (Hughes-d'Aeth 2019: 374), indicating a collapse of the colonizing exercise that the members of the Pearce family have fought at all costs, repeating the acts of depravity again and again and thus the trauma of convictism and colonialism 'by turning it inward' (Lowenstein 2005). However, the real and more immediate horror within *Dying Breed* comes from the connections supposedly 'modern' Australians have with the archaic violence and aberrations of the Pearce family. Rebecca realizes that the cannibal child Katie is the result of the rape of her sister and is therefore her niece, tying her forever to the family. The existence of this child as the next generation and a continuation of the cannibal legacy emphasizes the role of intergenerational trauma, symbolizing how horrible and violent legacies of the past continue to impact Australia in the present. Legends like that of Pearce exist in cultural memory, and are passed on to succeeding generations (Sinha and McSweeney 2012: 11), an insidious canker that grows over the years, encoded in each iteration with a different set of anxieties layered over those that came before. The potential for these traumatic memories to be perpetuated within modern Australia contributes to the air of horror that lingers around them.

As in the American backwoods horror film, which conventionally takes place in the South or West, the historicized depravity of *Dying Breed* can only exist in certain isolated areas. Tasmania's claustrophobic bush plays the same role as Western Australia's Outback in *Wolf Creek*, the Georgian wilderness in *Deliverance* and the Nevada desert in *The Hills Have Eyes*. The invocation of these rural locations reflects the negative perception and cultural attributes ascribed to the area by the rest of the nation (Murphy 2013: 136). Like the 'nightmarish' American South or its arid, unpopulated West, Tasmania is a place where national audiences could 'localize certain anxieties – without feeling threatened themselves' (Murphy 2013: 137). Like the American South, the state has even been described as 'Australia's geographical unconscious, a place where repressed national histories, fears, self-loathings and insecurities might be displaced' (Bullock 2011: 73). However, Tasmania, like Australia, generally lacked highly stratified social structures, which resulted in the establishment of privileged upper classes and their reliance on slavery, causing the denigration of the rural poor as it had done in the United States (Murphy 2013). In contrast to the American South, Tasmania, formerly known as Van Diemen's Land, was 'the only state which systematically set about erasing its first half-century; under a new name, it was determined to be born again' (Davidson 1989: 307). The horrific potential of this history was fully realized cinematically in the early twentieth century with films such as *For the Term of His Natural Life* (1927), filmed partially in Tasmania's Port Arthur and other locations, despite the huge practical challenges of filming in a place that could be so inhospitable (Bullock 2011: 72). The unfamiliar rigours of wilderness survival had led some of Pearce's fellow escapees to decide that 'chains, flogging, and labours were preferable to that living death of misery' (Bonick 1857) – the misery, that is, of attempting to exist in the Tasmanian bush. However, Tasmania's history and landscape are too complex for it to be merely symbolically utilized 'to project the protagonist's psychic state' (Stadler 2012) or to encapsulate within its boundaries all the problematic issues of Australian history. The perception of Tasmania's wilderness as a landscape on the margins and a location of repression was applied by early settlers to Australia generally, and in *Dying Breed* Tasmania marks the last outpost of this suppressed history. Australia has been ascribed with 'a sense of spiritual darkness emanating from the land itself, a feeling of primeval cruelty fed ... by the guilty sense that man has forced his will upon the earth without the hallowing of ritual' (Phillips 1966: 81). This begs the question whether the Pearce family of *Dying Breed* is a product of this spiritual darkness, or a cause of it. Are their cruelty and violence a result of their historic imposition on the land, however unwitting that was initially, or have they been engendered by this land? In Dwyer's rendition, the question remains hanging in the oppressive air of the Tasmanian bush.

Australian national trauma exposed

Dying Breed was released at a time when filmmakers had begun engaging with alternative discourses regarding Australian identity and national history while exploring the possibilities of genre-based storytelling. Previously, the industry was dominated by nationalist cultural policy (Turner 1993) and exploitation films of a different kind – the Ozploitation film of the 1970s and 1980s (Ryan 2009b). Despite Gothic antecedents such as *Picnic at Hanging Rock* (1975), or 'Ozploitation horror' films such as *Night of Fear* (1972), *Turkey Shoot* (1982) and *Razorback* (1984), horror was a mode 'rarely associated with Australian cinema' until its rebirth in the twenty-first century (Ryan 2009a). Since then and despite attempts to box it within Australian Gothic or Ozploitation categories, Australian horror has experienced significant growth, to become an entertainment staple within the nation's film tradition (Ryan 2021) – proof, perhaps, that there are indeed 'deep seams of horror in the Australian psyche' (Moran and Vieth 2006: 106). Outside the horror genre, twenty-first-century filmmakers appear less concerned than their predecessors about the international reputational implications of 'publicizing Australia's shameful convict history' (Stadler 2012). And, films from very different moments in Australia's recent history, from *Rabbit-Proof Fence* (2002) to *The Nightingale* (2018), sought to '[provoke] a public reckoning with Australia's violent settler-colonial past' (Arrow and Findlay 2020: 4), even when that engagement was at odds with prevailing public discourses about convict and settler legacies. That these contradictory histories were being depicted and probed on screen signalled a shift in Australian cinema's response to its national history from one of 'compensation to confrontation' (Lowenstein

2005: 8). However, few Australian horror films directly engaged with the nation's convict past until *Dying Breed*.

While *Dying Breed* never reached quite the critical or commercial heights of other Australian horror outputs (Byrnes 2008), it represented a shift in the films in which government funding bodies would invest, with Film Finance Corporation Australia (now Screen Australia) investing $1 million towards its $2.9 million budget (Ryan 2009a) after a sharp decline in horror movie production during the 1990s as a result of bias among funding bodies (Ryan 2021). The commercial and/or critical potential for Australian films that did not portray a positive or flattering view of Australia's history was being realized. This underlined the growing internal confidence in Australian productions, and the recognition of Australian genre filmmaking within paracinema discourses, revealing 'a more secure cultural position that is less concerned with "Americanization" of Australian culture, and the imperative to construct nationalist notions of identity and difference' (Thomas 2010: 240). That is not to say that the American influence on Australian film had diminished, just that filmmakers were less self-conscious about borrowing from their US counterparts. *Dying Breed* nods to classic US horror with the obvious allusions to *The Texas Chainsaw Massacre* and *The Hills Have Eyes*, to the 'peeping tom' scene suggestive of the infamous sequence in *Psycho* (1960) and the aerial shots of the Tasmanian wilderness reminiscent of the Torrance family's road trip to the Overlook Hotel in Stanley Kubrick's *The Shining* (1980). Such moments resonate with the idea that 'the horror genre lends itself to … globalization as the motifs and narratives are not linked to a particular country' (Moran and Vieth 2006: 110). Director Jody Dwyer himself said in an interview in 2008:

> *Dying Breed* is culturally relevant without being parochial and that's important if it is to be commercially viable in overseas markets. It's kind of interesting and ironic that a lot of the praise in NYC (at the Tribeca Festival) was the fact that it wasn't 'typically Aussie'. That's a branding issue since distributors tend to categorise Australian as art house. Not so here – watch *Dying Breed* in your local Hoyts.
>
> (quoted in Appleyard 2008)

Working within a well-trodden genre ensures that themes, and even national and local histories, are penetrable to international audiences. This penetrability, however, should not be overstated. With regard to *The Nightingale*, released ten years after *Dying Breed*, international critics were accused of focusing on genre rather than subject matter, 'reflecting their bafflement and unfamiliarity with Australian colonial history' (Arrow and Findlay 2020: 10). *Dying Breed*, however, gives enough genre-based cues to international audiences to ensure they will understand the implications of tropes and portrayals even without a good grasp of Australian history. Working with the darker elements of Australia's history within the horror genre would have been inconceivable through much of the twentieth century. Not only was it unlikely to be a commercial hit, but it would also have been considered 'an affront to "quality" Australian cinema' (Ryan 2009b: 47). However, instead of 'reproducing images of Australia that audiences found familiar' (Turner 1989: 114) as a film within the horror and exploitation genres, *Dying Breed* is expected and even encouraged to work outside these national conventions. While partly repurposing well-understood and even homogenized film traditions, Australian filmmakers have been able to contribute to the richness of international horror by tapping into their own national and cultural anxieties. Within *Dying Breed*, conventions of Ozploitation films and historical dramas on which Australian film traditions have been built are subverted. The 'history' portrayed in the film is mythologized and unnatural, the result of the escape of a near-legendary convict figure, an almost supernatural encounter with a thylacine and the improbable survival of a clan of cannibalistic rapists for nearly 200 years in the wilds of Tasmania. Being unburdened of this wider political and cultural pressure to paint Australia in a positive light allows films such as *Dying Breed* to sensationalize the horror of reality and encourage a re-evaluation of Australian history that is perceived through and ingrained in a domestic culture, which itself has previously been simplified, repackaged and commodified for global consumption.

Conclusion

Dying Breed has been called an 'unapologetic genre film' (Millar 2008: 19), and its awareness of the historic and cinematic traditions from which it has evolved can at times be both its strength and its weakness. Australia's twenty-first-century wave of low-budget horror, of which *Dying Breed* is a part, coincided with a re-examination of national cultural identity, and has even led to the argument that the horror film has given a new lease of life to the Ozploitation-style film (Thomas 2010). If those Ozploitation films provided an opportunity to commercialize and define, in a limited and limiting way, the Australian experience for international audiences in the twentieth century, the horror genre in the twenty-first century allows this identity to be revisited, exposed and re-examined. It is a contested viewpoint, but scholars such as Linnie Blake (2008: 4) suggest that, as a genre that encourages engagement with historical trauma, to produce and watch a horror film can be considered an act of catharsis. While not going quite so far as to ascribe a cathartic effect, there is merit in questioning the historical arguments a film is making about the past it depicts and situating those films in the culture that produced them (Arrow and Findlay 2020: 5). Yet, in fictionalizing these histories, we run the risk of divorcing ourselves of the real-world implications and complexities of historical anxieties, including the intergenerational trauma of a complex colonial legacy. This is particularly pertinent question for 'cinema's second most censored' after pornography (Petley 2014: 130) – long critiqued for its engagement with superficial conventions such as jump scares or morbid and excessive violence. Australian film has become increasingly willing to engage with these dark histories that engage with convictism, the treatment of Aboriginal peoples and the rural poor. Representation has become a key issue in modern Australia following milestones such as the Reconciliation process and the 2017 Uluru Statement, both aimed at improved relations and representation of the Indigenous communities with the federal government and wider Australian communities (Elder 2020). As a result, attitudes have shifted even in the comparatively short time between the release of *Dying Breed* and today. But this and other films released in the 2000s join the ongoing and increasingly complex discourses about the lasting impact of some of the distasteful elements of Australia's history. Using warped historical truth and an interplay between myths, legends and reality, *Dying Breed* contributes to the iterative process of defining national identity in a globalized world, ultimately prompting a renegotiation of our understanding of the ongoing impacts of our turbulent and troubled history.

References

Alexander, A. (2005), 'Gender', in *The Companion to Tasmanian History*, edited by A. Alexander, 444–50, Hobart: Centre for Tasmanian Historical Studies, University of Tasmania.

Anon (1916), 'Memories of a White Cannibal', *Richmond River Herald and Northern Districts Advertiser*, 11 February, 7.

Appleyard, R. (2008), 'Behind the Scenes of Dying Breed', *If.com.au*, 10 November. Available online: https://if.com.au/behind-the-scenes-of-dying-breed (accessed 22 June 2023).

Arrow, M. and J. Findlay (2020), 'A Critical Introduction to *The Nightingale*: Gender, Race and Troubled Histories on Screen', *Studies in Australasian Cinema*, 14 (1): 3–14.

Baker, A.W. (1984), *Death Is a Good Solution: The Convict Experience in Early Australia*, Brisbane: University of Queensland Press.

Biber, K. (2005), 'Cannibals and Colonialism', *Sydney Law Review*, 27 (4): 623–37.

Blake, L. (2008), *The Wounds of Nations: Horror Cinema, Historical Trauma and National Identity*, Manchester: Manchester University Press.

Bonick, J. (1857), 'The Bushrangers, Illustrating the Early Days of Van Diemen's Land', *Northern Times* (Newcastle, NSW), 3 January, 3.

Brown, J. (2013), *Cannibalism in Literature and Film*, Basingstoke: Palgrave Macmillan.

Bullock, E. (2011), 'Rumblings from Australia's Deep South: Tasmanian Gothic On-screen', *Studies in Australasian Cinema*, 5 (1): 71–80.

Byard, R.W. and H. Maxwell-Stewart (2017), 'Cannibalism amongst Penitentiary Escapees from Sarah Island in Nineteenth Century Van Diemen's Land', *Forensic Science, Medicine and Pathology*, 14: 410–15.

Byrnes, P. (2008), 'Dying Breed', *Sydney Morning Herald*, 7 November. Available online: https://www.smh.com.au/entertainment/movies/dying-breed-20081107-gdt1ui.html (accessed 22 June 2023).

Clover, C.J. (2015 [1992]), *Men Women and Chainsaws: Gender in the Modern Horror Film*, Princeton, NJ: Princeton University Press.

Craven, I. (2012), *Australian Cinema in the 1990s*, London: Frank Cass.

Daniel, C. (2003), 'Hairy on the Inside: From Cannibals to Paedophiles', *Papers: Explorations into Children's Literature*, 13 (December): 5–21.

Davidson, J. (1989), 'Tasmanian Gothic', *Meanjin*, 48: 307–24.

Elder, C. (2020), '"Brutal" and "Grisly": Exploring the (Non-Indigenous) Critical Reception to Two Australian Postcolonial Films of the Frontier', *The Nightingale* (2018) and *The Proposition* (2005)', *Studies in Australasian Cinema*, 14 (1): 47–62.

Freeland, C. (1995), 'Realist Horror', in *Philosophy and Film*, edited by C. Freeland and T.E. Wartenberg, 126–42. London: Routledge.

Haugtvedt, E. (2016), 'Sweeney Todd as Victorian Transmedial Storyworld', *Victorian Periodicals Review*, 49 (3): 443–60.

Hirst, J. (2010), *Looking for Australia: Historical Essays*, Melbourne: Black Inc.

Hughes-d'Aeth, T. (2019), 'Settlers of the Marsh: Settler Desire and Its Vicissitudes', *Settler Colonial Studies*, 9 (3): 341–57.

Lowenstein, A. (2005), *Shocking Representation: Historical Trauma, National Cinema, and the Modern Horror Film*, New York: Columbia University Press.

Maxwell-Stewart, H. and M. Quinlan (2022), *Unfree Workers: Insubordination and Resistance in Convict Australia, 1788–1860*, Singapore: Palgrave Macmillan.

Millar, C. (2008), 'The Horror! The Horror! Tasmania's Cannibal History on the Silver Screen', *Metro Magazine*, 159: 17–21.

Moran, A. and E. Vieth (2006), *Film in Australia: An Introduction*, Cambridge: Cambridge University Press.

Murphy, B.M. (2013), *The Rural Gothic in American Popular Culture: Backwoods Horror and Terror in the Wilderness*, Basingstoke: Palgrave Macmillan.

Murphy, B.M. (2020), 'Place, Space, and the Reconfiguration of "White Trash" Monstrosity', in *Jordan Peele's Get Out: Political Horror*, edited by D. Keetley, 72–86, Columbus, OH: Ohio State University Press.

Petley, J. (2014), 'Horror and the Censors', in *A Companion to the Horror Film*, edited by H.M. Benshoff, 130–48. Chichester: Wiley.

Phillips, A.A. (1966), *The Australian Tradition: Studies in a Colonial Culture*, Melbourne: Longman Cheshire.

Rafter, N., C. Posick and M. Rocque (2016), *The Criminal Brain: Understanding Biological Theories of Crime*, New York: New York University Press.

Rayner, J. (2022), *Australian Gothic: A Cinema of Horrors*, Cardiff: University of Wales Press.

Ryan, M.D. (2009a), 'A Dark New World: Anatomy of Australian Horror films', PhD thesis, Queensland University of Technology.

Ryan, M.D. (2009b), 'Whither Culture? Australian Horror Films and the Limitations of Cultural Policy', *Media International Australia*, 133 (1): 43–55.

Ryan, M.D. (2021), 'A Monstrous Landscape Filled with Killer Animals and Madmen: Tropes of Contemporary Australian Horror Movie', in *Australian Genre Film*, edited by K. McWilliam and M.D. Ryan, 90–108, New York: Routledge.

Shelley, P. (2012), *Australian Horror Films, 1973–2010*, Jefferson, NC: McFarland & Company.

Sinha, A. and T. McSweeney (2012), *Millennial Cinema: Memory in Global Film*, New York: Columbia University Press.

Stadler, J. (2012), 'Mapping the Cinematic Journey of Alexander Pearce, Cannibal Convict', *Screening the Past*, 34: 1–23.

'The Supreme Court of Van Dieman's Land' (1824), *Hobart Town Gazette and Van Diemen's Land Advertiser*, 25 June, 2.

Thomas, D. (2010), 'Ozploitation', in *Directory of World Cinema*, edited by B. Goldsmith and G. Lealand, 6–15. Bristol: Intellect.

Turcotte, G. (1998), 'Australian Gothic', in *The Handbook of Gothic Literature*, edited by M.M. Roberts, 10–19, Basingstoke: Palgrave Macmillan.

Turner, G. (1989), 'Art Directing History: The Period Film', in *The Australian Screen*, edited by A. Moran and T. O'Regan, 99–117, Ringwood: Penguin.

Turner, G. (1993), 'The Genres Are American: Australian Narrative, Australian Film and the Problem of Genre (The Australian Cinema)', *Literature-Film Quarterly*, 21: 102–10.

Films

The Blair Witch Project (1999), directed by Daniel Myrick and Eduardo Sánchez [film], United States: Haxan Films.
Candyman (1992), directed by Bernard Rose [film], United States: Propaganda Films and Polygram Filmed Entertainment.
The Cars That Ate Paris (1974), directed by Peter Weir [film], Australia: Royce Smeal Film Productions and Salt Pan Films.
Deliverance (1972), directed by John Boorman [film], United States: Warner Bros.
Dying Breed (2008), directed by J. Dwyer [film], Australia: Ambience Entertainment.
For the Term of His Natural Life (1927), directed by Norman Dawn [film], Australia: Australasian Films.
The Hills Have Eyes (1977), directed by Wes Craven [film], United States: Blood Relations Company.
The Last Confession of Alexander Pearce (2009), directed by Michael James Rowland [film], Australia: Hopscotch Films.
Night of Fear (1972), directed by Terry Bourke [film], Australia: Terryrod.
The Nightingale (2018), directed by Jennifer Kent [film], Australia: Causeway Films.
Picnic at Hanging Rock (1975), directed by Peter Weir [film], Australia: McElroy and McElroy.
Psycho (1960), directed by Alfred Hitchcock [film], United States: Shamley Productions.
Rabbit-Proof Fence (2002), directed by Phillip Noyce [film], Australia: Rumalara Films.
Razorback (1984), directed by Russell Mulcahy [film], Australia: McElroy and McElroy.
The Shining (1980), directed by Stanley Kubrick [film], United States and United Kingdom: Hawk Films and The Producer Circle Company.
The Texas Chainsaw Massacre (1974), directed by Tobe Hooper [film], United States: Vortex.
Turkey Shoot (1982), directed by Brian Trenchard-Smith [film], Australia: Hemdale.
Van Diemen's Land (2009), directed by Jonathan Auf der Heide [film], Australia: Noise & Light Pty Ltd
Wolf Creek (2006), directed by Greg McLean [film], Australia: 403 Productions.

13

Killing Private Zombie: *Overlord* and the twenty-first-century military horror film

Brian E. Crim

Overlord (2018) begins with Winston Churchill, Adolf Hitler and the commanding voice of General Dwight Eisenhower narrating what is ostensibly a dramatic recreation of the invasion of Normandy. In an edited version of his 'Order of the Day' speech, Eisenhower (1944) announces 'the great crusade' to destroy 'Nazi tyranny' and the German war machine.[1] As the credits fade, we enter the interior of a Douglas C-47 troop transport hurtling across the English Channel on the night of 5 June 1944. Two rows of paratroopers nervously eye one another and make small talk until the menacing Sergeant Rensin (Bokeem Woodbine) barks commands and fiery condemnations of the enemy. A shell pierces the C-47, killing a dozen men instantly and sending the plane into a tailspin. Rensin drags a handful of survivors with him and jumps into the void as the C-47 explodes above them. We plummet into the unknown with the unit and experience the action through the eyes of the affable and very green Private Boyce (Jovan Adepo). We know from history (and previous war films) that the 101st Airborne became scattered across Normandy, often landing miles from their intended drop zones. Survivors of the fictional airborne unit depicted in *Overlord* seemingly face the same dangers as the real paratroopers on that fateful night. Once on the ground, the unit's mission evolves from taking out a radio tower in a small French village to destroying a secret Nazi lab perilously close to creating indestructible zombie super soldiers. What begins as a stunning cinematic recreation of the airborne operations preceding D-Day, displaying all the hallmarks of the World War II combat film, gradually shifts into a horror film.

Like the paratroopers converging on their target, *Overlord*'s audience anticipates conventional dangers from conventional enemies. The first twenty minutes of *Saving Private Ryan* (1998) conditioned us to expect that any subsequent depiction of D-Day would include the worst sort of body horror imaginable. Ultimately, *Overlord* integrates several genres: Nazisploitation, military horror (including Gothic horror) and the Second World War combat film. Military horror is a hybrid genre defined by Steffen Hantke in which the horrors of war collide with the supernatural. 'The bottom line of war films – "war is hell" – applies to military horror films as well', Hantke (2010: 702) notes. 'The only difference is that, in military horror films, it really is.' Using Hantke's article and Jeanine Basinger's (2003) work on the Second World War film as a point of departure, this chapter first argues that *Overlord* represents an evolution in the military horror film by rejecting the genre's typically anti-war messaging and depicting a 'post-racial' integrated American military capable of defeating a supernatural force. As I demonstrate, *Overlord* depicts a fantasy of patriotic racial unity to combat the normalization of white supremacist rhetoric during the Trump presidency. Black and Jewish protagonists saving the day offers a reimagined version of American greatness, one that stands in stark contrast to the vision of the 'Unite the Right' rioters in Charlottesville in August 2017. Previous military horror films typically feature immoral and incompetent military organizations systematically butchered by a monstrous foe. By contrast, the enemy is not us in *Overlord* – as is usually the subtext of military horror – but the murderous fascist ideology responsible for the horror scenario. Private Boyce is transformed into a heroic figure, one with free will and a healthy cynicism to authority, while those around him, including his superior, Corporal Ford (Wyatt Russell), devolve into monsters.

After discussing *Overlord*'s relationship with military horror and the combat film, I argue that *Overlord* pays homage to the 'Nazisploitation' films of the 1960s and 1970s, but without trivializing the Holocaust and Nazi war crimes. 'Where Nazisploitation was once taboo', Daniel Magilow (2012: 6) writes in the introduction to a volume evaluating its cultural and historical legacies, 'today its motifs and narrative conceits have permeated big budget studio productions and mainstream pop culture'. Nazisploitation films often depict vampires, zombies and other monstrosities stalking Europe, either during the war or in the present. In the case of *Overlord*, I maintain the film is noteworthy for its unequivocal anti-fascist message and its portrayal of a diverse group of protagonists who destroy an existential threat. While most reviewers dismiss *Overlord* as no more than a serviceable military horror film thanks in large part to producer J.J. Abrams' special effects budget, I interpret it as a cultural response to the rise of far-right extremism in the United States since the election of Donald Trump, demonstrated by the 'Unite the Right' rally. *Overlord* does not condemn war or even expose America's racial hypocrisy; instead, it offers an alternative fantasy of the past, a mythic America that defeated an evil, white supremacist ideology capable of turning its followers into actual monsters. Thus, *Overlord* drapes itself in the trappings of Nazisploitation (monsters, hyperviolence and the trope of the mad scientist), but it also endeavours to appeal to our latent patriotism through its revision of the US combat film by reminding us that Nazi ideology never truly dies. If we were able to beat it before, we can beat it again.

The opposing worldviews represented by the MAGA-inspired white supremacy present in Charlottesville on one hand and *Overlord*'s fantasy of patriotic racial unity on the other can be viewed in terms of Svetlana Boym's (2001: 41–50) distinctions between 'restorative' and 'reflective' nostalgia. Restorative nostalgia 'obliterates history' and seeks 'truth' in a comforting national mythology (Boym 2011). Restorative nostalgics are drawn to conspiracies, such as 'The Great Replacement Theory' or George Soros's supposed sinister plots to erode American sovereignty.[2] 'Ambivalence, the complexity of history and the specificity of modern circumstances are thus erased', writes Boym (2001: 43), 'and modern history is seen as a fulfilment of ancient prophecy'. Traditional World War II combat films contribute to restorative nostalgia by imagining a united, patriotic and selfless – and predominantly white – nation defeating evil forces. *Overlord* includes elements of the combat film to be sure, but it does so with irony and dark humour, two characteristics of reflective nostalgia. *Overlord*'s premise – Nazi zombies unleashed on D-Day – is absurd but, as I argue here, that makes it all the more subversive. Usefully, Boym (2001: 49) notes that the focus of reflective nostalgia:

> is not on recovery of what is perceived to be an absolute truth but on the meditation on history and passage of time. Reflective nostalgia has the potential to cast doubt on comforting myths and celebrates the 'multitude of potentialities' when revisiting the past.

Reflective nostalgics appreciate that apocryphal cultural representation, such as Black and Jewish heroes playing central roles in a Second World War-era film, to disrupt restorative nostalgia's absolutist worldview.

Overlord's critical reception split between those who appreciated its timely and unsubtle sub-text and those who regarded it as another forgettable piece of Nazisploitation. William Lowery (2018) seems to present the consensus opinion, writing that *Overlord* is an entertaining mash-up of previous films, especially *Saving Private Ryan* and *Inglourious Basterds* (2009), and video-games like *Wolfenstein* (2009) and *Call of Duty* (2003–). *Overlord*, he writes, combines 'the heroism of classic war movies [with] campy horror'. Andrew Cripes (2018) is offended by *Overlord* and its cavalier treatment of real historical trauma, calling it 'an ill-advised creation, one that isn't intentionally insulting but rather cringe-inducingly unaware of its irresponsibility'. Cripes believes *Overlord* 'doesn't want its viewers to be troubled by history' and regards the graphic experiments on human subjects too close to reality to 'mine for fantasy'. Papers of record like the *New York Times* and *The Guardian* were underwhelmed by *Overlord* and chose not to comment on its dramatic rewrite of American racial history. Bilge Ebiri (2018) notes, 'The film doesn't try to surprise us with narrative revelations so much as it tries to jolt us with gore'. *The Guardian*'s Charles Bramesco (2018) declares *Overlord* an 'apolitical movie about Nazis' that 'doesn't have much to say … other than they were decidedly bad folks, tinkering with the laws of nature and science behind the scenes of combat'. This chapter disputes Bramesco's (2018) dismissive review, particularly its closing remark: '*Overlord* has no discernible interest in making a statement, and at present, that feels less like a creative choice and more like an omission'. The *Chicago Tribune*'s Amy Nicholson (2018) critiques *Overlord*, yet also points to how it contributes to political discourse during the Trump years, describing it as 'a jingoistic throwback to a time of moral clarity when there weren't very fine people on both sides'. Referencing Charlottesville, Nicholson concludes that *Overlord* might have the potential to shock those 'who mistakenly think white supremacy is a lark' back into reality: 'If it peels a few [trolls] away from buying tiki torches, it deserves a Nobel Peace Prize. Otherwise, it's junk food patriotism – but there's a grumbling hunger for it' (2018).

Overlord as military horror

Overlord is easily recognizable as military horror with some important differences, but it also adheres faithfully to the formula of the World War II combat film as defined by film historian Jeanine Basinger (2003). Having screened hundreds of films spanning five decades, Basinger (2003: 124) recognized that the combat film 'has a curious affinity for the horror movie' because of how filmmakers introduce the enemy on screen and create suspense. Why does every generation continue to revisit the Second World War? As Basinger writes, 'World War II seems to be the combat that speaks to the American soul. Perhaps it is our total victory, or the sense of righteousness, or the conviction that it wasn't our fault' (2003: 75). Basinger traces the genre's evolution from the first films produced just months after Pearl Harbor to *Saving Private Ryan* in 1998, noting that, despite shifting ideological and commercial considerations, every combat film deploys three elements: hero, group and objective: 'What we see from the evolutionary process is that a useful container has been built – a set of characters and situations that are familiar and that can be used to teach us new things we need to know' (2003: 198). Basinger concludes, 'If the new ideologies, problems, and pressures can fit into the old genre, it will remain alive' (2003: 198). *Overlord* passes what Basinger terms 'the Kilroy Test', a signature 'everyone recognizes and accepts' when viewing a combat film (2003: 16). Basinger outlines five waves of the World War II combat film before 2000, each reflecting the unique political and social context of the era in which the films were produced. To these I believe we should add a sixth wave, marking a change in the genre since the cultural rupture after 9/11. Films like *Fury* (2014), for example, are influenced by a decade of brutal and endless conflicts in Iraq and Afghanistan. The protagonists in *Fury* are certainly conventional characters rooted in the combat genre, but their behaviour disturbs and shocks audiences conditioned to seeing their World War II heroes bend but not break (Crim 2018a: 4–14).

Overlord, on the other hand, is a throwback to older films like *Bataan* (1943), which Basinger credits as the archetypical World War II combat film. Both feature uncomplicated characters meant to represent a diverse and principled American military. The Office of War Information's 1942 *Government Information Manual for the Motion Picture Industry* instructed Hollywood to represent the country as 'a melting pot, a nation of many races and creeds', whose citizens 'have demonstrated that they can live together and progress' (Locke 2008: 12). *Bataan*'s band of ill-fated soldiers includes Americans from all walks of life, but the breakthrough characters are Private Wesley Epps (Kenneth Spencer), a Black soldier with a substantive role in the plot, and Yankee Salazar (Alex Havier), a Filipino anxious to fight the Japanese alongside Americans. As Brian Locke (2008: 10) writes, like the Nazis in *Overlord*, the Japanese are represented as monstrous and unrelenting, 'a strange mix of sub- and superhuman'. Locke (2008: 16) demonstrates that *Bataan*'s 'melting pot' platoon served the agenda of the Office of War Information by deflecting attention from America's own racism and imperialism while foregrounding the savage bigotry of the Asian enemy. This 'scapegoat effect' is a staple of World War II combat films, specifically those set in the Pacific. *Bataan*'s 'tokenism' is intended to 'dispel the notion of American hypocrisy about democracy' while still maintaining the existing racial hierarchy. According to a 1943 OWI poll evaluating racial attitudes, 'whites overwhelmingly endorse segregation' (quoted in Locke 2008: 13). Equality certainly has its limits in *Bataan*, as evidenced by the particularly graphic and brutal deaths of Epps and Salazar. *Bataan*'s multiracial casting is a cynical tool for restorative nostalgia, appropriating the myth of racial unity to demonize the Asian enemy while extolling American virtue at a time when segregation was still the American armed forces' official policy.

Overlord leans more towards reflective nostalgia in the way it redeploys and reinvents the same myth of racial unity. The principal hero is Boyce, who represents another stock character in the genre – the inexperienced recruit who has leadership thrust upon him. Boyce overcomes fear and doubt while remaining true to his own morality. Boyce is tested and rises to the occasion. And unlike both Wesley Epps in *Bataan* and the typical Black supporting character in white horror films, he survives. The platoon is a varied cast of characters representing a diverse cross-section of society. Boyce is Black; Rosenfeld (Dominic Applewhite) is Jewish; Ford is a grizzled veteran of indeterminate origin; Tibbett (Joe Magaro) is a surly Brooklynite; and Chloe (Mathilde Ollivier) is a courageous French woman. This rag-tag band of undesirables simultaneously vanquishes supernatural Nazi evil and accomplishes the original objective. 'Genre is alive', Basinger (2003: 5) reminds us, and combat films 'don't always behave the way they are supposed to'. Casting Black actors in roles they did not normally perform during the Second World War underscores *Overlord*'s investment in reflective nostalgia. Resnin, a powerful Black sergeant, inspires an integrated airborne unit to action on the eve of one of the most important battles in history. There were certainly Black soldiers and non-commissioned officers in the US military, but very few integrated units in the European theatre. The only motivation for integrating at all was the terrible casualty rate during the Battle of the Bulge (December 1944). In *Overlord*, Boyce and other Black soldiers bond with their white comrades and share common dangers in a show of unity against a racist enemy. Director Julius Avery and screenwriters Billy Ray and Mark L. Smith foreground the Nazi menace, an enemy that seems to cast a long shadow from the perspective of 2018. Producer J.J. Abrams dismissed questions about casting. 'Although there might not have been Black soldiers mixed into a unit like this in real life', he said, 'there weren't any monsters lurking under churches either' (Leon 2022). *Overlord* shares at least one commonality with restorative nostalgia: it is not interested in moral ambiguity any more than it is in historical accuracy.

In the military horror films examined by Steffen Hantke (2010), the military as a social body is placed under the microscope and found wanting. Both the traditional combat film and military horror 'examine the coercive power of hierarchic institutions to generate and foster social relations, and the price that individuals pay and the trade-offs they must accept in order to attain and maintain desirable positions within them' (2010: 714). The extraordinary nature of the danger found in horror films forces total strangers and even mortal enemies to come together and eliminate the threat. Like soldiers in war, protagonists in horror films either discover untapped reservoirs of strength and courage or sink into cowardice and mendacity. The relationships forged during extreme duress are authentic and resilient. Hantke (2010: 715) writes: 'Social bonds are genuine because they have undergone trial by fire.' Threats in horror films strengthen the social body and imply 'that all social bonding is a (self-)protective response to danger' (2010: 715).

The similarities between the combat film and horror's narrative arcs explain the ease with which the genres converge to create military horror. Both have their own Kilroy Test, but Hantke (2010) describes an important difference. Where the unit coalesces and perseveres in a traditional battlefield scenario, the social body in military horror tends to disintegrate soon after the threat emerges. Whether it is 'supernatural or an externalization of psychological forces, it always appears beyond the group's power to vanquish it' (2010: 216). Hantke limits his analysis to three representative films – *The Bunker* (2001), *Dog Soldiers* (2002) and *Deathwatch* (2002) – but his overview of the genre is accurate. In most military horror films, the military does not 'provide any authentic social kinship, security from the external threat, or any useful strategies for how to combat this threat. Weapons are commonly as useless as fortifications, training, or courage under fire. Only a turning away from the military seems to promise a measure of safety' (2010: 716). Repressive social bodies – especially the military – 'must be discarded before genuine sociality can emerge – this is the essential narrative of the military horror film' (2010: 716). *Overlord*, by contrast, stays true to Basinger's (2003) formula and challenges Hantke's by vindicating the military unit. Boyce and his comrades defeat the supernatural threat as US soldiers, not individuals.

It is worth examining *Overlord* in relation to *Saving Private Ryan*, since director Julius Avery intends audiences to see his film as an extension of

Spielberg's immensely popular production. Both pass the Kilroy Test, valorize American soldiers and the nobility of their respective missions, and exploit the deep emotional connection between the audience and D-Day. James Creel (2020: 216) makes a convincing case for analysing *Saving Private Ryan* as a classic horror film that embraces all the hallmarks of the genre, building on Hantke's initial thoughts on military horror as a hybrid genre. By manipulating horror tropes, Creel argues, *Saving Private Ryan* effectively conveys to audiences 'what is monstrous, what is heroic, and how to appropriately react because it retains its veneer of historical realism while at the same time trading in the fantastical – and fantastically effective – rhetorical appeals of traditional horror films'. The famous first segment of *Saving Private Ryan* is an exercise in pure body horror as a faceless external force, 'a sort of Nazi fog that suffuses the landscape but defies embodiment', savages vulnerable and exposed bodies, literally creating an ocean of blood in its wake (2020: 224). Creel suggests the 'final girl' trope integral to slasher films plays out in *Saving Private Ryan* with the unlikely survival of Corporal Timothy Upham (Jeremy Davies), a weaker and thus 'traditionally feminine' character compared with the rest of the cast.[3] Further, Creel posits that *Saving Private Ryan* 'preys on both individual and national bodily anxiety through the systematic destruction and dismemberment of several variations of the ideal masculine body' (2020: 217). The best men are slaughtered on the beaches or in service of accomplishing the mission. Upham, who demonstrates cowardice and indecision, survives.

Like the first wave of soldiers at Omaha Beach, the paratroopers flying over France in *Overlord* experience a similarly traumatic introduction to combat when dozens of aircraft are shot down, and men are blown apart, set ablaze, drowned and left hanging from trees. In a film like *Bataan*, the minority characters die first and more horrifically than their white counterparts. Epps is decapitated by a samurai sword and Salazar is lynched. In *Overlord*, Boyce, Rosenfeld and Chloe don't just survive to the end, confounding the conventions of both combat and horror films; they destroy the Nazi monsters. Boyce and Rosenfeld, who would likely be 'tokens' in earlier combat films, behave heroically when tested and we never get the sense that they represent anything other than the best version of American masculinity. Like *Saving Private Ryan*, *Overlord* teaches audiences what is monstrous and what is valiant. It also deploys just enough historical realism to maximize the horror and promote a progressive brand of American patriotism. Both *Overlord* and *Saving Private Ryan* denote Nazism as evil, combine elements of the combat film and horror genres, and reflect an idealized view of the nation that speaks to contemporary concerns. Steven Spielberg resurrected the combat war film from a relative lull in popularity, paying homage to the 'greatest generation' with *Saving Private Ryan*. Twenty years later, *Overlord* exploits these pre-existing positive associations and audience expectations. The historical background of *Overlord* is sacrosanct because of *Saving Private Ryan*; only the 'details' are fanciful, indicative of a reflective, rather than strictly restorative, nostalgia.

Overlord as Nazisploitation

Overlord evokes elements of Nazisploitation and Gothic horror with its outlandish plot and caricatures of Nazis, specifically the mad scientist trope, but it stops short of replicating Nazisploitation's worst features. The Nazisploitation genre originated with such infamous films as *Ilsa: She Wolf of the SS* (1975) and others that trafficked in perverse sexual scenarios set in concentration camps or prison camps, sadism and gruesome medical experimentation (Magilow 2012: 2).[4] *Overlord* aspires to more than just shocking audiences with tired tropes about Nazi doctors and monstrous creations. Like *Saving Private Ryan*, the film appeals to audience's patriotism and demonstrates support for a multicultural society, but *Overlord* also references *Inglourious Basterds*' mise-en-scène and skewed perspective on history. Not all critics agree that *Overlord* distinguishes itself from crude Nazisploitation films, nor do they consider its Tarantinoesque flourishes anything more than superficial mimicry. However, to its credit, *Overlord* attacks racism and fascism as explicitly as it borrows from other films.

The relationship between war and Gothic horror dates back to the early nineteenth century. 'War Gothic' became an identifiable mode of cultural representation after the First World War with the popularity of expressionist films rooted in unresolved national trauma in France and Germany in particular (Poole 2018). The horrors of industrial killing and genocide increased exponentially during the Second World War, as Agnieszka Monnet and Hantke (2016: xvi) note, resulting in 'a rich harvest of Gothic nightmares in literature, film, and other emergent media' that are still playing out today. Nazis in particular populate the War Gothic by manifesting as monsters with centuries of lineage – zombies, vampires and ghosts (Kooyman 2016: 117). Ben Kooyman (2016: 122) notes that cinematic Nazis 'with their occult interests, their scientific hubris, and their technologies of death, extend and build upon [Gothic] tropes, straddling eras as both monsters of the past and monsters of modernity'. Nazis also haunt settings one normally associates with Gothic horror, such as castles, caves or, in the case of *Overlord*, a medieval church. The key to the setting is that the characters feel far removed from the 'existential comforts of civilization' and experience intense psychological pressure that brings out their true nature, whether that is noble, cowardly or sinister (Hantke 2010: 706). Hantke (2010: 705) argues military horror films that revolve around combat units tend to treat historical background as simply a 'dramatic backdrop against which ... questions of individual ethics and psychology can be projected' and 'elaborate shoot out scenes, sequences of stalking, chasing, and physically outmanoeuvring an enemy' unfold. In *Overlord*, Chloe's village evokes a 'once upon a time in occupied France' feeling analogous to the setting of *Inglourious Basterds*. This is likely by design, since in both films history is essentially another fictional character, a projection of 'what might have been', which highlights their reflective approach to nostalgic reconstruction. However, as the title *Overlord* suggests, the film is also grounded in one of America's most hallowed victories and costly national sacrifices. Hantke is correct to characterize historical background in military horror as tangential, but this is not entirely true of *Overlord*, which takes care to remind audiences that on 6 June 1944 good triumphed over evil. *Inglourious Basterds* similarly takes place on the eve of D-Day, but its grisly resolution meant the costly invasion never occurred.

Ultimately, *Overlord*'s treatment of race and anti-fascist messaging is a fantasy about American greatness diametrically opposed to the white supremacist version offered by the 'Unite the Right' crowd in Charlottesville. *Overlord* may be guilty of indulging in restorative nostalgia in its return to a heroic representation of the World War II combat unit, but its means and motives for doing so suggest that the film is more reflective than restorative. The imagined America of *Overlord* is the America of Basinger's World War II combat film, an idealized analogue for the country that overcomes its differences to vanquish pure evil. However, *Overlord* deliberately defies the racist tendencies of both the combat film and the horror film, which typically kill off Black and ethnic protagonists first (Basinger 2003: 52).[5] In the first few minutes of the film, Resnin strides up and down the aisle of the C-47, dismissing the Nazis' humanity in the same way Brad Pitt's Aldo Raines does with his unit of Basterds. What the paratroopers do this fateful night is crucial for the success of the invasion. 'There's going to be 120,000 Allied soldiers fighting on a French beach for all that is good and pure in this world', Resnin explains (*Overlord* 2018). As if to affirm this, a nervous

Rosenfeld states the obvious to his friend Boyce, 'We both know what the Nazis are going to do to a guy named Rosenfeld' (*Overlord* 2018).

It is no surprise, then, that Rosenfeld is discovered later in the church basement converted into a Nazi laboratory, just another Jew subjected to inhumane experimentation. Resnin calls the Germans they will face on the ground 'rotten sons of bitches. Because rotten sons of bitches will do anything they have to, to destroy everything that is good in this world. That is why we have to be as rotten as they are' (*Overlord* 2018). Ford will take this to heart when he tortures SS Captain Wafner (Pilou Asbæck) for answers concerning the serum that creates the monsters. Boyce, the embodiment of a more decent America untainted by Abu Ghraib and Guantanamo Bay, protests Ford's abusive actions, 'We're not him!' Ford delivers a hard truth, 'You want to beat them, play just as dirty as they do' (*Overlord* 2018). Ford becomes like Wafner in every sense during the climactic confrontation at the end of the film, injecting the same serum the Nazis do, but Boyce never loses his moral compass. Significantly, Resnin's murder in the woods soon after landing is explicitly racialized as he stands unarmed and defiant before a group of German soldiers who take pleasure in gunning him down. The camera zooms out to reveal a series of bodies caught in the trees, swinging. Their parachutes have snagged on branches, but the scene, with its dark silhouetted corpses in the trees, resembles a mass lynching. At this moment, between the fiery skies, dense woods and racial violence, *Overlord* might pass for Southern Gothic instead of military horror. This visual allusion to America's own history of racism during a pivotal battle to eradicate Nazi racism suggests the need for eternal vigilance and longer historical memories. After all, audiences had just witnessed a neo-Nazi riot on American soil in 2017.

Another pervasive theme in Nazisploitation and military horror concerns the spectre of the 'mad scientist'. A legacy of Gothic horror since *Frankenstein* (1818), scientists emerge as even more potentially villainous figures in the twentieth century in the wake of two total wars. Scientists serving under the Third Reich performed horrific experiments on concentration camp inmates, developed sophisticated weaponry designed to kill civilians, such as Wernher von Braun's V-2 missile, and organized and abused slave labour. Nazi scientists on screen mirror their antecedents from Weimar cinema, specifically Rotwang in *Metropolis* (1927), a character driven by vengeance and nihilism who unleashes a seductive gynoid to destroy the city's fragile social order (Crim 2020: 84).[6] Infamous figures like Josef Mengele, most famously depicted in *The Boys from Brazil* (1978) as essentially the same monster as he was in real life, inspired mad scientist caricatures in several genres (Crim 2020: 84). The Nazi doctor closely mirrored the mad scientist archetype popular in the 1930s and 1940s by 'indulging sadism in the guise of dispassionate science' and engaging in 'pointless and atrocious medical research', as noted by David Skal (2004: 80). Post-war trials and Robert Lifton's important work on the psychology of medical professionals involved in atrocities increased audiences' fascination and disgust with the Nazi doctor (Lifton 1998). Nazi scientists captivated Western audiences in the post-war period in part because so many of them continued their nefarious work for new masters, the United States especially (Crim 2018b). The Cold War, which offered tainted scientists a clean slate on both sides of the Iron Curtain, understandably introduced new existential anxiety about science run amok as nuclear weapons grew in number and destructiveness.

In Nazisploitation, scientists are often hard at work creating zombies or some other subservient cyborg driven by an ideological will that does not die. *Shock Waves* (1977) is an early example of the Nazi zombie film and inspired countless others, including *Overlord*. British actor Peter Cushing plays the only substantive character in the film, a Nazi scientist who lost control over his super soldiers created thirty years earlier to win the war. Living alone on a Caribbean island, Cushing's nameless character is ultimately killed by his own 'Death Corps' as they stalk and murder hapless tourists. James Ward interprets the zombified soldiers as defective weapons, 'the equivalent of V-2 rockets that fell short of their targets or of experimental jet fighters that downed more German test pilots than Allied bombers' (Ward 2012: 95). *Frankenstein's Army* (2013) brings the mad scientist full circle, as the titular character is none other than a scientist descended from the original Dr Frankenstein, who creates 'zombots' out of dead German and Russian soldiers. *Overlord* does not spend much time developing the character of Dr Schmidt (Erich Redman) precisely because the stock character is so well established by decades of representation. Schmidt is cold, indifferent to suffering and fascinated by the potential of the serum. 'He calls it his "science"', Chloe sneers, trying to explain the monstrous version of her grandmother locked upstairs to her new American friends (*Overlord* 2018). Schmidt harvested an 'ancient tar' from the medieval French village and began the injection experiments on villagers, but Wafner provides the ideological 'vision' for Dr Schmidt's technocratic worldview. Wafner beams with pride: 'They've been given a purpose', he says. 'For once in their pathetic lives they have value ... the blood and bodies of this village will contribute in ways you can only imagine' (*Overlord* 2018). During Ford and Wafner's climactic battle, Wafner declares, 'I am a god, Corporal', and injects himself multiple times. 'Germany will have an invincible army. This Reich, Hitler's one thousand year empire is going to take over the world' (*Overlord* 2018). However, like the Death Corps in *Shock Waves* and Frankenstein's zombots, the creatures in *Overlord* adhere to no ideology. They are just another defective weapon.

How does *Overlord* fit into Hantke's (2010) conception of the military horror genre, and what is its relationship to Nazisploitation? The most significant point of departure from Hantke's definition is that in *Overlord* the military social body perseveres. The brush with the supernatural emboldens the paratroopers. Kim Newman (2018: 68) argues that it is important to acknowledge that the US Army in *Overlord* is 'ahistorical' and 'revisionist' because it depicts a racially integrated unit. He observes a trend in which 'WWII has become what the Wild West used to be – a nebulous past of actual peril and limitless possibility' (2018: 69). The *Los Angeles Times* accuses *Overlord* of aping *Inglourious Basterds* by deploying 'prestige' war flick trappings to vandalize history books with a wild rewriting. It's gory, utopian fan fiction that imagines, 'What if the night before D-Day, a bunch of black and Jewish American soldiers fought off Nazi zombies?' (Walsh 2018). *Overlord*'s protagonists are imperfect and, in the case of Ford, capable of great darkness, but the stress of combat and the more extreme horrors lurking in the village only strengthen the bonds they presumably established during basic training. Tibbet's rough exterior and cynicism mask decency and grudging respect for Boyce and Chloe, the random French woman on whom he must rely to save himself. Boyce, like so many similar archetypal characters in combat films, takes his cues from seasoned veterans like Resnin and Ford to become a confident and capable soldier. Rosenfeld seems destined for a quick death, but winds up becoming a one-man killing machine in the same vein as his *Inglourious Basterds* counterparts. Chloe, who has opposed the Nazi menace for years, falls right in with the American interlopers in her village and ends the film tending to wounded soldiers on the beaches of Normandy. The military depicted in *Overlord* is not repressive, does not disintegrate upon first contact with the supernatural and, most importantly, comprises the best the nation has to offer. Ford, the unknown quantity in the unit with a penchant for violence, perishes alongside Wafner and the serum. The only suggestion that the US military could be tempted to 'play God' like the Nazis comes at the end of the film when Boyce is debriefed about the last eight hours. The officer questions Boyce about 'rumours' concerning the lab: 'If there was anything down there worth digging through all that rubble, you'd let us know, right?' (*Overlord* 2018). Boyce honours Ford's self-sacrifice and denies that there is anything other than the collapsed radio tower.

Conclusion

Overlord speaks to American audiences' anxiety and anger at the state of the nation just a year after the 'Unite the Right' rally. The deceptively simplistic plot and uncomplicated depiction of the protagonists hold the potential for catharsis. The Nazi menace is not so remote since hundreds of neo-Nazis had recently marched openly in a major university town. For many, the 2016 election and Charlottesville were traumatic. Two scholars in particular reflect on the symbiotic relationship between horror film and national trauma, effectively arguing that the genre simultaneously allows nations to process trauma or deflect it. Linnie Blake (2008: 2) argues, 'Horror cinema is ideally positioned to expose the psychological, social, and cultural ramifications of the ideologically expedient will to bind up the nation's wounds.' Adam Lowenstein (2005: 13) takes a similar approach, writing that to 'speak of history's horrors, or historical trauma, is to recognize events as wounds'. Whether it is Auschwitz, Vietnam or Hiroshima, wounds like these represent profound allegorical moments in which cultural production plays a significant role. Lowenstein (2005: 1–2) defines allegorical moments as the 'shocking collision of film, spectator, and history where registers of bodily space and historical time are disrupted, confronted, and intertwined'. Charlottesville is not Auschwitz or Hiroshima, but it is an open wound and *Overlord* stages a collision between unrepentant Nazis seeking eternal life and their victims – racial, ethnic and national minorities. Blake (2008) notes that popular culture does more to interrogate trauma than 'high-modernist' cultural artefacts since the former is 'consumed by millions'. Horror films expose 'dominant ideologies' prevalent in a given nation and, in the case of *Overlord*, that ideology is anti-fascism (2008: 4–6). In this 'bloody cacophony', Katie Walsh (2008) writes, Americans stand up to Nazis: it is 'significant that in this vision of revisionist revenge, the ones who prevail against the Nazis are those who would be marginalized and targeted by them … *Overlord* doesn't lose sight of its heroes.' It seems in 2018 many Americans needed to be reminded of this.

Overlord is more than a prominent recent addition to the military horror genre; it is a cultural response to the open wound that is Charlottesville and the Trump presidency. In *Planet Auschwitz* (Crim 2020), I note that the enduring popularity of Nazisploitation and military horror suggests Americans remain traumatized by Nazism. 'If we accept the premise monsters are political entities reflecting our collective ideas about good and evil', as I reflect elsewhere, 'then we must ask ourselves why contemporary culture is replete with the Nazi menace seventy-five years after its defeat' (2020: 82). Nazis may no longer stalk the planet in Hugo Boss uniforms, but the ideology never dies. *Overlord*'s facile patriotism harkens back to the first wave of the World War II combat films, but that is precisely why it is a fascinating cultural product for 2018. *Overlord* highlights continuity between the horrors of the Third Reich and our own time and place. There are in fact aspiring Nazis in church basements, small towns, big cities and government offices. *Overlord* is an enjoyable spectacle unconcerned with historical context, but not basic concepts such as good and evil. Perhaps more than most genres, military horror films like *Overlord* encourage us to pay heed to Jean Baudrillard's (1990: 92) observation (or warning): 'What has disappeared has every chance of reappearing.'

Notes

1. See https://www.archives.gov/milestone-documents/general-eisenhowers-order-of-the-day (accessed 15 August 2023).
2. The Great Replacement Theory is a white nationalist conspiracy theory originating with French author Renaud Camus, which maintains that white people in Europe and North America are being replaced by immigrants, migrants and refugees from non-white regions. American white supremacists use the theory to promote the danger of 'white genocide' supposedly orchestrated by Jews and other 'elites'. Protesters at the 'Unite the Right' rally famously chanted, 'You will not replace us' and 'Jews will not replace us', indicating familiarity with the theory. See Farivar (2022).
3. Carol Clover (2015 [1992]) explores the 'final girl' trope.
4. See also Crim (2015).
5. See also Means Coleman (2011). I am grateful to Amanda Howell for making this observation.
6. For more on Rotwang and Metropolis, see Frayling (2005: 62–3).

References

Basinger, J. (2003), *The World War II Combat Film: Anatomy of a Genre: Updated Filmography*, Middletown, CT: Wesleyan University Press.

Baudrillard, J. (1990), *Cool Memories*, London: Verso.
Blake, L. (2008), *The Wounds of Nations: Horror Cinema, Historical Trauma and National Identity*, Manchester: Manchester University Press.
Boym, S. (2001), *The Future of Nostalgia*, New York: Basic Books.
Boym, S. (2011) 'Nostalgia', *Atlas of Transformation*. Available online: http://monumenttotransformation.org/atlas-of-transformation/html/n/nostalgia/nostalgia-svetlana-boym.html (accessed 20 December 2022).
Bramesco, C. (2018), 'War Is Hell: Overlord and the History of Battle-set Horror Movies', *The Guardian*, 9 November.
Clover, C.J. (2015 [1992]), *Men, Women, and Chain Saws: Gender in the Modern Horror Film*, Princeton, NJ: Princeton University Press.
Creel, J. (2020), 'Gender, Horror, and War: Reading *Saving Private Ryan* as Horror Film', *Journal of Popular Culture*, 5 (31): 215–34.
Crim, B.E. (2015), 'She Wolves: The Monstrous Women of Nazisploitation Cinema', in *Selling Sex on Screen: From Weimar Cinema to Zombie Porn*, edited by K. Ritzenhoff and C. McAvoy, 95–110, Lanham, MD: Rowman & Littlefield.
Crim, B.E. (2018a), '"I Got No Problem Killing My Kin": *Fury* (2014) and the Evolution of the World War II Combat Film', *Film & History*, 48 (1): 4–14.
Crim, B.E. (2018b), *Our Germans: Project Paperclip and the National Security State*, Baltimore, MD: Johns Hopkins University Press.
Crim, B.E. (2020), *Planet Auschwitz: Holocaust Representation in Science Fiction and Horror Film and Television*, New Brunswick, NJ: Rutgers University Press.
Cripes, A. (2018), 'Overlord, a Reflection of Humanity's Darkest Moments', *UWIRE*, 20 November. Available online: link.gale.com/apps/doc/A562815835/AONE?u=viva_lynch&sid=bookmark-AONE&xid=c5546060 (accessed 26 January 2022).
Ebiri, B. (2018), 'Old-Fashioned Nazi-Killing, with a Gory Twist', *New York Times*, 8 November. Available online: https://www.nytimes.com/2018/11/08/movies/overlord-review.html (accessed 10 January 2024).
Eisenhower, General D.D. (1944), 'Order of the Day' [speech], *National Archives*. Available online: https://www.archives.gov/milestone-documents/general-eisenhowers-order-of-the-day (accessed 5 February 2023).
Farivar, M. (2022), 'What Is the Great Replacement Theory?', *Voice of America*, 18 May. Available online: https://www.voanews.com/a/what-is-the-great-replacement-theory-/6578349.html (accessed 4 January 2023).
Frayling, C. (2005), *Mad, Bad, and Dangerous? The Scientists and the Cinema*, London: Reaktion Books.
Hantke, S. (2010), 'The Military Horror Film: Speculations on a Hybrid Genre', *The Journal of Popular Culture*, 43 (4): 701–19.

Kooyman, B. (2016), 'Snow Nazis Must Die: Gothic Tropes and Hollywood Genre-Fication in Nazisploitation Horror', in *War Gothic in Literature and Culture*, edited by A. Soltysik Monnet and S. Hantke, 117–35, London: Routledge.

Leon, M. (2018), 'Inside J.J. Abrams' *Overlord*: A Bonkers Horror Movie with Bloodthirsty Nazi Zombies', *The Daily Beast*, 10 November. Available online: https://www.thedailybeast.com/inside-jj-abrams-overlord-a-bonkers-horror-movie-with-bloodthirsty-nazi-zombies (accessed 13 May 2022).

Lifton, R.J. (1998), *The Nazi Doctors: Medical Killing and the Psychology of Genocide*, New York: Basic Books.

Locke, B. (2008), 'Strange Fruit: White, Black, and Asian in the World War II Combat Film *Bataan*', *Journal of Popular Film and Television*, 36 (1): 9–20.

Lowenstein, A. (2005), *Shocking Representation: Historical Trauma, National Cinema, and the Modern Horror Film*, New York: Columbia University Press.

Lowery, W. (2018), '*Overlord* Is One of 2018's Biggest Surprises', *UWIRE*, 18 November. Available online: link.gale.com/apps/doc/A562193193/AONE?u=viva_lynch&sid=bookmark-AONE&xid=5cdd1750 (accessed 26 January 2022).

Magilow, D.H. (2012), 'Introduction', in *Nazisploitation! The Nazi Image in Low-Brow Cinema and Culture*, edited by D.H. Magilow, E. Bridges and K.T. Vander Lugt, 1–19, New York: Continuum.

Means Coleman, R.R. (2011), *Horror Noire: Blacks in American Horror Films from the 1890s to the Present*, London: Routledge.

Monnet, A.S. and S. Hantke (2016), 'Ghosts from the Battlefields: A Short Historical Introduction to the War Gothic', in *War Gothic in Literature and Culture*, edited by A. Soltysik Monnet and S. Hantke, xi–xxv, London: Routledge.

Newman, K. (2018), '*Overlord*', *Sight and Sound*, December, 68–9.

Nicholson, A. (2018), '*Overlord* Review: The Nazi Undead Battle U.S. Soldiers in J.J. Abrams-Produced WWII Thriller', *Chicago Tribune*, 8 November. Available online: https://www.chicagotribune.com/entertainment/movies/sc-mov-overlord-rev-1108-20181107-story.html (accessed 15 August 2023).

Poole, W.S. (2018), *Wasteland: The Great War and the Origins of Modern Horror*, Berkeley, CA: Counterpoint.

Skal, D.J. (2004), 'The Horrors of War', in *The Horror Film*, edited by S. Prince, 70–81, New Brunswick, NJ: Rutgers University Press.

Walsh, K. (2018), 'Review: *Overlord* Turns a Fight against Nazis into an Energetic B-movie Splatterfest', *Los Angeles Times*, 8 November.

Ward, J.J. (2012), 'Utterly without Redeeming Social Value? "Nazi Science" Beyond Exploitation Cinema', in *Nazisploitation! the Nazi Image in Low-brow Cinema and Culture*, edited by D.H. Magilow, E. Bridges and K.T. Vander Lugt, 92–112, London: Bloomsbury.

Films

Bataan (1943), directed by Tay Garnett [film], United States: Metro Goldwyn Mayer.

The Boys from Brazil (1978), directed by Franklin J. Schaffner [film], United Kingdom and United States: TC Entertainment and Producer Circle.

The Bunker (2001), directed by Rob Green [film], United Kingdom: Millennium Pictures.

Deathwatch (2002), directed by M.J. Bassett [film], United Kingdom and Germany: Apollo Media and Bavaria Film.

Dog Soldiers (2002) directed by Neil Marshall [film], United Kingdom: Kismet Entertainment Group.

Frankenstein's Army (2013), directed by Richard Raaphorst [film], United States: Dark Sky Films.

Fury (2014), directed by David Ayer [film], United States: Columbia Pictures.

Ilsa: She Wolf of the SS (1975), directed by Don Edmonds [film], Canada: Cinépix Film Properties.

Inglourious Basterds (2009), directed by Quentin Tarantino [film], United States: The Weinstein Company.

Metropolis (1927), directed by Fritz Lang [film], Germany: UFA.

Overlord (2018), directed by Julius Avery [film], United States: Paramount Pictures.

Saving Private Ryan (1998), directed by Steven Spielberg [film], United States: Amblin Entertainment.

Shock Waves (1977), directed by Ken Wiederhorn [film], United States: Lawrence Friedricks Enterprises.

14

Post-socialist body horror(s): On exhaustion and social death in *The Life and Death of a Porno Gang* and *A Serbian Film*

Andrija Filipović

One often hears that citizens of Serbia live with the excess of history. Just the fact that one has travelled without moving, to use Deleuze's expression, through four states in less than fifty years – the Socialist Federal Republic of Yugoslavia, the Socialist Republic of Yugoslavia, the Republic of Serbia and Montenegro and the Republic of Serbia – together with several wars that tore apart every single one of those republics, speaks in favour of this sentiment. The consequence of such historical excess is that every single point in space and time turns out to be a multi-layered palimpsest. Such a state of thickly layered meaning can easily lead to the collective feeling that wherever one goes in space and time there is a viscous historical matter that glues itself to bodies and subjectivities like sticky quicksand. And, like quicksand, it quickly tires out the bodies that are being sucked into it, the bodies that are in danger of suffocating. This social affective atmosphere of historical excess, then, creates a feeling of exhaustion in individuals perhaps even to the point of social and even visceral death for some.

Serbian society in the years preceding *The Life and Death of a Porno Gang* (2009) and *A Serbian Film* (2010) was marked by deep historical changes. Slobodan Milošević, the dictator of more than a decade, was removed from his post after the NATO military campaign in 1999 and mass protests against election fraud in 2000. Milošević was replaced by a group of centre and centre-right democratic parties, which began the process of structural reforms with the aim of joining the European Union and an even faster push towards neoliberal economy together with austerity measures since the world economic crisis in 2008. Set against this history, *The Life and Death of a Porno Gang* is increasingly grim as its narrative progresses, extinguishing (rather than culminating) in an act of double suicide. Along the narrative descent of the porno gang into a situation that is beyond any hope, while performing vaudeville acts for villagers and snuff shows for foreign clientele across Serbia, we steal glances into the lives of the marginal. Gay men, transgender people, sex workers, drug addicts, the elderly, peasants, war survivors and the poor are both the subjects and perpetrators of snuff shows. The porno gang, with its constitutive multiplicity, works as a sort of desiring machine connecting all the wretched of the world. We also see in all its gory glory the reason the wretched are made such – a long history of economic exploitation, political oppression and cultural marginalization. Similarly, in *A Serbian Film* the main character is Miloš, a porn star, who is drugged and forced to take part in torture-porn snuff films, and ultimately ends the nightmare with collective family suicide. Both films, using the metaphor of snuff – a film that shows or purports to show scenes of an actual homicide or death by suicide – work to show how the bodies are exhausted and led into (social) death in postsocialist times.

The impact of these two films was not equal, however. Although they were released within a year of each other and responded to the general atmosphere of disappointment in social progress after the fall of the dictator Slobodan Milošević, as explained in more detail in the next section, their reception was diametrically opposite. While Mladen Đorđević's *The Life and Death of a Porno Gang* won twelve awards including the Special Jury Prize at the Boston Underground Film Festival, Best Film at the Buenos Aires Rojo Sangre and Best Film at the Fantaspoa International Fantastic Film Festival, it received almost no domestic critical attention except for what is referenced in this essay. On the other hand, *A Serbian Film* has caused both domestic and international uproar and received accolades, depending on the cultural values spectrum of the critical voices.

The reason for this difference in reception lies partly with their conditions of production, as well as in the placement of the films themselves by their directors. Đorđević worked with the micro budget and a cast of relatively unknown actors, whereas Spasojević's *A Serbian Film* aimed at higher production values with a more famous cast. Spasojević also courted notoriety, particularly by choosing this title for the film. However, while these reasons contributed to their uneven domestic reception, these two films – despite their shared investment in extreme horror and central role of the snuff film – cannot be more different when it comes to their critical stance. While *A Serbian Film* depicts the horrors befalling a Serbian *paterfamilias* and thus a particular kind of masculinity that grounds white cisheterosexual patriarchal society, *The Life and Death of a Porno Gang* looks into the violence performed by such society in order to maintain itself throughout (post-)socialist history. There is thus an important sociopolitical difference between the two films, as demonstrated by how and which bodies are exhausted and killed, and the historical valence of their respective recourse to body horror.

The post-socialist condition and the life amid ruins

The period after the Second World War in the Socialist Federative Republic of Yugoslavia, and especially the period during the late 1950s and 1960s, was marked by thorough modernization when a large part of the most important infrastructure that the people of Serbia know today was made (for a general overview of the history of Yugoslavia, see Calic 2019). An excellent example of this is Novi Beograd, which was built by draining the river swamps between the Danube and Sava and quickly became the symbol of Yugoslav modernity (Normand 2014: 103–46). Today, it is the largest and the most populated municipality of Belgrade, which is still undergoing development. It is, for example, the municipality where one of the more expensive residential blocks is being built. The period of the late 1950s was also marked by economic reforms together with a turning away from the Soviet model of planned economy. Yugoslavia started opening towards the West, both culturally and economically, which led to the creation of a specific kind of socialist consumerist society. Darko Suvin (2014: 333) claims that by proclaiming care for everyday needs, the Party programme from 1958 strengthened the self-governing aspect of Yugoslav socialism. It marked the transformation of state bodies into self-governing bodies, which is especially important considering the Yugoslav distinction from the rest of the Eastern as well as Western political forms of government.

Later decades, the 1960s and 1970s, were marked by definitive formation of socialist consumerist society with the presence of numerous Western brands and products. What this shows, besides being a historical curio, is that there was a lived collective feeling of optimism within the self-governing socialism (Bennett 1995: 246–7; Kirn 2019: 190) regarding the disappearance of nationalism and the self-management system replacing capitalism and statism (Denitch 1990: 63) – so much so that many of the Yugoslav Communist Party ideologues saw consumerism not as something antagonistic to the self-governing project but as an indelible part of it (Dimitrijević 2016: 60). There was hope that self-governing socialism would lead to the abolition of classes, ethnicities and, finally, the state itself. However, this project of perpetual modernization and increasingly rich consumerism – the hope that the future was secured and that it would be ever brighter – would implode in the wars between the constitutive states that started in 1991.

The wars in Bosnia and Herzegovina and Croatia ended in 1995 and with them not only Yugoslavia but any trace of self-governing consumerist socialism and optimism that Yugoslav society was based on. The 1990s in Serbia were marked by the dictatorship of Slobodan Milošević, economic sanctions, cultural isolation and, finally, the Kosovo War and NATO bombing campaign in 1999. Milošević was ousted after massive protests against the election fraud in 2000. The ex-Yugoslav states entered a period of post-socialism, each in its own way. Nancy Fraser (1997: 1) uses the concept of post-socialism to name 'the general horizon within which political thought necessarily moves', and defines the post-socialist condition as 'an absence of any credible overarching emancipatory project despite the proliferation of struggle; a general decoupling of the cultural politics of recognition from the social politics of redistribution; and a decentring of claims for equality in the face of aggressive marketization and sharply rising material inequality' (1997: 3). Of particular importance for this chapter and for the local context about which I write are the problems of social redistribution, aggressive marketization and the rise of material inequality, and perhaps most importantly, the lack of an overarching emancipatory project. In that regard, it is necessary to differentiate between the post-socialist condition in general, as used by Nancy Fraser, and the post-socialist condition in a narrower sense, as in the case of those societies that possess historical experience of socialism – in this case, Yugoslav self-governing socialism.

I would take the beginning of economic reforms and its restructuring after the year 2000 as the post-socialist condition's moment of birth in Serbia (Bideleux and Jeffries 2007: 320–8), especially the privatization aspect together with the precarization of the workforce as one of the movements towards free market economy in an attempt to bring the Serbian economy closer to the European and global economies. To the post-socialist condition as historical experience, I would also add the 'infrastructural aspect' – that is, the insight that all those historical strata of experience, from the diverse material practices such as road building, waterways, etc. to those strata in the 'superstructure' such as policies, laws and politics, at least partially define and condition current, contemporary experience and forms of (non-)life. As such, this historical 'infrastructural' aspect is of key importance for the materialization of various material-semiotic flows and relations between individuals and historical forces.

Hopes were once again raised with the election, but were quickly thwarted with the assassination of the first democratic prime minister, Zoran Đinđić, in 2003 and the disappointment with the experience of economic transition to a market economy that left many without work in the period of privatization of previously state-owned companies. The years that followed, as depicted in *The Life and Death of a Porno Gang* and *A Serbian Film*, were and are still at the time of writing this essay at the beginning of 2023, marked by the complete disillusionment and utter lack of hope for a better future. As Aleksandar Radivojević, the scriptwriter of *A Serbian Film*, said when alluding to the prevailing social atmosphere after Đinđić's assassination, 'it's difficult to be optimistic ... We killed the last man who had any kind of value' (Iarlori 2011).

Both *The Life and Death of a Porno Gang* and *A Serbian Film* respond to the age of post-socialism with its social and economic precarity and other social issues adding to a growing palimpsest-like accumulation of historical horror. *The Life and Death of a Porno Gang* is perhaps even more substantial than *A Serbian Film* in its treatment of the ruination of the Serbian state, society and individual lives, as will be shown. What is common to both is the critical stance towards the given state of affairs, and the depiction of the way post-socialist conditions affect individuals. Both films show the horrors that bodies undergo in the age of post-socialism, and the horrors of history that sediment violent stratum by violent stratum. Each film in its own way tries to find a way out for the characters, and these films are markedly different in their approach to this. *The Life and Death of a Porno Gang* emphasizes how queer bodies are exhausted by the historical forces, while *A Serbian Film* projects a paranoid social death of the heterosexual family in the age of post-socialism. Both, finally, move towards a conceptual and affective space of ruin, where bodies devoid of hope are directly exposed to various forms of violence.

Post-socialist death in *A Serbian Film*

A Serbian Film shares the shocking content with *The Life and Death of a Porno Gang* and adds some more, including necrophilia, incest and paedophilia, while showcasing a very different, high production aesthetic compared with the latter's semi-documentary video-diary style. Hyper-realistic style coupled with more famous cast worked together with the intentionally shocking story to spectacularize the suffering of heterosexual masculinity, the cisheteronormative family and the Serbian nation. In contradistinction to the collective suffering of the gang, it is Miloš (Srđan Todorović), the main character in *A Serbian Film*, who is the focus of all the bodily horrors. He is a retired porn actor who is lured out of retirement with the promise of earning a large amount of money and the possibility of leaving Serbia, where he finds the future of his family untenable for various socio-economic reasons. However, as the film shoot progresses, Miloš falls down a rabbit hole of increasingly gruesome scenes. The film culminates in a scene of Miloš unwittingly raping his own son and, in desperation – because it seems there will be no end to the horrors that befall him and his family – making a suicide pact with his wife, killing himself, her and their son with a single bullet. According to director, Srđan Spasojević, *A Serbian Film* is 'a family drama which turns into hell' (Kapka 2014; also quoted by Batori 2017: 3), 'an allegory of Serbian national cinema; the European film order; the post-Yugoslav disintegration; as well as contemporary Serbian politics' (Batori 2017: 3). This 'family drama turning into hell' is here explicitly connected to the post-Yugoslav, post-socialist condition as well as to contemporary Serbian politics. And, as will become clear, *A Serbian Film* sets a clear association between Miloš's family and Serbian society.

Miloš is depicted as a porn legend, well-endowed and potent, a man who earns a living for his family. He is the *paterfamilias*, a typical form of Serbian heterosexual masculinity. But when things take a bad turn for him, he tries to save not only his masculinity but also the sacredness of his family and, metonymically, Serbian society as a whole. This is the key to the final scene of collective suicide, contrary to what Tatjana Aleksić (2016: 190) writes about the profanation of 'the precious paternal authority at the foundation of the sacred family', where according to Aleksić, Miloš challenges the sacredness of the family in Serbian society by destroying it. But Miloš does not kill himself and his family any which way, he does that with *a single bullet*. Hence, it is not just any murder-suicide, but the most *ideal* and the *cleanest* one. With this clean exit from the horrors, he and his family are suffering, Miloš saves his masculinity, his family and therefore the nation from the threats that are coming from outside.

The affective politics of *A Serbian Film* aims to maintain the status quo in Serbian society, safeguarding the heteronormative order and with it the political and economic structures that support it. *A Serbian Film* incites viewers to identify as heterosexual, scaring them into identifying with the heteronorm through the threat of violence. However, it is not only the fear of violence that does so, but also the promise that heterosexual masculinity, family and the social order are sacred and untouchable, even in the ideal sense of being beyond life, as all (heteronormative) ideals are in the last instance. The film ends with a suggestion that the body of the family is not even safe in its own death. It appears that the threatening outside does not respect any kind of boundary – or, rather, that the boundaries set up as traditional forms of sociality are being violently re-formed under the pressure of contemporaneity.

The threat from outside is represented by the producer and the other people gathered around the film's production. It is not clear who exactly participates in the making of this torture-porn snuff film, but it is suggested that at least some of them are foreigners. As Aleksić (2016: 189) writes, 'the camera crew is directed by the Politician who, we realize finally, is ranked higher in the clique of puppeteers but is still only the one who provides services for the anonymous clientele'. If we take the film to be an allegory of the Serbian political situation – and both director and scriptwriter insist on that – this threat from outside can be taken as both a paranoid projection and the denial of historical agency and responsibility. Scriptwriter Aleksandar Radivojević says:

> He [Miloš] is in a way like a metaphorical stand-in for the country of Serbia – humiliatingly impoverished and easily manipulated by the powers that be (the European Union) and the people [politicians] in charge ... He is drugged, molested, raped and so on. And that is precisely what happens with some of the employees here who work in the private sector, with marketing or virtually any job you can get. This is a film about the neo-sociopolitical industry in which any kind of monetary exchange or any kind of emotional exchange comes off as porn.
>
> (quoted in Ognjanović 2017: 65)

Radivojević finds the mirror image in Miloš of the torture-pornification of everyday life in the age of post-socialism, but we can see the lure of the forfeiture of agency in an allegorical reading of the film, this time raised to the level of the state and society at large. The denial of agency to Miloš, and through him to Serbian society in general, masks the fact that the violence is produced within the heteronormative and patriarchal system of contemporary Serbian society, as described earlier. Both Miloš and Serbian society are projected as innocent victims of someone and something coming from outside, without any responsibility for their actions, while it is their actions which inflict suffering by erasing even the possibility of an existence that is otherwise than heteropatriarchal. Also, what is purposively avoided is any sense of historical agency. By insisting on heroization of Miloš's victimhood, the film refuses to recognize the entanglement of Serbian political and economic elites and the common people in their racism and nationalism, which resulted in violent dissolution of Yugoslavia and all the war horrors until the very end of the twentieth century.

According to the logic of *A Serbian Film*, it is the heteronormative order that suffers the violence coming from outside, while that outside is defined as contemporary European society. Miloš, from this perspective, not only symbolically saves the Serbian family, but shows to the viewers that his suicide and familicide – as final acts of agency, the only ones capable of reaching for an ideal – is the only way out from the horrors befalling the heteropatriarchy at the beginning of the twenty-first century, at a time when Serbian society is transitioning increasingly rapidly towards the contemporaneity marked by the liberalization of both economy and social norms. *A Serbian Film*, then, shows a particular kind of post-socialist death – or, rather, fear of such death. Given the nature of the final act of collective suicide and the projection of perpetual victimhood where responsibility for the horrors of history belongs only to others and not oneself, one can understand the film as a plea for the heterosexual family in the post-socialist age. While the film locates the reasons for socio-economic ills in shady local elites and the exploitative nature of foreign capital, it shies away from broadening its critical reach to include other groups and classes of people in danger of social death. Instead, what suffers the painful death – or rather, what we as viewers are made to be fearful of – is the destruction of the heteronormative social structure. Thus, Spasojević does nothing other than offer support to the norm amid the re-traditionalization of post-socialist Serbian society at the beginning of the twenty-first century. Spasojević, finally, only repeats the prevailing political narrative from the 1990s onward of the Serbian nation being the innocent victim of historical horrors that befall it without any responsibility of its own.

Exhausting the body in *The Life and Death of a Porno Gang*

According to Steven Shaviro (2011), history for Serbia includes a

> sense of exhaustion and depletion ... The feeling of having come too late, of being post-everything (postmodern, posthuman, post-historical) is probably

a worldwide pathology at this point. But it is felt with a particular acuteness in postwar and post-socialist Serbia, torn as it is between a past of vanishing traditions, and a globalized future that somehow never manages to arrive.

It is, in this light, particularly productive to engage with *The Life and Death of a Porno Gang* as a political text, especially as one imagining what the extinguished future of queer politics may look like in Serbia and perhaps elsewhere. A never arriving future, exhaustion, depletion and pessimism are the attributes of its overarching affective atmosphere, and there is a strange horror after the implosion of the gang because there is nothing that can be observed behind it. This post-exhaustion void is more provocative as *The Life and Death of a Porno Gang* asks the fundamental question of whether there is life after social death – that is, how to think beyond representation.

The most important points of historical excess that lead towards the absolute bodily exhaustion of the post-socialist condition are mapped by the porno cabaret's village and snuff shows, peeling off layers upon layers of decades of social, economic and political ruin, neglect and marginalization. The porno gang consists of director Marko (Mihajlo Jovanović), failed theatre actress Una (Ana Aćimović), HIV-positive gay couple Džoni (Radivoj Knežević) and Maks (Srđan Jovanović), married heroin addicts Rade (Aleksandar Gligorić) and Darinka (Mariana Aranđelović), two porn actors Dragan (Bojan Zogović) and Sofija (Nataša Aksentijević) and voyeuristic cameraman Vanja (Predrag Damjanović) – and they set out with the first porno theatre show in the Balkans. 'Serbs watch out, patriarchy is going out of fashion' proclaims one line of the cabaret. The film is set in late 2000 and early 2001, and the call of ousting patriarchy cannot be understood otherwise than ironically on the part of porno theatre troupe as the events that follow will show.

Another aspect of the porno theatre troupe's undertaking that reflects the failure of 'ousting' the excesses of post-socialist history is the use of the road movie genre trope. All packed together, they set off from Belgrade to their village porno cabaret shows in a pink van painted in flowers and lively colours, immediately bringing to mind the 1960s hippie flower power movement. Associations with the hippie movement become even stronger with the scene when the porno gang takes psychedelics in a forest along the way. That scene is also the most utopian one in the film, opening potentially revolutionary vistas in relations between human and non-human beings, as some of the porno gang members sensually touch trees and plants around them and each other. It all, as the title of the film says, ends in death. Instead of taking us to the space of futurity, as the road movie has historically conjured 'an array of utopian connotations (most generally, "possibility" itself)' (Laderman 2002: 2), *The Life and Death of a Porno Gang* takes another route. Although 'the road secures us with direction and purpose' (Laderman 2002: 2), the porno gang's trip leads to utter hopelessness. This use of the road movie genre trope is in accordance with the historical journey of the road movie itself, as Timothy Corrigan (1994: 153) notices when he writes that

> in the mid-seventies and eighties, the genre has made its very action and subject its own historical hysteria: if genre is the prototype of classification and interpretation, it now becomes the *mise-en-abyme* reflection of an audience that can no longer imagine a naturalized history. The environment, conditions and actions of the road movie have become a borderless refuse bin.

Indeed, the audience watching the 'adventures' of the porno gang troupe cannot imagine 'a naturalized history' as both the troupe and the audience move through the historically produced 'refuse bin' of poor, marginalized, discarded, maimed and, finally, killed individuals. Laderman (2002: 19) writes that it is 'a utopian vision of social reform' that 'drives the road movie beyond society's limits', adding that 'the inability to realize such a vision often turns the journey in an aimless, forlorn and somewhat bitter direction'. The affect that dominates *The Life and Death of a Porno Gang* is much more complex than mere bitterness. While the use of the road movie genre trope is, if not cynical, then at least ironic, the possibility of any future whatsoever, let alone a utopian one, is radically foreclosed, exhausted by the immanence of post-socialist conditions and thus made unrepresentable.

Their first village porno cabaret show is a success, but seemingly out of nowhere a German ex-journalist, Frantz (Srboljub Milin), appears and offers money for the troupe to perform snuff shows for the international black market. The next day, the villagers chase the porno gang out and Ceca (Ivan Đorđević), a transgender woman from the village, joins them on the run. Ceca, however, first kills her favourite goat. A few scenes later, we learn more about Ceca when, in a porn cabaret show, she recounts her life in the village, and we find out that she had her first sexual experience with a sheep. She ends her performance by fellating a horse, shocking the audience into silence. Besides Želimir Žilnik's *Marble Ass* from 1995, this is a rare instance of giving substantial space to a representation of a transgender woman that is intended by the director to be neither mocking nor damning, even though the characters of villagers assume such an attitude. Ceca is shown as a victim of cisheteropatriarchy and socio-economic marginalization, all leading to ultimate exhaustion marked by death and suicide. She is only able to relate to animals, while even those affective relations are made under the shadow of violence. She kills her favourite animal because she did not want it to fall into the hands of her violent father, who molested her. The film suggests that trans people in rural communities are able to form emotional bonds only with animals, while even those bonds appear precarious within the cisheteropatriarchal system. In other words, the bodily horror of a sex with an animal shows us the horror of being a trans person in the cisheteropatriarchal environment of village life.

The members of the porno gang, beaten and raped by the villagers, accept Frantz's offer and begin shooting snuff plays. There are several, and each shows a particular aspect of post-socialist body horror. In almost every case, the subjects of snuff plays are volunteers, which underlines the overwhelming collective feeling of despair. The first volunteer comes from a nearby village. His scar-covered body is exposed to the gaze of the camera, and grinning maniacally he cuts himself on the stomach and chest several times, finally slitting his own throat in an abandoned train wagon. We are not given any explanation for his condition and the reason for his extreme death wish. We are left to speculate whether it was the oppressive atmosphere of the village life that made him such, or perhaps the war trauma. Whatever the case, we are shown the spectacle of bloody self-destruction, an image of the body in pain beyond any possibility of healing.

The next volunteer is from a different village, an ex-sniper and veteran of the wars in Bosnia and Croatia. He recounts his combat experiences, and we learn that he is dying from liver cancer related to AIDS, which he got from a needle exchange during the war. He feels remorse for killing soldiers, civilians, women and children alike. The money from the snuff performance will help his family to survive. He is killed by Sofija, who bludgeons him over the head with a huge mallet. This snuff play points to the deep historical trauma that wars in Bosnia and Croatia were for all ex-Yugoslav nations (on the wars, see Wilmer 2005; for the ways in which this trauma has been represented in ex-Yugoslav cinema, see Jelača 2016: 27–58; for the ways in which war in Bosnia was represented in film, see Harper 2017: 121–42). The dissolution of the Socialist Federal Republic of Yugoslavia into constitutive republics was enacted through ethno-nationalist projects of the individual states. The wars that led to genocide, mass killings, ethnic cleansing, isolation and international sanctions rendered poor the lives of those who survived, including queer people.

The gang's last snuff play is *lapot*, a ritual killing of the oldest family member, the origins of which – historical or mythical – are still unclear. *Lapot* was supposedly performed at times when families did not have the means to support all of their members, so their eldest were ceremoniously killed when they became a burden. The gang's *lapot* was supposed to be performed on an old man who chose to die to fund treatment for his granddaughter who was born disfigured by enriched uranium left by the NATO bombing campaign to end the Kosovo war. The 1999 NATO campaign left deep marks in the Serbian national body, especially because it led to the secession of Kosovo and Metohija, the mythic source of nationhood for ethnic Serbs. From the perspective of the second half of 2020 when this text was being written, the wounds of the Kosovo war, NATO bombing and Kosovo secession appear deeper than ever, locking the whole nation into a deep historical trauma that occasionally bursts out in violent acting out.

Though the gang is disbanded, there is one final snuff film to be made. The last snuff episode involves just Marko and Una. After finding out that those porno gang members who did not die or were killed along the way have died in a car crash, Marko and Una kill Frantz. The murder of Frantz – and it is the only murder by the gang members given that snuff subjects gave their consent for their deaths – could be understood in at least two ways. First, Marko and Una react to the threat of the international snuff cabal that Frantz represents, and they also want revenge for their porno gang members who more or less directly died because of the involvement in snuff production. But Marko and Una also perform the last snuff film, as the segment of the film is called. 'I'm taking you to a romantic place', says Marko. 'Honeymoon', Una adds. 'Something like that',Marko responds. Marko and Una commit suicide in the ruins of a Roman shrine, cutting open their veins while the video camera keeps recording.

And thus the story of the porno gang quietly extinguishes. However, that is not the end. The viewers are left with a feeling not of some kind of Aristotelian catharsis but rather complete devastation, faced with the extinguishment of the porno gang. The fact that the film ends with a whimper points to the fact that we are in terrain beyond representation. What is unrepresentable is the possibility of life beyond the horror of not only (post-)socialist history but beyond the violent cisheteronormative patriarchal society as such, especially for those who are marginalized, violated and killed. One can ask whether there is another kind of queer life-after-death with all the violence that is being incessantly perpetrated within the space that is produced as (social) life. Could something like a radically queer resistance strategy of (non-)life beyond the social death and representation be imagined? Can the violence of representation and social life be refused? As

Lowenstein (2005: 1) writes, 'to speak of history's horrors, or historical trauma, is to recognize events as wounds', but what if the wounds are fatal? In this context, the murder of Frantz can be read as one last attempt to lash out against the whole system of (social) life that created the conditions of life and death for the porno gang members, snuff subjects and other characters in the film. But the pair's suicide points to the fact that no person and no thing is redeemed through the spectacle of the grand finale – that is, on the one hand, there is no grand gesture with which to extricate oneself and others from the (post-)socialist histories that implicate even the most marginalized in the violence. On the other, thinking from the point of view of a radical foreclosure of the possibility of life within such histories leads not towards historical traumas as unpresentable (they are shown in quite bloody detail), but towards imagining a space-time beyond life and non-life.

The post-socialist body horror of *The Life and Death of a Porno Gang* shows us the ways in which history, and the post-socialist condition in particular, perpetrates violence against the body in all its horrific goriness. Once the body is violated, traumatized and exhausted, there opens a devastated landscape of (non)life beyond representation in the sense that, while post-socialist histories produce conditions inimical to life and productive of death, what appears on the grounds of persisting to think within the immanence is the third term – (non) life – signifying those forms that include the wounds, the exhaustion and the death, and that exist in those devastated (non-)worlds. In short, the forms of (non-)life that appear at the end of the road. However, those forms cannot be represented by the subject as it is traditionally imagined in classical political theory, hence the insistence on that which is beyond representation. What kind of (non-)living existents are beyond but defined by post-socialist immanent conditions of life and death and how to imagine an exhausted form of (non-)life remain a challenge – although a necessary one if a radically queer post-socialist politics are to be conceptualized. The quiet extinguishment at the end of the film, the absence of cathartic relation between the characters and the audience, certainly gestures towards the (im)possible (non-)spectacular (non-)life amid the ruins of cisheteronormative post-socialism.

Conclusion

The excess of history in the age of post-socialism kills. That could be one way of summarizing the analysis in previous parts of the chapter. However, not all bodies are killed, nor do these bodies suffer the horrors of history in the same way. *The*

Life and Death of a Porno Gang shows us the ways in which historical horrors open bodies up through excessive violence, but these bodies are queer bodies. It is those bodies that are socially and economically marginalized that suffer post-socialist body horrors in the most direct way, through rape, dismemberment, suicide and slaughter. Historical horrors focus in a particularly intensive way on these marginalized, queer bodies, showing the ways these horrors are embodied through disembowelment. Post-socialism and the excess of history in Serbia turn queer bodies into bodies of horror. *A Serbian Film* paints a different picture. While insisting on body horror perhaps even more than *The Life and Death of a Porno Gang*, the bodily violence works in a wholly different register. While in *The Life and Death of a Porno Gang* it is the most marginalized who suffer the historical horrors, in *A Serbian Film* the ultimate victim of the post-socialist condition turns out to be a heterosexual cis man and his heteronormative family. The post-socialist condition is the source of the social death of heterosexuality, especially in the form of 'foreign' Western influence. The gruesomeness of the rape and murder serves to strengthen the hold of heteronormativity, which is seen as threatened by the horrors of Serbian history.

Thus, we have two models for understanding the horrors of history in Serbia as well as body horror as a film genre. One shows the unspeakable violence suffered by the utter margins of society, while the other offers a paranoid framework of heteronormativity in danger. Considering the social, economic and political changes since these two films were made, the rise of nationalism, xenophobia, homophobia, transphobia and the re-traditionalization of gender roles in general, the past horrors seem to be just a prelude to what is to come (Bieber 2019). It seems that the only possible way out is a radically queer resistance strategy of (non-)life beyond social death and representation. *The Life and Death of a Porno Gang* offers us more than enough of inspiration in that regard.

References

Aleksić, T. (2016), 'Of Families and Other Sacred Cows on the Serbian Screen', in *Scholarship as the Art of Life: Contributions on Serbian Literature, Culture, and Society by Friends of Radmila (Rajka) Gorup*, edited by S. Vladiv-Glover, 175–93, Bloomington, IN: Slavica.

Batori, A. (2017), 'Newborn-Porn and the Wannabe-Art Film of the Future: Srđan Spasojević's *A Serbian Film* (Srpski Film, 2010)', *East European Film Bulletin*, 78 (October): 1–6.

Bennett, C. (1995), *Yugoslavia's Bloody Collapse: Causes, Course and Consequences*, New York: New York University Press.

Bideleux, R. and I. Jeffries (2007), *The Balkans: A Post-Communist history*, London: Routledge.

Bieber, F. (2019), *The Rise of Authoritarianism in the Western Balkans*, Basingstoke: Palgrave Macmillan.

Calic, M.-J. (2019), *A History of Yugoslavia*, West Lafayette, IN: Purdue University Press.

Corrigan, T. (1994), *A Cinema without Walls*, New Brunswick, NJ: Rutgers University Press.

Denitch, B. (1990), *Limits and Possibilities: The Crisis of Yugoslav Socialism and Stater Socialist Systems*, Minneapolis: University of Minnesota Press.

Dimitrijević, B. (2016), *Potrošeni socijalizam: Kultura, konzumerizam i društvena imaginacija u Jugoslaviji (1950–1974)* [*Socialism Consumed: Culture, Consumerism and Social Imagination in Yugoslavia (1950-1974)*], Beograd: Fabrika knjiga.

Fraser, N. (1997), *Justice Interruptus: Critical Reflections on the 'Postsocialist' Condition*, London: Routledge.

Harper, S. (2017), *Screening Bosnia: Geopolitics, Gender and Nationalism in Film and Television Images of the 1992–95 War*, London: Bloomsbury.

Iarlori, F. (2011), 'Aleksandar Radivojevic of "A Serbian Film": It's Catharsis More than 'Torture Porn', *Cafebabel*. Available online: https://cafebabel.com/en/article/aleksandar-radivojevic-of-a-serbian-film-its-catharsis-more-than-torture-porn-5ae0078ef723b35a145e20b4 (accessed 12 July 2020).

Jelača, D. (2016), *Dislocated Screen Memory: Narrating Trauma in Post-Yugoslav Cinema*, Basingstoke: Palgrave Macmillan.

Kapka, A. (2014), 'Understanding *A Serbian Film*: The Effects of Censorship and File-sharing on Critical Reception and Perceptions of Serbian National Identity in the UK', *Frames Cinema Journal*, 6. Available online: http://framescinemajournal.com/article/understanding-a-serbian-film-the-effects-of-censorship-and-file-sharing-on-critical-reception-and-perceptions-of-serbian-national-identity-in-the-uk (accessed 15 July 2020).

Kirn, G. (2019), *Partisan Ruptures: Self-Management, Market Reform and the Spectre of Socialist Yugoslavia*, London: Pluto Press, 2019.

Laderman, D. (2002), *Driving Visions: Exploring the Road Movie*, Austin, TX: University of Texas Press.

Lowenstein, A. (2005), *Shocking Representation: Historical Trauma, National Cinema, and the Modern Horror Film*, New York: Columbia University Press.

Normand, B.L. (2014), *Designing Tito's Capital: Urban Planning, Modernism, and Socialism in Belgrade*, Pittsburgh, PA: University of Pittsburgh Press.

Ognjanović, D. (2017), 'No Escape from the Body: Bleak Landscapes of Serbian Horror Film', *Humanistika*, 1 (1): 49–66.

Shaviro, S. (2011), 'After Hope: *The Life and Death of a Porno Gang*', *ACIDEMIC Journal of Film and Media*. Available online: http://www.acidemic.com/id137.html (accessed 12 July 2020).

Suvin, D. (2014), *Samo jednom se ljubi: Radiografija SFR Jugoslavije [Splendour, Misery, and Potentialities: An X-ray of Socialist Yugoslavia]*, Beograd: Rosa Luxemburg Stiftung.

Wilmer, F. (2005), *The Social Construction of Man, the State, and War: Identity, Conflict, and Violence in Former Yugoslavia*, London: Routledge.

Films

The Life and Death of a Porno Gang (2009), directed by Mladen Đorđević [film], Serbia: Film House Bas Celik.

A Serbian Film (2010), directed by Srđan Spasojević [film], Serbia: Contra Film.

Index

#MeToo movement 188, 195

Abdul-Jabbar, Kareem 3
abject 1, 11, 156, 157, 213
    abject woman 72–3
Aboriginal 23–35, 208, 210, 212, 220
    see also Indigenous
Abrams, J.J. 216
affect 1, 84, 86, 188, 194, 195, 199, 200, 243, 247, 248, 251–3
agonistic politics 24, 25
Aleksìc, Tatjana 248–9
allegory 6, 33, 79–80
    allegorical deployment of children 60
    allegorical imperative 75
    allegorical moments 93, 96
    allegorical mortification of time 75
    allegorical truth 32–4
    allegorical vision 74
    and allusion 169–73
    and social protest 178–80
allusion 12, 14, 23, 24, 25, 27, 28, 29, 30, 32, 34, 35, 208, 210, 212, 215, 220, 169–73, 178–80, 218, 235
America 3–4, 30, 109, 117, 120, 167–81
    African American 3–4, 168, 170
    American history 145, 175
American Dream 168–71, 181
Amityville Horror 170
Ancient Aliens 5
Anderson, M. 80
anger, feminist 192–8
Anvari, Babak 2, 9, 12, 55–66
apocalypse 14, 15, 109–10, 112, 115, 123, 149, 179, 190
Apollo 18 76–7
Arnold, Sarah 175
art house horror 9
atomic testing 156–60
    see also Hiroshima and Nagasaki
Australia 12, 24–35, 207–20
Australian Gothic 217

backwoods horror movie 207, 211, 216
Badalamenti, Angelo 145–6
bakemono 74
Baker, A.W. 207
Baker, Lucy 167
Balmain, C. 74–5, 84–5
Basinger, Jeanine 228–9, 231
Bataan 229–30
Baudrillard, Jean 239
Bean, Sawney 207
Beardsley, Aubrey 113
beDevil 24–5
Benjamin, Walter 6, 33, 75, 81–2
Beville, Maria 134
Biber, Katherine 210
Blair Witch Project, The 72, 76, 77, 78, 97, 101, 209
Blak Wave 12, 24–6
Blake, Linnie 6, 10, 79–81, 96, 147–8, 160–1, 181, 211, 220, 238
Blanchett, Cate 32, 35
Blood Window 7
Blow, Richard 179
body horror 10, 14, 171, 205, 211, 226, 232, 245, 253, 255, 256
Bowser, Benjamin 171
Boym, Svetlana 227
Bradbury, Ray 120
Bramesco, Charles 228
Branagh, Kenneth 191
Bride of Frankenstein, The 191, 192
Briefel, A. 6
Britt, Ryan 118, 120
Brogan, Patricia Burke 95
Buck-Morss, Susan 33
Buckley, Chloe 197
Bullock, Heather E. 180–1
Bunker, The 231
Burton, Tim 114

Call of Duty 228
Cannibal Holocaust 78
cannibalism 215

capitalism 25, 122, 146, 147–9, 152, 155, 190, 245
   patriarchal 188, 190
Carroll, Lewis 120
Cars That Ate Paris, The 213
Cave, Nick 23
Charles, Jack 26, 28–9
children
   abandoned 91, 94, 100
   imperilled 173–8
   intergenerational trauma 42, 43, 48
   lost 168–9
   memories of childhood 55–6, 59–60
   poverty and 172, 179
   protagonists 9, 11, 59
   remains 97
   stolen 32
Churchill, Winston 225
cinéma verité 99
Clare, John 118
Clarke, Aislinn 2, 8, 13, 92, 97–103
Clarke, Marcus 208
class 167–81, 216
   consciousness 151–2
   underclass 168, 171–2, 176, 181
Clover, Carol 39–40, 211
Cloverfield 99
Cold War 159
Cole, Beck 30
colonialism 7, 30, 42, 52, 79, 112, 208–9, 215, 220
   Japanese 82
   postcolonialism 93, 130, 207
   settler 24–6, 35, 217
Colour of Paradise, The 60
convergence culture 2
convicts 207–20
Corrigan, Timothy 252
Council of Europe
   Eurimages 8
counter-history 13, 110
Creed, Barbara 72, 193–4, 197
Creel, James 232
Creepwave 7
Cursed Violent People 78
Cushing, Peter 236

Daly, Mary 190
D'Amore, Laura M. 198

Dark Waters 41
Darkside, The 12, 23, 24, 25, 26–9
De Groot, Jerome 5–6
De Martinis, Louis 122–3
Dear Daughter 95
Deathwatch 231
del Toro, Guillermo 2, 9
   Spanish Civil War films 10–2
Deliverance 207
Deodato, Ruggero 78
Devil's Backbone, The 9, 10–2
Devil's Doorway, The 8, 13, 92, 97–101
   critiques 102–3
Devil's Woods, The 92
diasporic
   filmmaking 55
   mobility 57–60
Dickens, Charles 119
Đinđić, Zoran 247
Dines, Martin 114
Dixie, Florence 122
djinn 12, 55–66
   haunting 61–3
documentary 75–6
Dog Soldiers 231
doppelgänger 14, 49, 149, 167–81
Đorđević, Mladen 19, 244
Doré, Gustave 112
Dracula 63, 91, 110–12, 119, 123, 187
Dumas, Raechel 158, 160
Dwyer, Jody 208, 209
Dying Breed 14, 207–20

Eichhorn, Kate 189
Eisenhower, General Dwight 225
Ellis, Mathew 147
Ellis, Warren 23
Eppard, Lawrence M. 180–1
Eraserhead 158
Erll, Astrid 112, 131
exilic filmmaking 55
Exorcist, The 97

Fahs, Breanne 189, 190, 195, 200
family
   American 167–81
   bloodlines 39
   heritage 40, 43, 48, 52, 208, 211–18
   in Japan 85

see also children, intergenerational trauma
female horror filmmaker-fan 8
female monsters 14, 191, 193, 199
  see also monstrous feminine
feminism
  feminist killjoys 19
  feminist revolt 193
  feminist snap 192–8
  radical 187–200
  vigilante 188, 198, 200
  see also gender-based violence, monstrous feminine
festivals
  GenreBlast 8
  A Night of Horror 8
  Nightmares Film Festival 8
  ScreamFest LA 8
Figal, Gerald 73–4
Film Finance Corporation Australia 218
final girl trope 211, 232
Firebite 12, 23, 24, 29–32
Firestone, Shulamith 190
First Australians 30
Fischer, Clara 93–4
Fletcher, Brendan 23, 26
Flynn, Roddy 95–6
folk 74
folklore 42, 60, 63, 65, 80, 82–3, 130
For the Term of His Natural Life 216
found footage horror 12–13, 75–9, 98–9
Frankenstein (James Whale) 119
Frankenstein, Lily 187–200
Frankenstein: or, The Modern Prometheus 111, 118, 187, 191
Frankenstein, Victor 116, 118–19, 123, 191
Fraser, Nancy 189, 246
Freud, Sigmund 40–1
Frost, Mark 145, 152
fugitive energies 30–2
Fukayama, Francis 145
Fury 229

G-boom 7
Galt, Rosalind 9–10
Game of Thrones 130
gender-based violence 212

Get Out 3–4, 11, 170, 181
ghost 10, 11, 23–9, 34–5, 41–3, 47–8, 50, 71, 75, 80–1, 84, 86, 97, 99
  ghost modernism 146
Godzilla 74–5, 79
'good mother' archetype of horror 173–8
Goslett, Phillipa 114, 115
Gothic Americana 148–52
Gothic fiction 110, 112, 132–5
  penny dreadful novel 114
  steampunk 110
Gothic time-travel films 109–23
  archetypes 111
  literary features 118–22
  literary transformations 117–18, 122–3
  recursive adaptation 111
  recycling of originary texts 112, 117
  use of motifs and tropes 110
Grand, Sarah 122
Gray, Jonathan 153
Green, Stephanie 132–3, 194–6
Greer, Germaine 190, 195
Grey, Zane 119
Grossman, Julie 153

Halberstam, Jack 196
Hallam, Lindsay 153
Halloween 58, 171
'Hands across America' 178–80
Hantke, Steffen 231, 233, 237
Harrington, Michael 171
Hart, A.C. 100
haunted histories 12, 116–17, 135–40
Haunting, A 24
Haut, Mavis 190
Hawkins, Joan 9
Hawley, Erica 191
Heller, Dana 190
Hills Have Eyes, The 171, 207–8, 209
Hills, M. 86
Hiroshima and Nagasaki atomic bombing 72, 74, 79, 80, 82
Hirsch, Alexander 30–1
Hissrich, Lauren Schmidt 132
historical
  imagination of horror 1, 4–7
  revisionism 132–5
  truth 134
historical culture 7

historiography 1–15
  horror as popular 2–3
history
  commodification 2
  repetition 160
  see also counter-history
History Channel 5
Hitler, Adolf 225
Hole in the Ground, The 92
home
  concept of 12, 55, 56–7, 58, 61, 63
  haunted 55, 57
  homeland 55–6
  homelessness 169, 179–80, 181
  mobility 62
  space of conflict 65
Honig, Bonnie 25
Horler, Sacha 26, 27
Howling Village 12, 39, 40, 42–4

Iles, T. 74
impure women 93–4
Indigenous 12, 14, 23–5, 27–30, 32, 34–5, 208, 210, 212, 215, 220
Inglourious Basterds 228, 233, 234, 237
intergenerational criminality 213–17
Iran 55–66
Ireland
  church–state relationship 94
  institutional abuse 91, 93–7
Irish horror cinema 91–103
Ives, Vanessa 113

J-Horror 41
Jack the Ripper 120–1
Jameson, Fredric 79
Japan
  historical revisionism 72–3
  Japanese Spirit, 74
  modernity 80
  national trauma 39–53
  Shintōism 41, 85
  shrine mergers 73–4, 83–4
  Yasukuni Shrine 82–3
  see also *kaidan*, *kam*
Jeffries, Stuart 146–48, 246
Jenkins, Henry 2, 112
Jetztzeit 6

Joyce, Ashlee 156–8
Ju-On franchise 39, 41

Kääpä, Pietari 95
Kaczor, Katarzyna 130
kaidan 41
kami 41–2, 44, 45, 74
Kay, Jilly Boyce 188
Kazuhiko, Komatsu 74
Kent, Jennifer 2
Khosroshahi, Zahra 65
Kilroy Test 229, 231–2
King, Frederick D. 116–17
King, Stephen 175
Kingston, Jeremy 13
Koizumi, Meiro 71–86
Kouzas, Chrisanne 195, 198
Kubrick, Stanley 173, 175, 218
Kurosawa, Kiyoshi 80

Laderman, D. 252
Lagerwey, Jorie 13
Landy, Marcia 13, 110
Langford, Michelle 60
Last Confession of Alexander Pearce, The 208
Latour, Bruno 111
Le Fanu, Joseph Thomas Sheridan 93
Lee, Alison 116–17
legends 112, 133, 209
  bushranger 211
  convict 215
  urban 12, 42, 46, 48–9, 52
Let the Right One In 9
Life and Death of a Porno Gang, The 10, 14–15, 243, 250–5, 256
  awards 244
  body horror 243, 255
Lim, B.C. 86
Linsley, Brent 122
Logan, John 2, 114
loss 1, 40, 79, 80, 83, 117, 132, 136, 139, 140
Louttit, Chris 114, 116, 123
Lovecraft, H.P. 13, 152, 155–6
  see also phantasmagoria
Lowenstein, Adam 6, 10, 74, 79, 82, 84, 93, 96, 136, 170, 181, 208, 215, 217, 238, 255

Lowery, William 227
Lusty, Natalya 189, 200
Lynch, David 145, 147, 149, 153, 157–59

Mabo decision 24, 210
MacKenzie, Colin 27–8
mad scientist trope 3, 168, 235–6
Magdalene Laundries 13, 91–103
Magdalene Sisters, The 95
Magilow, Daniel 226
Mahood, Kim 25
Majkowski, T.K. 133
Manea, D. 110, 112
Mangan, Lucy 115
Marble Ass 252
Marcus, Greil 10
Martin, George R.R. 130
Mary Shelley's Frankenstein 191
Maza, Sarah 5
McCarthy, Donald 153
memorial 57, 136, 138, 213
    Holocaust 41
memorialization 74, 80, 83, 177
memory
    location memory 136–8
    modes of remembering 140
    politics of 130
    sense-memory 56
    traumatic memory 95
Mengele, Josef 235–6
Mighall, Robert 139
Miike, Takashi 72, 80
Miller, S.J. 6
Milošević, Slobodan 243, 244, 246
Moffatt, Tracey 24–6
Monnet, Agnieszka 233
monstrous feminine 72, 192–8
Monstrous Possibilities 167
Monterrubio-Ibáñez, L. 117
Moreton, Romaine 26, 27–8
mothers 14, 31, 47–8, 50, 51, 57, 61–3, 66, 91, 167–81
Mullan, Peter 95
Myrick, Daniel 78
myth 42, 44–8, 52, 63, 78, 92, 117, 119–20, 121, 133, 145, 150, 155, 172, 188, 193, 207, 208–13, 219, 227, 230, 254

Naficy, Hamid 55–6, 62
Nagasaki 72, 74, 79, 80, 82, 83, 158
Nakata, Hideo 72
national identity 10, 78, 93, 207, 211, 220
nationalism 51
    Japanese 72–4, 80, 82, 85, 209, 250, 256
Nazism 225–31
    neo-Nazi 235, 238
Nazisploitation films 226, 233–7
nensha 77
neoliberalism 7, 147–8, 151, 160, 168, 243
Nevers, The 13, 109, 111, 114–16, 117–18, 123
New Boy, The 12, 23, 24, 32–4
New Women 109, 121–2, 197
Newman, Kim 237
Ni Houlihan, Kathleen 93
Nice Coloured Girls 24
Nicholson, Amy 228
Nieland, Justus 148–9
Night Cries: A Rural Tragedy 24
Night of Fear 217
Nightingale, The 217, 218–19
Nightmare on Elm Street 171
Nochimson, Martha 147
Noroi: The Curse 8, 13, 71–86
Nosferatu 47
nostalgia 86, 102, 145, 169, 227, 230–1, 233, 234
Noyce, Phillip 33
Nyong'o, Lupita 167

Occult 78
Och, Dana 7–8
Olmstead, Kathryn S. 154
One Missed Call 72, 80
onryou 80
Overlord 14, 225–31
    critical reception 227–8
    as military horror 228–33
    as Nazisploitation 233–7
Ox-Head Village 12, 39, 40, 48–51
Ozploitation films 217, 219

Pan's Labyrinth 8–9, 10–2
parafictional film 76
Paranormal Activity 99

paratext 56, 145, 152–6, 158–9
Park-Finch, H. 111–12
Pacat, C.S. 115–16
past
    fear of 1
    monstrous nature 1
    relationship with present 1
patriarchy 39, 91, 103, 119, 175, 177, 181, 188–90, 194, 195, 197, 198, 212, 245, 249, 251
    heteropatriarchy 250, 254, 252–3
Pearce, Alexander 208, 209, 211
    see also Dying Breed
Peck, Raoul 3
Pedro, Dina 197
Peele, Jordan 2, 3, 11, 14, 167–81
Penderecki, Ashlee 156
Penny Dreadful 13, 109, 111, 113–14, 117–18, 187–200
    story franchise 122–3
performative recollection 71, 75
Perkins, Rachel 30
Pescucci, Gabriella 113
phantasmagoria 152–6
Picnic at Hanging Rock 217
Picture of Dorian Gray, The 112, 118, 193
Pike, David L 159
Pine, Emilie 95
Pitt, Brad 234
Poltergeist 169, 171, 173, 175
porn 244
    porno 243, 244, 245, 247–9, 252–6
    pornography 220
Portals 24
post-socialism 245–7
post-truth culture 146
postcolonial filmmaking 55
postmodernism 13, 146–50, 155, 160
poverty 14, 112, 168, 169, 171–2, 177, 179, 180–1, 208, 213
Procházka, Martin 138
Proposition, The 24
Psycho 218
Pulse 41, 80

quality TV horror 13
queer perspectives 122, 193–4, 247–51, 253, 254, 255, 256

Rabbit-Proof Fence 24, 33, 217
racism 3, 170, 229, 233, 235, 250
Radivojević, Aleksandar 247, 249–50
Rank, Mark Robert 180–1
Rathbone, Basil 114
Reagan, Ronald 169, 171–2, 176
Redfern Now 25
repression 7, 11, 71–86, 167, 216
revolting women 14
Reyes, Xavier Aldana 97–9
Ringu 41, 72, 80
ritual 24, 32–3, 71–86, 116, 174, 254
Roddy, Lalor 100
Rosemary's Baby 3
Roszczynialska, Magdalena 130, 133
ruins 33, 72, 83–4, 132, 135–40
Rüsen, Jorn 7

Sapkowski, Andrzej 129–33, 137–39, 141
Saving Private Ryan 226, 229, 231–3
Sayad, Cecilia 98
Schaap, Andrew 25
Scheck, Frank 92
Scheibel, Will 153
Schoonover, Karl 9–10
Schreiner, Olive 121
Schubart, Rikke 122, 196
Scream 58
SCUM Manifesto 187, 188–91, 194
Secret Diary of Laura Palmer, The 153
Secret History of Twin Peaks, The 145, 152–5
sense of wonder 111–14
Serbia 243–56
    modernization 245–7
    post-socialist condition 245–7
Serbian Film, A 10, 14–15, 243, 244, 256
    post-socialist death in 247–50
Sex in a Cold Climate 95
Shaviro, Steven 250–1
Shea, Robert 155
Shelley, Mary 14, 187, 191, 193
Shimizu, Takashi 12
    Village trilogy 39–53
Shining, The 173, 175, 218
Shiraishi, Koji 8, 13, 75
Shirome 78
Shock Waves 236

slavery 3–4
Smith, James 91, 94, 95, 103
snuff films/shows 244, 249, 251–5
Sobchack, Vivian 2, 4, 5, 109, 117
socialism 245–7, 249, 255
societal monster 167
Solanas, Valerie 187, 188–91, 197, 200
Soros, George 227
Spasojević, Srđan 248
spectacle of the real 75–9
spectral encounters 12
spirits 12, 24, 25, 26, 41, 43, 44, 45, 51, 52, 57, 72, 74, 82–3, 155
Staley, David 5
Strayer, Kirsten 7–8
Stepford Wives, The 3
Stephan, Matthias 113, 169
Stoker, Bram 63, 92, 111, 119
Stolen Generations 24, 28–9, 32
Strange Case of Dr Jekyll and Mr Hyde, The 111
stranger relationality 34
Stranger Things 169
strangerhood 34
Subramanian, Janani 13
Suicide Forest Village 12, 39, 40, 45–8
Suvin, Darko 245
Sweeney Todd 114

Tasmania 207–20
    impact of isolation 216–17
Tennyson, Lord Alfred 118
terra nullius 210
Texas Chainsaw Massacre, The 171, 207, 218
Theus, Tyler 147
Third, Amanda 190, 195
Thornton, Warwick 2, 12, 23–35
Time Machine 181
tokkōtai 71, 72
torture 61, 63, 235, 244, 249
Towlson, Jon 8
Tracker, The 24
transnational horror trends 7–10
trauma
    in Australia 217–19
    collective 41
    historical 141–2

national 6–7, 39–53, 217–19
original 42–4
traumatic memory 95
Travers, Ben 115
Trump, Donald 146, 160, 226, 227, 238
Trumpian 29, 172
Turkey Shoot 217
Turner, Graeme 7
Tuttle, W.C. 119
Twin Peaks 145, 147, 151
Twin Peaks: Fire Walk with Me 153
Twin Peaks: The Final Dossier 145, 152, 158–60
Twin Peaks: The Return 9, 13–14, 145–61
    Las Vegas location 148–52

Uluru Statement from the Heart 24, 220
Under the Shadow 9, 12, 55–66
underclass 168, 171–2, 176, 181
Unite the Right rally 227, 234, 238
urban legends 12, 42, 46, 48–9, 52
Us 14, 167–81
    poverty discourses 168–9, 181
    use of allegory 169–73

vampire films 23
vampires 90, 116, 119, 121, 191, 226, 233
Van Diemen's Land 208
vigilantism 192–8, 200
village
    as symbol of monstrous past 39–42
Voice referendum 24–5, 29–30

Wallace, R. 75, 76–7
war 7
War Gothic 233
Warhol, Andy 189
welfare queen myth 172
Wells, H.G. 120, 122, 181
Western movies 119
Wetmore, Kevin 6, 169
Whale, James 119, 191
Whedon, Joss 114
Where the Silence Falls (Double Projection #1) 71, 76
White, Hayden 4, 6
Wik decision 210

Wilde, Oscar 112, 118
Wilson, Anton 155
Wilson-Cairns, Krysty 122–3
Witcher, The 8, 13, 129–41
    franchise 130
    intertextuality 130
    tourism 130
Without Name 92
Wolf Creek 207
Wolfenstein 228
women, *see* abject woman, female monsters, impure women, monstrous feminine, New Women, revolting women
Wordsworth, William 118

World War II combat film 225, 229–30
Wounds
    national 6–7, 74, 96
    open 79–85

Xavier, Ismail 33, 178, 180

Yeats, W. B. 112–13
Yoneyama, L. 82
Yugoslavia 243, 245–6, 253
    Balkan wars 246

Žilnik, Želimir 252
Zohar, Ayelet 13, 71, 75
zombies 33, 167, 225–31